# HAPPINESS IS
# OVERRATED

# HAPPINESS IS
# OVERRATED

## RAYMOND ANGELO BELLIOTTI

ROWMAN & LITTLEFIELD PUBLISHERS, INC.
*Lanham • Boulder • New York • Toronto • Oxford*

ROWMAN & LITTLEFIELD PUBLISHERS, INC.

Published in the United States of America
by Rowman & Littlefield Publishers, Inc.
A wholly owned subsidiary of The Rowman & Littlefield Publishing Group, Inc.
4501 Forbes Boulevard, Suite 200, Lanham, Maryland 20706
www.rowmanlittlefield.com

PO Box 317
Oxford
OX2 9RU, UK

British Library Cataloguing in Publication Information Available

**Library of Congress Cataloging-in-Publication Data**

Belliotti, Raymond A., 1948–
   Happiness is overrated / Raymond Angelo Belliotti.
      p.   cm.
   Includes bibliographical references and index.
   ISBN 0-7425-3361-1 (alk. paper)—ISBN 0-7425-3362-X (pbk. : alk. paper)
   1. Happiness.   2. Conduct of life.   I. Title.
BJ1481.B46   2003
170—dc21                                                    2003013626

Printed in the United States of America

The paper used in this publication meets the minimum requirements of American
National Standard for Information Sciences—Permanence of Paper for Printed Library
Materials, ANSI/NISO Z39.48-1992.

*For Marcia, Angelo, and Vittoria*

*Migliore vivere un giorno come leone
che mille anni come pecora.*

# CONTENTS

# PREFACE

Two decades ago, a colleague, Marvin Kohl, asked me what I would teach my children about happiness. He was convinced that happiness is a great, perhaps the greatest, good. At that time I had no children. I was not even married. I told Dr. Kohl that I would not teach my children anything about happiness. They would require more important lessons. They would need to learn how to embody appropriate values; how to lead meaningful, even exemplary, lives; how to stand against injustice; how to resist the allure of a soft world that prizes leisure time and a life of habit punctuated by diversion over creative labor and purposive accomplishment; and how to take responsibility for their choices, judgments, and actions instead of retreating to the consolations of easy excuses and denials. Why would I spend time teaching my children trivialities such as happiness? We do not pursue happiness directly. We pursue worthwhile, meaningful, valuable, exemplary lives. If we are reasonably successful in that quest, happiness may follow. If so, all the better. If not, we can still take pride and derive satisfaction from living well, from crafting interesting, worthwhile biographical narratives, and from maximizing the value of our time on earth. To exhaust time and energy lecturing my children about happiness would be counterproductive. They might draw the wrong impression that happiness, the pursuit of pleasure in a surrealistic setting of *la dolce vita*, is most important.

I was convinced then that happiness is overrated. Was I correct? The question lingered. I was not plagued by it, but at times I recalled the intensity of my response to a seemingly innocuous question from a well-intentioned colleague. In retrospect, my vitriol (or pompous diatribe) seemed out of place. Maybe I did not understand what he took happiness to be. Maybe I was under the spell of a particular notion of happiness that did not define the parameters of the term well.

I now have two children, born in 1988 and 1989. I still have taught them nothing about happiness. This book is a beginning.

## 1. TOPICS

I introduce numerous ancient Greek, Roman, and Christian understandings of happiness in chapter 1: Socrates and Plato, Aristotle, Cynicism, Epicureanism, Stoicism, Plotinus, St. Augustine, and St. Thomas Aquinas. Most classical notions are condition views of happiness in that they define happiness as an objective condition of the mind or soul. Condition views of happiness can have a paradoxical outcome: Human beings can attain the requisite objective condition yet be predominantly sad. To insist such people are happy rings false to contemporary ears.

Examining the historical development of the concept of happiness is crucial. Among other things, we learn the connections between happiness, personal identity, kinds of goods, human destiny, and value. In short, discussions of happiness revolve around how we should best live our lives. Much Greco-Roman philosophy and Judeo-Christian theology centered precisely on that question.

Modern philosophy retained the question but reconceived the answer. In chapter 2, I discuss the modern era during which happiness is closely identified with a relatively enduring, positive psychological state. The feelings of happiness take a more prominent role than in the classical era. I examine different notions of happiness in the work of Immanuel Kant, Georg W. F. Hegel, Jeremy Bentham, John Stuart Mill, Arthur Schopenhauer, and Friedrich Nietzsche. I then sketch the dominant notion of happiness among contemporary social scientists, a notion that defines happiness by the requisite feelings. Throughout this chapter, I explain in what sense happiness is overrated and distinguish the experience of happiness—as defined by predominant feelings of joy, peace, or exuberance—from worthwhile happiness.

From the discussions and historical surveys in the first two chapters emerge important lessons about happiness that form the ballast for the distinctions between worthwhile happiness that is tightly connected to value and happiness as a positive state of mind that is not necessarily linked to value. If happiness is to be the greatest personal good, a great good, or good at all, it must be joined to value in some way and to some extent.

Contemporary philosophical work on happiness is the focus of chapter 3. Some philosophers accept the social scientific view of happiness; others argue that happiness requires a positive self-appraisal; still others demand an accurate, positive self-appraisal; while a few recall the Platonic-Christian understanding of happiness as connected to an objective, preexisting good. In this chapter, I discuss the relationship between happy, minimally meaningful, robustly meaningful, significant, important, and exemplary lives. I conclude by addressing a series of philosophical puzzles: Can everyone be happy? Should everyone be happy? How much suffering, if any, is compatible with happiness?

In chapter 4, I describe the work of social scientists who have developed strategies for attaining a relatively enduring, positive state of mind. The extent to which our positive state of mind is the product of genetic inheritance and brain chemistry, and the extent to which it emerges from our choices, is crucial to this analysis. I conclude by reiterating that attaining a positive state of mind is not necessarily a great good, and happiness defined by uplifted feelings, while usually a good, is overrated.

The final chapter analyzes the meaning of human life. In chapter 5, I examine the relationship between meaning and theism. After briefly discussing attempts to dismiss the question of life's meaning on linguistic grounds, I sketch answers provided by Eastern and Western religions. The ability of religion to provide (highly contestable) answers to the meaning of life demonstrates that theism is more than its critics suspect. I then accept for the sake of argument the existentialist claim that the cosmos is inherently meaningless: that there is no meaning or value built into our world. The myth of Sisyphus is a rich metaphor encouraging discussion of the possible absurdity of human life. The question then becomes whether human beings can construct sufficient meaning and value. By analyzing the work of Nietzsche and Albert Camus, I distinguish the cosmic from personal perspectives and review numerous images of how we can best live our lives in the face of cosmic meaninglessness. I outline why and how human life is like a telescope and a slinky toy, and suggest how we can use the cosmic perspective artfully. I then highlight the role of struggle, suffering, and death in creating meaning.

I conclude that happiness, in most of its realizations, remains valuable; but it is far from the most important human aspiration. We should teach our children how to lead robustly meaningful, valuable lives. If they do, they will deserve worthwhile happiness and often realize it. But even if they are not predominantly happy, they will have created lives worth emulating.

This work has extravagant ambitions: to critically discuss classical, modern, and contemporary understandings of happiness; to apply the lessons of that discussion to the findings of social science; and to relate happiness to meaningful human lives. The marriage of grand aspirations to limited space is volatile. I often sacrifice technical sophistication for clarity. In the interest of saving space, I often cut off an argument that could have continued vigorously. Each of the chapters of this work and many of the subsections of the chapters merit book-length treatment. Accordingly, I regard this work as an introduction to the relevant material, not the final word. Hopefully, the work will inspire readers to continue their investigations. Readers, at least, will find meaning in struggling with the questions and paradoxes raised in the book. They may even find happiness.

## 2. ACKNOWLEDGEMENTS

I have numerous people to thank. Without the support of my wife Marcia this book would not have been completed. My children Angelo and Vittoria are the source of my motivation to write.

This book begins their instruction on the meaning of, relative worth of, and recipe for worthwhile happiness. That they will be forced to read this work constitutes a parental revenge that deeply consoles. That this book will long outlive its author and be available to haunt them in my absence renders me uncontrollably giddy.

Thanks also to Marvin Kohl, a wonderful colleague and dear friend, who exemplifies the grandest tradition of philosopher as seeker of practical wisdom. But for his interest in happiness and the meaning of life, the undergraduate courses on those topics he created at SUNY Fredonia, and his initial question to me about what I would teach my children about happiness, my passion for these issues might have remained dormant.

Eve DeVaro and John Wehmueller of Rowman & Littlefield's acquisitions department were prompt, supportive, and helpful from the start. John Calderone, production editor, ensured that my numerous typographical errors were corrected and my annoyingly stilted prose was softened. The two readers who evaluated the manuscript for Rowman & Littlefield provided uncommonly helpful suggestions and generous encouragement. Joanne Foeller provided extraordinary word processing skills, editorial acumen, and boundless good will. Stefanie Griffith, my undergraduate research assistant, went above and beyond the call of duty in locating and analyzing articles on happiness. More important, she maintained good cheer and optimism throughout the long, arduous process.

Finally, I thank the publishers of Editions Rodopi for permission to reprint and adapt material from my book, *What is the Meaning of Human Life?*

# 1

# GREEK, ROMAN, AND CHRISTIAN HAPPINESS

With the exception of love, no human experience is celebrated more than happiness. We pursue wealth, success, honor, relationships, education, and the like because we believe they will lead to our happiness. Parents often say that what they want most for their children is happiness. Typically, parents utter this bromide self-satisfied that they are open-minded and accepting of the paths their children choose: "I may disagree with what my children are doing, it is not for me, but if it makes them happy I cannot say they are wrong." The intuition is clear: Our accomplishments, careers, relationships, and the potentials we realize are hollow if they do not make us happy.

Happiness is often described as a great good, even the greatest good. To imagine someone sincerely denying the value of happiness is difficult: "We do not need happiness. We are better off without it. I am unhappy and proud of it." What unusual psychology, perverted sense of priorities, or bizarre vision of the world could motivate such a statement? For even those who take happiness to be elusive, perhaps impossible to achieve, embrace its value. Pessimists sense one of the tragedies of human life to be the impossibility of attaining the high value of happiness. The tragedy, though, is the failure to attain happiness. Even pessimists glorify the value of and long for happiness.

The issue may seem simple. We all want, perhaps even need, happiness. The only question remains how to attain it. What courses of action, which choices, what lifestyles are most likely to make us happy?

But matters are not this simple. Until we agree what "happiness" is we cannot begin to answer the major questions: Is happiness attainable? If so, how do I attain happiness? How great a good is happiness? Are the best lives happy lives? Is happiness necessary for a good life, a meaningful life, a worthwhile life? Does it matter how we achieve happiness?

Assessing remarks on happiness is difficult because the term is used in different ways. Aristotle understood happiness as human beings flourishing in their natural environment. Others speak of happiness as a joyful, pleasurable, exhilarating state or series of states. Still others view happiness as a global state of contentment, tranquility, and peace. Contemporary sociologists take happiness to be a psychological condition and insist that self-flattering illusions, not keen insight into reality, are necessary for happiness. The British utilitarians argued that maximizing happiness and pleasure was the foundation of morality. Yet Friedrich Nietzsche ridiculed happiness as the refuge of the mediocre.

Here are a few examples of definitions and assessments of happiness:

[Happiness is a] lasting state of affairs in which the most favorable ratio of satisfied desires to desires is realized, with the proviso that the satisfied desires can include satisfactions that are not *preceded* by specific desires for them, but come by surprise.[1]

True happiness is a profound, enduring feeling of contentment, capability and centeredness. It's a rich sense of well-being that comes from knowing you can deal productively and creatively with all that life offers—both the good and the bad. It's knowing your internal self and responding to your real needs, rather than the demands of others. And it's a deep sense of engagement—living in the moment and enjoying life's bounty.[2]

[To be happy] is to really enjoy the good things in life, if and when they come your way; to experience pleasure, enthusiasm, satisfaction . . . to be truly joyful, 'high,' when things go right for you.[3]

[Happiness] outlasts yesterday's moment of elation, today's buoyant mood, and tomorrow's hard time; it is an ongoing perception that this time of one's life, or even life as a whole, is fulfilling, meaningful, and pleasant. It is what some people experience as joy—not an ephemeral euphoria, but a deep and abiding sense that, despite the day's woes, all is, or will be, well.[4]

Happiness . . . involves realizing one's important values, where these are justified relative to the best standard of justification.[5]

To be happy is to be generally 'pleased with life.'[6]

Happiness: Characterized by luck or good fortune; prosperous; having or demonstrating pleasure or satisfaction; gratified; well adapted; appropriate; felicitous.[7]

Happiness is whatever individual political actors take it to be.[8]

To live happily I must be in harmony with the world. And that is what 'being happy' means.[9]

Happiness is a state of subjective well-being—an inner feeling of balance and contentment.[10]

When we say that someone is living happily, we imply that he has certain attitudes towards his life: he is very glad to be alive; he judges that on balance his deepest desires are being satisfied and that the circumstances of his life are turning out well.[11]

Happiness is composed of three related components: positive affect, absence of negative affect, and satisfaction with life as a whole.[12]

Happiness should be understood as being the result of a calculation. You appraise your circumstances and then compare these against what you had expected or wanted. The meaningful standard is just as important as the actual circumstance in deciding how happy you are.[13]

Happiness requires the having of a central purpose which guides one's life. It also requires that this purpose be end-specific, that it permit progressively increasing success, and that the individual find both joy and worth in this central task.[14]

These sound bites on happiness do not capture the range of musings on the subject. Like other fundamental terms such as "love," "justice," and "virtue," "happiness" has been used in numerous ways throughout recorded history. To proclaim one definition of happiness supreme begs the paramount questions—the definition we embrace will itself determine the answers to whether happiness is a great good, attainable by everyone, and embodied by the best lives. We could use our definition of "happiness" to chide critics: "You simply do not understand what happiness is. That to which you refer is not happiness. We know this because we have discovered the true meaning of the term." Dissenters to our views would be silenced through definitional fiat. This technique is common in rhetorical skirmishes, but unsatisfying for people trying to learn how best to live their lives: "I do not care what you call it, happiness or shampiness or zappiness, what I am describing is a great good. Why should I be silenced because you claim to have uncovered the only true, necessary and sufficient conditions of a term?"

Accordingly, I have no stake in convincing readers that only one, true meaning of "happiness" exists. The term has been and is used legitimately in numerous ways. Instead, I will explain and examine the major classical and contemporary understandings of "happiness." I will analyze the insights and deficiencies of each understanding. My purpose is not conceptual and technical, not an arid dissection of the literature for the glory of analytic technique. My purpose is practical: What understandings of happiness can help us lead better lives? Is happiness the greatest good under any of its versions? What is the relationship of happiness to meaningful lives, worthwhile lives, exemplary lives? And how, if at all, is happiness overrated?

A *theory* of happiness usually includes three parts. First, it *defines* happiness—it tells us what happiness is, of what it consists. Next, the theory provides a *recipe* for happiness—it tells us what activities, relationships, and experiences make us happy. Finally, the theory *explains* why and how certain activities, relationships, and experiences make us happy.

Some thinkers, occasionally philosophers, are content to advance and defend definitions of happiness. They define happiness, perhaps in terms of mental states, satisfied desires, or aspects of well-being, and stop. Social scientists and popular discussions of happiness focus more on recipes for happiness that instruct us on what things make us happy. Such theories are often accompanied by explanations that delve into why those things make us happy. Every recipe for happiness, though, must take at least an implicit position on a definition of happiness. How can someone inform us about what things will make us happy unless he or she assumes some notion of what happiness is?

I will assume that happiness requires a predominantly positive state of mind. To say "Rossi is almost always sad, anxious and depressed, but she sure is happy," gravely violates language. While contemporary theorists, particularly social scientists, generally take a predominantly positive state of mind as the definition of happiness—they assume that having a predominantly positive state of mind is both a necessary and sufficient condition of being happy—I will assume only that the requisite state of mind is necessary for happiness. My strategy is to avoid, to the extent possible, begging the question against those versions of happiness that require more than a positive state of mind. I do not want to claim such visions are wrong by definition. On the contrary, they often pave the way for distinguishing types of worthwhile happiness from less valuable forms of happiness.

## 1. HAPPINESS AS MORAL AND INTELLECTUAL VIRTUE

Socrates (470–399 BC) and Plato (428–347 BC) are linked historically and philosophically. Although Socrates did not publish, his teachings and character reverberate in the writings of his contemporaries and followers, particularly in the prolific works of Plato. Plato wrote in the dialogue form with Socrates as the main interlocutor.

Socrates emerges from Plato's portrayal as a man with firm moral convictions. We should never harm or wrong others regardless of what they did to us. To retaliate—to act from the vengeful philosophy of an eye for an eye—is both to add wrongly to the amount of evil in the universe and also to harm oneself. The just person has a balanced soul and is in harmony with the world. A balanced, harmonious soul results from the domination of reason over appetites and desires. We have numerous desires, but should act only on a select few. We have aggressive instincts, but should exert them only in appropriate amounts on proper occasions. Reason is the faculty of the soul that distinguishes worthy from unworthy desires and appropriate from inappropriate aggression. Only the nurturing of a balanced soul can ensure a healthy psyche. The immortal soul, not the mortal body, defines who we are.

Socrates insisted that no evil can befall a good person. If the soul possesses moral goodness it cannot be made to suffer evil. The gravest evils are not those which affect the body, such as murders, rapes, and tortures, but evils that corrupt the soul. Others cannot make a good person ignorant or vicious. Not even false imprisonment or lies that destroy one's well-earned, glowing reputation can corrupt the well-ordered soul. Yes, good people can be physically harmed, defamed, and suffer the degradations of poverty, poor health, and peer disapproval. But none of these can corrupt a well-ordered soul unless its bearer is a collaborator: No person, no matter how evil or unrelenting, can unilaterally destroy the moral and intellectual virtue exemplified by a harmonious soul.

Happiness consists of moral action flowing from a virtuous character, which presupposes a refined, dominant rational faculty of the soul. Happiness is not merely a positive, enduring, subjective feeling. Instead, happiness is moral and intellectual virtue, an objective condition of the soul.

To call happiness an objective condition in this context means that whether a person attains happiness is a fact, not just a matter of the person's belief. Under this view, I could believe I was happy, perhaps because my predominant state of mind was peaceful or joyful, but not be happy if my objective internal condition failed the Socratic-Platonic test. A parallel case would be a person who thinks she is healthy because she is energetic and enthusiastic, but who unknowingly suffers from a serious brain tumor. She thinks she is physically healthy, she feels healthy, but she is gravely ill.

Socrates and Plato reacted to what they perceived as the increasing materialism and acquisitiveness of their fellow Athenians. The race for material aggrandizement, personal honors, martial recognitions, and literary awards was dwarfing the search for truth and virtue. Traveling teachers known as the Sophists were extolling the art of rhetoric and techniques of persuasion above the journey towards truth.

Plato assumed all human beings desired happiness, although they perceived different ways to attain it. Some people identified the good with material acquisition and thought that attaining that goal would ensure happiness; others took gymnastics, pleasure, or philosophy as the good and devised different routes to happiness. For Plato, happiness is the life of virtue. Because virtue requires knowledge, wisdom, courage, temperance, and the pursuit of truth are crucial. The highest happiness, the type most closely united with the good, flows from exercising the highest part of the human soul in pursuit of knowledge and truth. The highest happiness, perhaps beyond the reach of all human beings, would emerge from the greatest knowledge and wisdom—going beyond mundane understandings of knowing how to do things and knowing that certain things are true, to wisely using philosophical examinations and ascending to an apprehension of the definitions and essences of all things and concepts. Socrates never takes himself to have climbed this high, nor does he find anyone who has. We can identify, then, degrees of Socratic-Platonic happiness based on the distance a person has traveled on the ladder of ever-increasing knowledge, wisdom, and virtue.

Plato argued that the proper objects of knowledge must be fixed, eternal, and intelligible.[15] He observed that we call many different things by the same name. For example, objects of different color, shape, size, and material are accurately called "desks." But what is it by virtue of which this can be done? Plato concluded there must be a Form of deskness just as there is a Form of lines. The Form of deskness is the essence, or defining characteristics, of desk. The Form of "desk" is whatever an object must embody to be a desk. Forms, or universals, give particular objects their being and permit us to recognize particular objects as what they are. Forms exist even if the particulars on earth which exemplify them do not exist, but the reverse is not true. Put differently, Forms preexist particular objects, particular objects partake of or participate in Forms, and this participation is the cause of the particular object being what it is.

Plato believed that the transcendent world of Forms constituted a reality higher than this world. To explain the diversity of particular things on earth, he stated that Forms are not merely abstract ideas; instead, they comprise the highest reality in a transcendent realm. The greatest Form is the Form of the Good which is the final and highest reality, the foundation of all other Forms and all particular things. Whereas our world is material, changeable, transient, flawed and particular, the transcendent world of Forms is immaterial, changeless, eternal, perfect and universal.

At times, Plato, influenced by Eastern theism through his predecessor Pythagoras, suggests that at death the soul travels to the transcendent world and apprehends the forms directly, without use of sense perception.[16] The soul, if pure, then either remains in the transcendent world or, if impure, transmigrates into another human or animal body. Once reunited with body the soul forgets the grand knowledge it gained in the transcendent world. Learning and education in this world then becomes a process of dimly remembering what the soul once knew vividly while in the world of Forms.

The parallels between Platonism and mainstream religions are clear. Replace the Form of the Good with an anthropomorphic God or the Absolute, substitute a version of heaven or Nirvana for Plato's transcendent world, spice up the Platonic soul with religious metaphors, and the compatibility between Plato and the great religions is striking. This is unsurprising because the mainstream religions and Plato's notions are fueled by the same human aspirations: yearnings for a final culmination, a connection to enduring value, and a rational, just cosmos.

An extended critique of Plato's metaphysics is beyond the scope of this inquiry. Introducing his theory of Forms, though, is crucial for understanding Plato's theory of human happiness. The Forms constitute the greatest knowledge and virtue, and thus link human beings to the greatest good.

Socrates and Plato define happiness as a harmony of the soul such that reason moderates and controls aggressive appetites and desires. Their recipe for happiness is primarily virtuous living. Because they so closely link virtue and knowledge, intellectual activity is also required, at least for the higher forms of happiness. Health, wealth, physical beauty, friends, love, honor, and the like—those things or relationships commonly identified as good—are not viewed by Socrates as inherently good. But they can be instrumentally good if they are used wisely to facilitate the quest for knowledge, truth, and virtue. None of these potentially instrumental goods, though, is necessary for happiness. Socrates and Plato explain why fulfilling this recipe will make us happy by appealing to dualism and destiny—human beings consist of a body and soul, but the soul defines who we are and its care is primary. Our earthly mission is to purify the soul in preparation for a disembodied afterlife. The Socratic-Platonic slogan that "philosophy is preparation for death" does not mean that philosophers are suicidal deviants, but that philosophy, understood as the cultivation of intellectual and moral virtues, best purifies the soul and prepares it for a higher destiny. Socrates and Plato represent an unyielding, unusual position: Moral and intellectual virtues are necessary and sufficient for happiness. At first blush, the position is preposterous. Are we guaranteed happiness through moral and intellectual virtues? Are moral and intellectual virtues required for happiness? If we take a positive, subjective psychological state—extended joy, contentment, exuberance, or peace—as necessary for happiness, the Socratic account is unpersuasive. Imagine a moral and intellectual paragon who suffers greatly from debilitating illness, the slings and arrows of outrageous fortune, disastrous relationships, and extreme maliciousness of peers. Draw this picture as bleakly and starkly as you are able. (Voltaire's *Candide* may help.) How can such a beleaguered soul be happy? Do we not reach a point where the moral and intellectual virtues are insufficient ballast for happiness?

Analyzed from another angle, that moral and intellectual virtues are necessary for happiness is also doubtful. Imagine someone who falls far short of a moral and intellectual paragon, but who enjoys robust health, uncommon good luck, satisfying relationships, and lavish honors from peers. Draw this picture as vividly and extravagantly as you are able. Must such a fortunate pilgrim be unhappy? Does he or she not reach a point where extremely good fortune, adaptation to one's environment, and personal success carry the day and produce happiness regardless of moral and intellectual deficiencies?

Achieving the Socratic-Platonic conception of happiness, then, does not guarantee that a person will be predominantly joyful, peaceful, or exuberant; nor is attaining a balanced, harmonious soul required to attain those states of mind.

Socrates and Plato, however, are not out of philosophical ammunition. First, they could argue that my objections miss the mark. I am explicitly taking a positive, subjective psychological state—extended joy, contentment, exuberance, or peace—as at least necessary for happiness. They understand happiness as an objective condition of the soul. Why should we be surprised that the account of Socrates and Plato does not fulfill criteria appropriate to a different understanding of happiness? Viewed in this light, my objections are irrelevant to their account.

This response is powerful, but invites further questions. Have Socrates and Plato ruled critics out of order by definitional fiat only? Have they provided an account of happiness that is unpersuasive to contemporary users of the term? Even if happiness is an objective condition of the soul, cannot that condition be undermined by extremely adverse states of affairs? Finally, if all Socrates and Plato mean by happiness is "moral and intellectual virtues," then why even use the term? Why not simply proselytize for more and better moral and intellectual virtues among people? What is added by calling this happiness? Are not Socrates and Plato tacitly smuggling in the praiseworthy and highly desired qualities of happiness—those flowing from enduring, positive psychological states—while simultaneously denying the need for those subjective qualities in the definition of happiness?

Second, a defender of the Socratic and Platonic position could argue that I have misconstrued that account from the outset. Even for Socrates, moral and intellectual virtues are not always enough to shield people from the degradations and indignities that render life no longer worth living. To burden Socrates with the position that if people are morally and intellectually virtuous then they must be happy is uncharitable, unnecessary, and misguided. Socrates and Plato were keenly aware that morally and intellectually virtuous people could be harmed in countless ways other than the corruption of their souls. Granted, such harms are physical, and therefore lesser wrongs than corruptions of the soul, but they nevertheless jeopardize happiness.

Maybe. But the clear direction of Socrates' philosophy is to privilege the soul over the body, to stress the immortality of the soul, to insist that the soul is constitutive of personal identity, to underscore that mental and moral pursuits are paramount to well-being, to advise human beings to rise above the vicissitudes and material fortunes of the world. Although defenders of Socrates may have a point, his instruction is unequivocal: Virtuous sufferers of the world's harshest tribulations can, indeed *should*, maintain the felicitous condition of their souls. If his defenders are correct, then Socrates must be relying on a subjective element in his definition of happiness. Such reliance does not coalesce easily with general Socratic principles.

Third, Socrates and Plato could challenge my suggestion that people falling far short of moral and intellectual paragons can be happy. They were firmly convinced that such people are slaves to their appetites and desires. The unjust soul is unhealthy due to internal disharmony. Unjust people are not happy regardless of external appearances that suggest otherwise. In the same way that physically unhealthy people may seem healthy to their acquaintances, unhealthy souls cannot always be detected by the naked eye. Injustice, nevertheless, manifests an illness that is never in the interests of the perpetrator. Justice is always in our interests because it manifests and nurtures the health of our souls. A person's health, whether physical or spiritual, is an objective condition not subject to popular plebiscite.

Socrates and Plato are correct if we are assessing a thoroughly and morally depraved, intellectually bankrupt tyrant. Most such people are unlikely to be happy. Their excesses are themselves often attributable to their unhappiness and inability to adapt to their social environments. Even their episodic satisfactions evaporate quickly. Socrates and Plato are less convincing if we are assessing the vast majority of human beings who are neither moral paragons nor unrepentant tyrants. That people can be reasonably happy while falling far short of being moral and intellectual paragons remains plausible. Consult your own lives and those of your peers.

Accordingly, that relentless commitment to moral and intellectual virtues is necessary and sufficient for happiness that requires an enduring, positive, subjective psychological state, such as extended joy, contentment, exuberance, or peace, is highly doubtful. Socrates and Plato, however, highlight numerous features of the relationship of happiness to value:

- Happiness is desired for its own sake, not for the sake of anything else.
- The direct pursuit of pleasure, a project later called hedonism, cannot be the greatest good.
- Different pleasures can be ranked in terms of quality, quantity, intensity, duration, and purity.
- Happiness must be connected to moral and intellectual virtues if it is to embody maximum value.
- Happiness that embodies maximum value must be more than merely an enduring, positive, subjective psychological state, such as extended joy, contentment, exuberance, or peace.
- Although passions for justice, knowledge, truth, and virtues have no excess, moderating the passions is often a reliable path to happiness.
- To achieve a happiness that embodies maximum value we must enjoy and use other goods wisely.

Such lessons will appear throughout my discussions of historical renderings of happiness. They are conclusions about happiness suggested by the discussions that precede them. I do not claim to have proved them with deductive certainty at the time they first appear. Additional analysis of the most important lessons continues throughout the work. The lessons we may draw from the work of Socrates and Plato on happiness are crucial. If happiness is to embody maximum value, if happiness is to be a great good, special attention must be paid to how it is connected to other values. The mere presence of joy, contentment, exuberance, or peace is often considered happiness. But such happiness need not be a great good, depending upon the way it was attained, the activities to which it is connected, the degree of meaningfulness of the life to which it attaches, and its general relationship to value. This ancient wisdom, often ignored in petty, technical disputes over the proper definition of happiness, endures. It suggests reasons, which I will examine later, why happiness understood in the popular, contemporary fashion is over-rated.

## 2. HAPPINESS AS FLOURISHING

Aristotle (384–322 BC) understood happiness as an activity of the soul in accord with excellence.[17] He heralded happiness as the greatest good because it is desired for its own sake, not desired for the sake of anything else, and the end toward which all other goods aim.

> If, then, there is some end of the things we do, which we desire for its own sake (everything else being desired for the sake of this), and if we do not choose everything for the sake of something else (for at that rate the process would go on to infinity, so that our desire would be empty and vain), clearly this must be the good and the chief good . . . there is very general agreement; for both the general run of men and people of superior refinement say that it is happiness, and identify living well and faring well with being happy.[18]

Aristotle was firmly convinced that we need a greatest good to prevent an infinite logical regress. If we desired X because it produced Y, and desired Y because it produced Z, and desired Z because it produced A, and so on, an infinite regress would occur: an unending series of partial causal descriptions from which no ultimate explanation emerges. Happiness prevents a vicious infinite regress because it stands as the ultimate explanation that accounts for the chain of human desires. As the end toward which all other goods and desires aim, happiness is the greatest good.

As an activity, happiness (*eudaemonia*) is not merely a state or disposition. While Socrates and Plato were dualists whose philosophies were constructed from the premise that immortal souls were distinct from and superior to mortal bodies, Aristotle was not. He took souls to be inseparable from bodies. Achieving happiness, then, requires, among other things, fulfilling the needs of the body.

Aristotle's epistemology is connected to his rejection of mind-body dualism. He rejects the transcendent world of Platonic Forms, but accepts Plato's view of knowledge grounded in Forms. For Aristotle the universal notion of desk, for example, is extracted by the human mind as the essence, or common qualities, observed in numerous particular desks. The qualities all these particulars share by virtue of which they can legitimately be called desks comprise the universal notion of desk. No Form of desk, however, resides in a transcendent world. The existence of numerous particular desks in this world is necessary and sufficient for the existence of the universal notion of desk.

Aristotle argued that happiness consisted of living well and faring well. Living well consists of understanding and acting on the intellectual and moral virtues: wisdom, understanding, prudence, temperance, generosity. The recurrent Greek themes and metaphors of moderation, harmony, striking the proper chord, and knowing the appropriate measure animate Aristotle's conviction that living well requires virtuous activity in accordance with the Doctrine of the Mean: understanding virtues generally as means lying between two extremes. For example, if we are extremely aggressive and adventuresome we will be foolhardy, if we are insufficiently aggressive and adventuresome we will be timid and cowardly, and if we are appropriately aggressive and adventuresome we will be courageous.

Virtues, though, are not always found halfway between extremes; the mean need not be located at the same point for each person; and some virtues are not means between extremes at all. For example, murders and betrayals are always wrong. Exemplifying virtues also involves a disposition to choose according to a rule embodied by those of practical moral wisdom, the judgment of the enlightened. The contemplative life, one embracing the intellectual and moral virtues, is more self-sufficient, leisurely, pleasant, and happy than other lives because it is devoted to the highest objects of human concern.

Faring well consists of a host of practical factors: a measure of material well-being, a congenial family life, friends, leisure time for contemplation, freedom, health, and a not repulsive physical appearance. Like Socrates and Plato, Aristotle thought that a well-ordered, stable state was necessary to provide the opportunities and preconditions for happiness.

> [Happiness] needs the external goods as well; for it is impossible, or not easy, to do noble acts without the proper equipment. In many actions we use friends and riches and political power as instruments; and there are some things the lack of which takes the luster from happiness—good birth, goodly children, beauty; for the man who is very ugly in appearance or ill-born or solitary and childless is not very likely to be happy, and perhaps a man would be still less likely if he had thoroughly bad children or friends or had lost good children or friends by death . . . happiness seems to need this sort of prosperity . . . for which reason some identify happiness with good fortune, though others identify it with virtue.[19]

This version of Aristotle's *eudaemonia* is *inclusive*: it consists of rational contemplation, the moral virtues, and the conditions of faring well. At times,

Aristotle seemingly conjures an *exclusive* version of *eudaemonia*, one consisting only of rational contemplation.[20] Aristotle concluded that theoretical reason is the most distinctive and highest part of the human soul; that the objects of theoretical reason such as philosophical analysis, mathematical and logical principles, and scientific truths are eternal and thus embody highest value; and that the objective yearning for knowledge is more self-sufficient than even the activity of moral virtue because we can rationally contemplate in solitude, while exercising moral virtue requires other people.

I interpret the exclusive version of *eudaemonia* not as a rival to the inclusive version, but as an expression of Aristotle's veneration of and preference for rational contemplation and the intellectual virtues. The inclusive version defines happiness. But the highest activities, the most self-sufficient life, the most valuable objects of human concern center on rational contemplation. A person could be supremely happy if he or she could focus exclusively on rational contemplation, but human beings are social animals—we require moral virtues and the conditions of faring well to achieve *eudaemonia* in our collective context. Accordingly, no inconsistency need be found between the inclusive and exclusive descriptions of *eudaemonia*.

By functioning effectively in our world, along intellectual, moral, and practical dimensions, we will find happiness. But not all of us. Women and slaves, for Aristotle, lacked the requisite rational capability, freedom, leisure time, and material well-being for happiness. Most males were tethered to manual labor, which Aristotle thought desensitized the soul, impaired contemplative possibilities, limited leisure time, and prevented civic participation. Accordingly, Aristotle thought women, slaves, and most males could not be happy because they lacked, by virtue of their social positions or natures, the necessary intellectual ability or the conditions for faring well. Although we typically judge spans of life as happy or unhappy, Aristotle insists that happiness is most appropriately judged over an entire lifetime.

For Aristotle happiness is neither a mood nor an emotion. Instead, it is an objective condition that arises from leading a certain type of life. Under this view, it often makes sense to say, "Jane thinks she is leading a happy life, but she is not." Aristotelian happiness involves judgments about a person's success in obtaining the most valuable aspects of life. Because happiness is not merely a truthful report of a person's current or predominant state of mind, Jane could *feel* happy even though she was mistaken about what was most valuable and whether she had achieved it. Under these circumstances, Jane would think that she was happy, while she was in fact unhappy in Aristotelian terms.

Aristotle's definition of happiness is living well and faring well: having and exercising the moral and intellectual virtues, while enjoying a measure of material, worldly, and personal success. His recipe for happiness includes attaining, or at least approximating, wisdom, understanding, prudence, temperance, and generosity, while benefiting from a congenial home life, friends, leisure time, freedom, health, an acceptable physical appearance, and material prosperity. Aristotle explains how and why achieving this recipe makes us happy by referring to our *telos*—our natural goal based on our distinctive human function: Because of our biological constitution we are fulfilled only through the requisite intellectual and moral activities, exercised within a successful social context.

Aristotle's account of happiness differs from Plato's in several respects. For Plato, as I have interpreted him, virtue is necessary and sufficient for happiness, while for Aristotle virtue is only necessary for happiness. Plato's view of happiness has a decidedly mystical and otherworldly quality. Human life well lived is preparation for a better, enduring existence in a transcendent world. A human soul, purified by conviction and action energized by moral and intellectual virtues, is freed from the shackles of the body at death. Because the soul is immortal it elevates to the other world, where through apprehension of the Form of the Good, it attains boundless happiness. Socrates' statement that the philosopher's life is preparation for death expresses concisely how the afterlife prolongs and perfects happiness. Plato casts a suspicious eye toward our world, citing its transitoriness, imperfections, and perishability. While this world must prepare us for the next and can yield a faint image of reality, only the transcendental world of Forms offers Reality, Goodness, and ultimate Happiness. Rejecting Plato's mind-body dualism, Aristotle's *eudaemonia* applies to this world and is attainable only by a few.

Although Aristotle's position was hotly contested by medieval Arabic, Jewish, and Latin philosophers, he seems to have rejected personal immortality. Accordingly, Aristotle does not appeal to another world nor can he identify ultimate Happiness with a transcendent Form. Such Forms are eternal, fixed, immutable, and nonmaterial. Aristotelian happiness requires activity of the soul, while Forms are inactive. For Aristotle, the soul's mysterious process of apprehending immutable Forms is not active enough.

Plato described the human soul as having three parts: reason, spirit, and desire. He viewed desire and reason as warring elements whose conflicting demands threatened internal harmony. A well-ordered soul required the triumph of reason over the other elements. Aristotle perceived a deeper problem: Desire and reason could not be polar opposites because acting on the demands of reason requires motivation. Aristotle rejected the Platonic doctrine that virtue is knowledge, that if human beings knew the good they would pursue it. Reason, taken by itself, is insufficient. Knowing the right course of action is not enough to pursue that action. We must be motivated—have the requisite desires—to act on our knowledge. Thus, for Aristotle, reason and desire are, at best, complementary, not contradictory.

Assessing Aristotle's *eudaemonia* is tricky. We easily slip into the quicksand of anachronism and ahistoricism. Given our contemporary, popular usage of "happiness" as extended joy, contentment, exuberance, or peace, Aristotle's conception of happiness as human flourishing seems odd.

Aristotle's convictions about the intellectual inferiority of women, slaves, and manual laborers can be quickly dismissed. Throughout history, the favored classes have rationalized the subordination of disenfranchised peoples by claiming, often in good faith but with poor science, that the underclasses are mentally deficient and thus their plight is mandated by nature. That Aristotle falls prey to this ruse is unfortunate, but this should not prevent us from appreciating the insights about happiness his work contains.

He also fails to address adequately the tragedy of human life and its relationship to happiness. Why are we born to suffer and die? Socrates and Plato provided an answer that related to ultimate happiness: This life, if lived well, is preparation for the dissolution of the soul from the body, the rise of the immortal soul to a transcendental world of Forms, and its experience of eternal bliss as the soul apprehends the Form of the Good. We die because the dissolution of the soul from the body is a necessary part of the process. We suffer because the soul's union with a body brings forth physical debilities. We need not suffer the greatest harms, those that corrupt the soul, unless we are collaborators. Leading a good life, then, moderates our suffering. Regardless of whether readers today find this account persuasive, Socrates and Plato understood that explanations of why we suffer and die, and how the tragedies of life relate to human happiness, are important. Aristotle rejects the dualism of mind-body and the immortality of the soul, but fails to provide the explanations we seek about suffering, death, and their relationship to happiness. Instead, he offers a picture of a middle-class, male citizen who enjoys leisure, contemplation, civic participation, relatively good luck, and congenial social and family relations. Still, we wonder, how are suffering and death related, if at all, to happiness?

Aristotle derives his notions of the human good from his conviction that human beings have a fixed nature, a *telos*. He evaluates the claims we lodge about our happiness in accordance with normative standards grounded on our fixed human natures. Whether such a *telos* exists, though, is highly contestable. Much of what seems fixed and natural is merely historically typical. The nineteenth-century masters of suspicion, Friedrich Nietzsche, Karl Marx, and Sigmund Freud, demonstrated how historically grounded social needs could give rise to a structure of rewards that nurtured particular behaviors that could become so common that they seemed natural, appropriate, even inevitable. By forgetting the contingent social needs that energized the behaviors, we could wrongly conclude that we were observing part of a fixed human nature.

Moreover, even if human beings do have a fixed human nature the normative consequences are unclear. A common argument against an action charges that it is unnatural, against human nature. The term "natural," however, admits several interpretations: what is statistically usual; statistically frequent; statistically possible; accomplished without human interference; and what is in accord with an entity's essential characteristics. None of these interpretations, however, establishes that an unnatural act is necessarily or generally wrong. Notions dependent upon statistical normalcy or statistical possibility, for example, lack necessary moral significance: The mere fact that human beings routinely or often engage in an act does not necessarily imply that the act embodies moral merit, nor does it necessarily imply that contrary actions are immoral. *A fortiori*, the fact that humans can engage in an act does not establish the act's moral credentials: Not everything an entity can do naturally is necessarily moral. Likewise, an interpretation such as "accomplished without human interference" is unhelpful. Numerous morally appropriate actions do require human agency, and numerous actions that are not generated by human agency are either without moral significance or are morally inappropriate.

A more promising interpretation of "natural" is "what is in accord with an entity's essential characteristics and what facilitates an entity's progress toward its rightful purpose." In this vein, sometimes the term "natural" is invoked tautologically to mean "what is right": Conferring the honorific title "natural" on an action becomes trivial for purposes of *determining* the action's moral merit because "natural" becomes just another way of *saying* "morally sound."

Most plausibly, the term "natural" is invoked functionally: Because an act is compatible with essential human characteristics and purposes it is natural, and because it is natural the act is morally sound. Nevertheless, this interpretation is fraught with grave difficulties. Natural laws, at best, merely describe events in the universe, but they bear no necessary moral significance: Even if it could be established that an act is "unnatural" it does not necessarily follow that the act is immoral. Moreover, attempts to bridge the descriptive and the normative depend invariably on a specialized picture of human nature, on a full account of the proper human *telos*, and on a particular rendering of the genesis of objective morality. These notions, themselves, rest on suspicious metaphysical underpinnings and, often, on question-begging assumptions. Thus, the term "natural" is most often used in conclusory fashion to express an antecedently held condemnation of a practice, rather than as a conceptual tool for *arriving* at a normative judgment. Furthermore, claims of "naturalness" often commit the error of reductionism by wrongly postulating that an action, for example sex, has only one permissible function or behavioral manifestation. Too often, such reductionism does not mirror the imperatives of an alleged objective morality, but the narrow conditioning and historical taboos of a particular culture. Accordingly, accusations of "unnaturalness" expose themselves as feckless analytic instruments for deriving normative conclusions. Aristotle's appeal to a fixed human *telos* as the link between happiness and value is less persuasive today than it was when Aristotle wrote.

A more pressing question remains: Would Aristotle's living well and faring well be enough for happiness if they did not bring the expected sense of extended joy, contentment, exuberance, or peace? Imagine showing someone that they embodied the prescribed intellectual and moral virtues, and the conditions for faring well. Suppose the person agreed but still insisted, "But I am not happy." If we respond "Oh, you are happy, you just don't know it," our words are odd. If I don't know that I am happy, how can I be happy?

Aristotle downplays the experience of happiness and, instead, favors happiness as a condition of the self. He is open to the charge that his flourishing is better understood as praiseworthy moral and intellectual activity punctuated with a fair amount of luck in practical matters. Without the appropriate state of mind, experience, or feelings, however, achieving Aristotle's condition of the self fails to capture the internal response necessary for happiness.

Few modern language users agree with Aristotle's conception of happiness as human flourishing. That a person could meet and know they met all the conditions of flourishing yet be predominantly sad or agitated is clear. Thus, that happiness, in the modern sense, is simply meeting a set of external conditions is unlikely. Aristotle severs happiness from feelings and attitudes, instead defining it in terms of meeting objective conditions. He also rules out from the start all possibility of the nonvirtuous being happy. Thus, for Aristotle, happiness is not a state of mind, but an evaluation of a person's life with regard to virtue, intellect, and the circumstances of faring well. Although meeting Aristotle's list increases our chances for happiness, functioning effectively or flourishing is not always enough. The moral of the story? An appropriate subjective response, a conscious condition—whether sustained joy, contentment, exuberance, or peace—is also necessary for happiness.

But are extended joy and pleasure, regardless of how they are attained, enough for happiness? Is extended joy even required for happiness? Could lingering contentment and overall satisfaction that lack apparent joy define happiness?

Remember, though, that happiness has numerous, legitimate historical meanings and usages. I am not seeking the essence of happiness as depicted in a Platonic transcendental world. I am not trying to discover the only true meaning of happiness. Such a meaning does not exist. Instead, I aspire to understand the relationship of different conceptions of happiness to value: What, if any, understanding of happiness connects it to significant value? Can happiness, in any sense, be the greatest human good? Is happiness in the contemporary sense of extended joy, contentment, exuberance, or peace overrated and overvalued? What kind of happiness is worth pursuing? How might we attain it?

Aristotle's *eudaemonia* inspires a rich tradition of answers to such questions. Aristotle crams everything that is inherently valuable, everything that is sought for its own sake, into his definition of *eudaemonia*. He also includes in that definition numerous practical goods that are instrumentally valuable to our exercise of the moral and intellectual virtues. While we would expect that most people who attain Aristotle's recipe for *eudaemonia* would also enjoy a predominantly positive state of mind, some people would not. Accordingly, Aristotle's *eudaemonia* is understood better as describing human well-being or human flourishing, instead of human happiness. Discussing Aristotle's *eudaemonia* yields the following lessons on the relationship of happiness and value:

- The only happiness worth pursuing must be connected to human good.
- A happiness worth pursuing requires more than extended joy, contentment, exuberance, or peace.
- A happiness worth pursuing shapes our entire lives.
- The character, behavior, and lifestyle that cause positive psychological states are paramount.
- Thus, a person's positive psychological state, how a person feels, cannot itself define a happiness worth pursuing.
- All claims to a happiness linked to human good must be evaluated: A person's good-faith self-report is insufficient.

- Such appraisals examine a person's character and social actions.
- Desirable psychological states are most valuable when they flow from the proper character, appropriate thought, and social action.

Aristotle's teachings reinforce the wisdom that subjective satisfactions can be wrongfully induced; that claims to a happiness linked to human good require normative appraisal; that such a happiness is a recommended lifestyle, not merely a description of how a person has lived; and that only a relatively stable, praiseworthy character embodies the dispositions necessary for the good life. Finally, Aristotle unsettles our confidence in our own efforts: Good fortune, or at least the absence of grave misfortune, is also required. Our happiness is not fully under our control. Whether Aristotle is correct about this and, if so, what consequences follow, are questions I will address throughout.

## 3. HAPPINESS AS RADICAL ASCETICISM

Antisthenes (445–360 BC) and Diogenes (400–325 BC), the most important Cynics, advanced one of the most extreme views of happiness on record. They admired, maybe too much, Socrates' linkage of virtue and happiness. The Cynics declared that pleasure is evil. We should resist our appetites and desires. We should pursue virtue, the greatest and only good. Virtue is attained by minimizing, even extinguishing, passion. We should nurture negative freedoms: freedom from need, want, desire, personal and social success, material well-being, and societal connections. Radical asceticism requires self-control, poverty, and the repudiation of societal conformity. Personal redemption is earned by internal discipline. Societal conformity, especially, is evil. We should dismiss conventional morality, patriotism, pursuit of wealth, courtesies and refinements, fame, honor, reputation, sexuality, and everything else reeking with the stench of social creation. Parting company with Socrates and Plato, the Cynics even regarded art, science, the pursuit of knowledge, and family relations matters of indifference. Cynics took refuge in the legend of Hercules, who symbolized overcoming burdens and labors through free, independent, self-fulfilling action.

The Cynics advocate such a thin program of action—triumph over desire and resistance to social conventions—that we might well wonder what activities riveted their concern. Granted, contemporary Americans often need to simplify their lives, but Cynics somberly turn the screws on this insight. How did they kill the day?

Some Cynics did have a madcap side:

> The Cynics set out deliberately to attract attention by shocking the middle classes. This was harder to do then than now, for the Greeks were sophisticated and tolerant. However, Diogenes managed. He masturbated publicly, remarking to spectators that he wished he could assuage his hunger for food by rubbing his belly. When Plato's Academy, laboring to define Man, produced the formula 'featherless biped,' Diogenes plucked a chicken and threw it into the lecture hall. It was he who went around with a lantern at midday, saying that he was looking for an honest man.[21]

In contrast to conventional norms and rules, the Cynics embraced tightly the Greek concept of natural law: Embedded in the universe are moral laws dictated by Reason itself. Natural laws are allegedly valid for everyone, everywhere, at all times. Societal understandings are artificial human creations contaminated by class interests, the effects of power struggles, uninformed passions, and wishful thinking.

The Cynics, though, were drawn to another version of natural behavior: what human beings are instinctively inclined to pursue freed from societal restraints. The two notions—universal moral laws embedded in the universe and our instinctive inclinations—do not easily coalesce. Surely, not all of our instinctive inclinations conform to moral imperatives.

What could lead people to a wildly counterintuitive view such as Cynicism? A fundamentally antisocial attitude is a good start. A person must be deeply alienated from the norms, customs, and institutions of his or her dominant social order. A thorough distrust of desires, particularly physical and material appetites, also helps. A limited sense of possibility, world-weariness, and a rugged individualism fuel the journey. A dose of self-loathing probably does not hurt.

The Cynics defined happiness as purity of the soul. Their recipe for happiness was nurturing virtue and self-sufficiency through austerity and self-discipline. Cynics explained that fulfilling this recipe leads to happiness because only thereby would our souls be in tune with the natural laws of the universe.

Cynicism, unsurprisingly, was never an influential school of thought and practice. Its demands were too severe, its joys lacked intensity, its effects were too divisive. The admirable individualism of the lone wolf too easily degenerates into the hostility of estrangement and the darkness of isolation. The policies that pleasure is evil and our desires are enemies can neither animate our spirits nor motivate our actions. As a theory and practice that large numbers could not adopt even in principle—as doing so would destroy cultures and civilizations—Cynicism is self-consciously pitched only to the few whose temperaments, social station, and prospects impel them to desperate measures. Cynicism is offered as an antidote to the maladies of a licentious society. But most people must find the cure stunningly worse than the supposed disease. Sincerity of belief is small consolation for an impoverished soul.

Aside from the dangers of fanaticism and the horrors of extreme self-denial, what lessons can we draw from the Cynics?

- Matters of personal concern such as our outlook on life are in our control. We have limited or no control over matters of social concern.
- The internal ordering of our own psyches should be our primary project.
- Norms that are merely conventional bear dubious authority.
- Self-discipline is necessary for the good life.
- A worthwhile happiness must be connected to value and virtue.

Cynicism accepted and refashioned some of the Socratic and Platonic legacy. What endures in Cynicism can be traced back to that legacy. Other philosophies, more powerful than Cynicism, such as Christian asceticism, Stoicism, and Epicureanism would further refine this legacy and shake the Greco-Roman world.


## 4. HAPPINESS AS HEDONISM

Aristippus (435–366 BC) was one of the earliest hedonists. He observed that the future is uncertain, while our subjective sensations are immediately knowable. Subjective sensations are the criterion for practical conduct. The goal of such conduct is pleasure. Bodily pleasures are superior to mental pleasures because they are more immediate, certain, knowable, intense, and powerful. Taking no account of the quality of different pleasures, Aristippus was not a toady to abstraction and intellectual contemplation. Even friends are only instrumentally valuable: Intense concern for the other is unwise because our access to their feelings is indirect, sketchy, and fallible.

Aristippus, who lived in Cyrene, and his followers comprised the Cyrenaic version of hedonism. Having been influenced by Socrates, the Cyrenaics cautioned that wise people should avoid unrestrained excess in their pursuit of

pleasure. Proper judgment is required to evaluate competing desires and pleasures. Short-term pleasure can lead to long-term pain. Despite their basic
disposition to distrust appeals to the future as uncertain, indirect, and speculative, the Cyrenaics conceded that proper judgment required evaluations
about the long-term effects of actions. These two inclinations coalesced uneasily. The Cyrenaics tacitly admitted that wise people were distinguished from
foolish people in part on the basis of their ability to evaluate the unknown.

Cyrenaic hedonism contained the seeds of its own destruction. We cannot
simply pursue physical and material pleasures. We must evaluate, probabilis-
tically, long-term effects. This evaluation, however, appeals to criteria other
than quantity of bodily pleasures. The unrestrained pleasure-seeker meets the
fate of Plato's tyrant: Immersed in the quicksand of ever-increasing desires,
the tyrant is never content and only sporadically satisfied. Cyrenaic hedonism
is insufficient and must look outside itself for guidance.

Worse, Cyrenaic hedonism failed to understand how the tragedy of life
provides opportunities for meaning and value. Pain and suffering are to be
avoided, not transformed into practical advantage. Given that in the world
they knew, perhaps the world as it has always been, most people suffer more
pain than experience enduring pleasure, Cyrenaic hedonism transmitted
implicitly a pessimistic message. If pleasure is the greatest good, if a life in
which pleasure predominates is inaccessible to most of us, what hope
remains?

Under a follower of Aristippus, Hegesias, the dark side of Cyrenaic hedonism, which had hitherto lain dormant, emerged.

[Hegesias] held that since pleasure is the good, no life is good on balance, for
pain always predominates in the long run. Therefore, the rational hedonist will
kill himself. Hegesias expounded this thesis with such eloquence that the
authorities found it necessary to suppress his lectures after many of his auditors
had committed suicide. Hegesias himself, we are told, lived to be a very old
man.[22]

Epicureanism was a more influential version of hedonism. Epicurus (341–
270 BC) and Lucretius (95–52 BC) were the most important Epicurean philosophers.[23] Liberating human beings from fear and maximizing their
prospects for happiness motivated Epicurus. Unlike the Cynics, he viewed
pleasure, which defined happiness, as the greatest good. But not just any
pleasure, only simple, sustainable ones. Worthy pleasures, those that define
happiness, do not include the tortured trinity of wine, women or men, and

song. The best pleasures preclude pain and produce a serene spirit. Epicurus's recipe for happiness was health, self-control, independence, moderation, simplicity, cheerfulness, friendship, prudence, intellectual and aesthetic values, and peace of mind. The calm, tranquil, harmonious life is the happy life. He explained why this is so by appealing to the conditions of the world, to human nature, and to natural law.

Epicurus devised a powerful strategy. First, he identified the beliefs and actions that caused human beings unnecessary pain and suffering: fear of the gods, anxiety about death and an afterlife, and the pursuit of self-defeating pleasures. Then, he reimagined and recreated a vision of human life that eliminated the main causes of human pain and suffering. Finally, he and his followers embodied and acted on this vision and drew supporters attracted to the charismatic exemplars of the Epicurean lifestyle.

If fear of the gods is a problem then what is the solution? Epicurus might have simply denied that gods exist: No gods, no fear. This solution, though, would have been unpersuasive to a Greco-Roman world that acknowledged and paid tribute to numerous, anthropomorphic deities with carefully circumscribed spheres of influence. Besides, Epicurus, uninformed by the nineteenth-century masters of suspicion whom he predated by over a millennium, was convinced that the universal belief in the gods could be explained only by their objective reality. The gods, then, existed.

Anticipating an enduring theological problem, Epicurus was puzzled by the amount of evil and suffering in the world. How could such enormous, unexplainable evil persist if divine providence ruled? Epicurus concluded that divine providence was a myth, a misunderstanding of the nature of the gods. Although the gods existed, the nature of their existence differed from the prevalent understanding. Epicurus brought forth the good news that the real nature of the existence of the gods should not engender fear. The gods existed as beautiful, happy, calm, merry, and indifferent to human life. The gods, fortuitously, are Epicureans! Indeed, they serve as divine ideals for the proper human life. Accordingly, human beings should not fear the gods because the gods do not punish or reward us. Instead, we should look to the lives of the gods as exemplars toward which to strive while on earth.

Having eliminated to his satisfaction the fear of gods, Epicurus took on his next target: fear of death and an afterlife. He observed that fear of death and anxiety over an afterlife disabled numerous human beings from full engagement in this world. Such suffering was unnecessary and grounded on philosophical errors.

Epicurus rejected mind-body dualism and belief in personal immortality.

Subscribing to the atomic theory developed by the pre-Socratic philosopher, Democritus (460–370 BC), Epicurus argued that the world is eternal and composed of atoms that produce everything by their infinitely variable combinations. Each human being is composed of atoms which dissolve entirely after the death of the body. No afterlife waits us.

Epicurus held that death is not an evil. He argued that death is irrelevant to us. For Epicurus, all good and evil consists in sensations: Pleasure is good, pain is evil. Death, however, is the end of all sensations, so death is nothing to us. We have no good reason to fear what is nothing to us.

Having eliminated to their satisfaction the fear of death and an afterlife, Epicureans took on their final target: dissatisfaction caused by pursuit of self-defeating pleasures. Epicurus, following the Socratic-Platonic tradition, disparaged physical and material pleasures as enslaving: The more we get, the more we want *ad infinitum*. We too easily become addicted to pleasures over which we have too little control and which jeopardize a well-ordered, harmonious internal condition. Such pleasures produce, at best, transitory pleasure that transforms into more enduring suffering. Epicurus, though, goes further. He disputes several of the projects that Aristotle thought necessary for *eudaemonia*. Epicurus observed that politics, marriage, family relations, and most passionate pursuits too often produced anxiety and ended badly. Avoiding pain, especially mental suffering, is even more important than pursuing pleasure. The absence of passion facilitates contentment. We must discard many of our desires or, at least, not act on them. The Epicurean program is explicitly for personal development, an egoistic hedonism grounded in withdrawal from public life.

'Live unknown' was the Epicurean motto—excellent advice no doubt, especially in so turbulent a period. One ought to abstain not only from politics and other ways of perhaps fatally attracting attention, but from sex also: 'Sexual intercourse never did anyone any good, and a man is lucky if it has not harmed him.' It is better not to marry and have children, for families are constant sources of anxiety. You should not overeat or drink much, for fear of indigestion and hangover. Epicurus deemed a little bread and cheese to constitute a banquet . . . 'plain living and moderately high thinking.'[24]

I will examine each part of the Epicurean strategy in turn. First, Epicurus's depiction of the gods. That universal belief in deities does not imply such deities exist is clear. Freudian, Marxist, and Nietzschean, as well as numerous other, explanations for the nearly universal belief in deities are available. But if gods do exist in the Epicurean fashion, their indifference to human life may not be consoling. Belief in divine providence, at least, provides human beings opportunities to earn the gods' favor. If the gods' responses correlate to our actions—if they respond to us in accord with our deserts—we have control over our fate. At least we have a fate. If the gods are indifferent to us and serve only as Epicurean exemplars, we lose hope along with the loss of fear. If the gods act providentially but capriciously, sometimes returning evil for our good deeds, Epicurus's point is sharper. But another alternative was available to him: gods who act toward human beings only in accord with retributive justice, perhaps tempered by mercy. Such gods model behavior appropriate for all of us and permit us to retain our hope.

The problem, though, for Epicurus is not merely one of strategy. The amount and nature of evil in the world precludes divine providence, but Epicurus was not an atheist. His belief in gods indifferent to human affairs was in good faith. The success of Epicureanism as a way of life—it ran a distant second to Stoicism as the dominant philosophy in the Greco-Roman world for four centuries—suggests that belief in nonprovidential gods was a reasonable possibility in Epicurus's historical context. Robust commitment to atheism was less possible. The power of monotheistic Judeo-Christianity would emerge later, co-opt some features of Epicureanism and Stoicism, and marginalize much of those philosophies.

The Epicurean view of death, however, is unpersuasive. Both Epicurus and Lucretius accept a hedonistic assumption: The sensations of pleasure and pain define what is good and bad for us. This assumption is unacceptable. We are sometimes harmed by events because they violate our rights or transgress against our just entitlements. But such events do not necessarily hurt us—do not cause us pain or suffering—if we are unaware of them. What we do not know may not hurt us, but it can still harm us. For example, if someone tells malicious lies about me to a third party behind my back, the lies may harm my reputation but I may never discover the betrayal. I am harmed because my interest in maintaining my deserved, high reputation is transgressed upon, but I am not hurt by the lies because I am unaware of them and thus am not pained by them. The hedonistic assumption, then, defines good and bad too narrowly. Even if death does not hurt us from an Epicurean perspective, it may well harm us. In the final chapter, I will describe why death is often a harm because it deprives us of the ongoing good that was our life.

Finally, I must address the Epicurean solution to the third cause of unnecessary human pain and suffering: dissatisfaction caused by pursuing self-defeating pleasures. Here egoistic hedonism disappoints. Its kernel of truth—

that physical and material pleasures, if taken to extremes, are self-defeating, and, even at their best, cannot be the sole, or even the main, source of happiness—is distorted into an admonishment against a host of interpersonal relations: sex, marriage, politics, engagement in civic life. The Epicureans observe accurately that interpersonal relations entangle and often bring mental suffering. They conclude unsoundly that the solution is avoidance. The Epicureans embody muted aspirations: fly beneath the radar, simplify your life, seek serenity, anesthetize yourself from pain, minimize your needs, resist your passions, avoid turbulence, moderate the vicissitudes of life.

We all can benefit from a dose of this advice. But like all medicines, if we consume too much of it we will aggravate our illness. If we take Epicureanism too seriously we dehumanize ourselves. Throughout history, writers have argued persuasively that existential tension is at the heart of human experience: Our yearning for intimate connection with others and the recognition that others are necessary for our identity and freedom coalesces uneasily with the fear and anxiety we experience as others approach. We simultaneously long for emotional attachment yet are horrified that our individuality may evaporate once we achieve it. This disharmony may never be fully reconciled; we find ourselves instead making uneasy compromises and adjustments as we oscillate along an existential continuum whose polar extremes are radical individuality and thorough immersion in community. This existential tension replicates itself at numerous levels: The individual confronts family, the family confronts village, villages confront wider society, and society confronts the state.

When we meet others at institutional levels, the stakes rise in some respects. Our need to retain individual freedom and resist coercion intensifies when our relations are impersonal, where we experience less direct control over our destiny, and when entrenched bureaucracies seem ready and able to usurp our autonomy. Circumscribed by socioeconomic reality, the relentless socializing of the established order, and the inherent inertia of the masses, our sense of possibility resists extinction and thereby honors the human craving for transcendence. Moreover, individuals confront several different, often conflicting communities. They face the intimate aspirations of family; the often conflicting ultimatums of ethnicity, gender, and race; the stirring, history-laden, patriotic implorations of country; and the more distant claims of the international order. The individual-community continuum expands in several dimensions. In fact, only in the simplest cases is it ever merely one-dimensional. As such, contexts such as family, ethnicity, gender, and politics multiply the tensions, exhilarations, fears, and hopes invariably embodied by the continuum.[25]

My general objection to Epicureanism is that it fails to capture the subtlety of the antinomies generated by the individual-community continuum. Epicureans deny our existential condition by trying to extinguish our need for robust community. Even friendship is reduced to instrumental value as its Epicurean justification is benefit to the self, not the other. Although it was a powerful philosophy in its historical setting, contemporary thinkers might well conclude that Epicurean austerity needs a measure of nineteenth-century romanticism for completion. Anesthetizing ourselves from social pain also prevents us from experiencing our greatest joys and triumphs. By denying the human need for transcendence, our quest to reimagine and recreate our selves and our contexts, the Epicurean version of egoistic hedonism severs us from paramount sources of human meaning and value: family, civic participation, grand social projects. Critics can cogently argue that steadfast devotion to Epicureanism offers much consolation but little growth. Accordingly, Epicureanism encourages human beings to settle for small enterprises and to be satisfied with mundane engagements. The romantic impulses toward robust context-smashing, self-transcendence, vigorous social engagement, and large-scale adventures wither away.

Although best viewed as an interesting historical artifact, Epicureanism reinforces crucial elements of ancient wisdom.

- Worthwhile happiness focuses on a person's internal condition.
- Physical and material pleasures are often self-defeating, especially if taken to extremes.
- Suffering caused by speculation about or anticipation of the unknown is unnecessary.
- To pursue happy, meaningful, valuable lives we must confront and come to terms with our mortality.
- Happiness results from distinguishing worthwhile from unworthy desires and acting only on the former.
- Deists must provide persuasive explanations for the amount and nature of evil in the world. We must all confront and come to terms with such evil.

Epicureanism attracted idealistic, refined people of a world ruled by militaristic, competitive strongmen. Although Epicurus's version of egoistic hedonism is severe, moderate versions, congenial to upper-class Romans, arose that softened his prescriptions for withdrawal from public life and social interactions. Epicurus's fundamental notion, that happiness is pleasure, could be taken in numerous directions. Our contemporary idea of Epicureans—those pursuing gustatory, sensual, and material pleasures—is one distorted example.

A rival view, one compatible with disciplined military valor and worldwide law, and with special appeal for the masses, soon emerged. Stoicism was the dominant philosophy and way of life in the Roman world for over five centuries.

## 5. HAPPINESS AS TRANQUILITY

Founded by Zeno of Citium (336–264 BC), Stoicism's most famous disciples were Chrysippus (280–207 BC), Cicero (106–43 BC), Seneca (4–65), Epictetus (50–138), and Marcus Aurelius (121–180).

Stoics were monotheists and adhered to natural law, a universal code. Everything happens as it must happen, according to fate. The World-Soul or God or Nature directs everything for the best. Happiness flows from reasonableness, from understanding the natural law, and from judging and acting compatibly with natural law. Although external events are fated, our attitudes toward and judgments about those events are in our control.

Stoics took happiness to be freedom from passion and the realization of inner peace. We should be indifferent to joy and grief, and flexible when facing life's changes. Virtue and right attitude are enough for happiness. By living according to nature, elevating reason over the passions, nurturing good habits, freeing ourselves from the desire to change the unalterable, and being indifferent to pleasure and pain, we can achieve the inner peace that defines happiness. The cardinal virtues are meditation, courage, self-control, and justice. Distinguishing things within our control from things beyond our control is paramount. Our judgments, attitudes, and evaluations are the only things solely under our control. By controlling these we can attain right will and virtue. The usual litany of desirables—love, honor, wealth, good health, worldly success, avoiding maltreatment from others, the well-being of friends and relatives, congenial family life, personal freedom—depends too much on external circumstances beyond our control, including the actions of others. Once we accept the slings, arrows, and seductions of life without rebellion or discontent, we are in control of our lives, and happiness is attainable.

Epictetus captured the gist of Stoicism:

> Some things are under our control, while others are not under our control. Under our control are conception, choice, desire, aversion, and in a word, every-

thing that is our own doing; not under our control are our body, our property, reputation, office and, in a word, everything that is not our own doing. Furthermore, the things under our control are by nature free, unhindered, and unimpeded; while the things not under our control are weak, servile, subject to hindrance, and not our own . . . if it has to do with some one of the things not under your control, have ready to hand the answer, 'It is nothing to me.' [26]

Stoicism differed from Epicureanism in several ways. First, Stoics regarded pleasure, along with sorrow, desire, and fear, as an evil. We must be indifferent to both pain and pleasure if passion is to be purged. Second, Stoics advocated social engagement. They recognized a brotherhood and sisterhood of human beings and denied the currency of class distinctions and social hierarchies. We have a duty to promote a world that mirrors the rationality embedded in the universe. Third, Stoics thought marriage and family facilitated inner peace. Fourth, Stoics were monotheists who believed in one supreme, universal Deity as creator and sustainer of the universe. They accepted the Roman deities as media for the worship of God. Fifth, Stoics believed our fate to be determined by the mechanistic laws governing all natural phenomena.

The Stoics defined happiness as inner peace. Their recipe for attaining happiness included minimizing desire, controlling our own judgments and attitudes, and acting in accord with natural law. Stoics explained how and why following this recipe makes us happy by analyzing human desire and our relationship to the world.

Stoicism invented the happiness quotient: Divide what you have by what you want—the higher the figure, the happier you will be. The best recipe for happiness is limiting what you want. The happiness quotient is still unveiled breathlessly, without attribution to the Stoics, in popular self-help books today: Divide your satisfactions by your desires—the higher the figure, the greater the happiness; limiting your desires is the surest road to success.

The happiness quotient is unsuccessful. It fails to distinguish the satisfaction of worthy from unworthy desires. If hundreds of our unworthy but relatively few of our worthy desires are satisfied we will still be unhappy regardless of a high average on the happiness quotient. If we correct this problem by stipulating that only worthy desires are candidates for the quotient, other difficulties appear. The happiness quotient would still fail to distinguish the intensity of our desires: We want some things much more than we want other things. Even if most of our weaker desires are fulfilled we will be unsatisfied if some of our stronger desires remain unsatisfied. The happiness quotient also does not distinguish between needs and wants. If most of our wants are satisfied but a few of our needs are unfilled, we will have a high score on the quotient but an unhappy life. The happiness quotient also makes no mention of how our desires are satisfied. If our desires are satisfied through simulated instead of real accomplishments, a worthy happiness cannot result.

Let us brush these objections aside. I will now play my trump criticism: Even if all of our desires are satisfied and we achieve a perfect score on the happiness quotient, we will still be unhappy. This is true even if we stipulate that all our satisfied desires are worthy. We would still be unhappy because our life would be inhuman. We would have nothing further to strive for, no unsatisfied projects to address, no future toward which to aspire. We would be a saturated sponge of desire. Unless we could quickly devise new desires, immediately driving our happiness quotient down, boredom and anomie would result. Accordingly, the happiness quotient requires considerable refinement.

The broader critique of Stoicism is by now a cliché. While Stoicism can bring consolation to those struggling under harsh conditions, its expectations are too low for general use. The expansive richness and creativity of human experience are sacrificed on the altar of accommodation. Although it does not insist on passivity, Stoicism inclines in that direction.

Can we, should we, be indifferent to poverty, disease, natural disasters, suffering, and evil in the universe? Imagine going home today for lunch. Under the first scenario, you are met by a loved one, engage in a wonderful social interaction (fill in your own details, make them as wonderful as you can), and return to work with maximum fulfillment. Under the second scenario, you discover your loved one has been brutally murdered (fill in your own details, make them as gruesome and upsetting as you can). How can a person be indifferent as to which of these scenarios occurs? Or in his or her reactions to these two scenarios? If someone were indifferent we would stigmatize them as psychologically impaired. To be indifferent is to relinquish what we value most.

Stoics draw a distinction between preferences and goods. They would understand that we would prefer one scenario, the loving lunch, over the other, the brutal murder. They would deny that one scenario is better than the other. They would understand that we would prefer a gourmet Italian dinner to hunger. They would deny that the Italian dinner is better than hunger. Nothing is inherently good or evil. Human beings label events as such. Eliminate the labels and we remove much needless anxiety and suffering. Stoics can thereby account for our preferences—we are not antecedently or posteriorily indifferent to numerous events—but retain their view that outcomes are inherently neutral. By focusing on the inherent neutrality of events, Stoics aspire to mute our reactions and judgments to them.

Why, though, would we prefer one scenario over another? Because we take the preferred scenario to be better or to be good, because we value one scenario over another. Stoics have a heavy burden that goes unaddressed: to account for why we prefer X over Y without referring to our values. Some preferences have their genesis in mere personal tastes or whims. Other preferences exist only because a value judgment, a labeling, has occurred. The Stoic bow to common sense, which acknowledges that we do prefer some events over others, is purchased at a stiff price: a spectacularly unpersuasive view of the relationship between preferences and goods. We prefer the loving lunch to the brutal murder because we judge, accurately, that the loving lunch is a good while the brutal murder is a monumental evil.

The Stoics were wrong. Grieving, sorrow, and suffering are not inherently evil. Human beings are by nature valuing creatures. We cannot be stonily indifferent and retain our humanity. To value something is to make it an object of concern. We cannot coherently value everything. We partially construct who we are through what we value. If we remain indifferent to the loss of what we value we call into question the intensity of our commitment, we hedge our bet. Because our evaluations, convictions, and actions define our lives, we cannot be indifferent to our defeats, disappointments, and losses. We stake our being on and experience life most directly through our values. Grief, sorrow, and suffering are appropriate responses to the tragedies of life. The Stoics were correct in thinking that sorrow and suffering are too often exaggerated, that they can impinge on a worthwhile life, that we can obsess inappropriately on our losses. To remain indifferent to everything not fully under our control, however, is unwarranted. We should not cry over spilled milk. We should cry over spilled blood.

Outlooks, such as Stoicism, that appeal to fate have trouble accounting for robust action. If I aspire to change the world I am focusing on things outside my control and trying to alter fate. I have judged the status quo deficient and taken steps to change it. If that aspiration and the results attendant to my actions are themselves fated then my judgments about external events—how I evaluated the state of the world prior to my actions—are not under my control. I was fated to a negative view of the world and the motivation to try to change it. Rendering compatible my freedom and control over my own judgments and actions, the pervasive direction of the World-Soul, and vigorous social action is no simple chore.

Even if we eliminate the presence of the World-Soul and natural law, are my judgments and attitudes about events totally within my control? They are probably more in my control than most social and natural conditions in the world. But many influences, my socialization in a broad sense, contribute to my outlook. That my conscious judgments and evaluations arise fully from my freedom is far from obvious.

The presence of natural laws that are both descriptive and prescriptive complicates matters. Following the natural law, which binds all human beings in all places at all times, is reasonable, proper, and enhances prospects for happiness. According to Stoicism, such laws are antecedently external to those things within our control, but we should not be indifferent to them. We should understand and abide by them because they are good. Although outside our control, they provide the ground for our action. If so, then "good" and "evil" are more than labels that human beings wrongly attach to events. Events and actions that violate the prescriptions of natural law are evil as such. To regard such events and actions indifferently would itself not be in accord with natural law. Again, we see that fundamental Stoical doctrines do not coalesce easily.

Stoicism's kernel of insight—do not dwell on misfortune, put suffering behind you, do not become intoxicated with unimportant pursuits or frivolous desires—is obscured by its demand that nothing else matters that much. Even on its own terms it fails to distinguish earned tranquility from simulated tranquility. Aristotle's keen observation that a person could be mistaken about whether he is happy bears currency. If Bob is peaceful because he has been hypnotized into thinking his life is other than what it is or because he has been drugged, then his tranquility does not translate into a worthy happiness. Instead, it is merely a simulated, unearned state of mind. Bob has been tricked into thinking his unsatisfying life is satisfying. Aristotle's intuition that happiness must in an important sense be earned, not merely induced, rings true.

In another respect, Stoicism provides a corrective to Aristotle's view of happiness. It points out that happiness is not simply achieving a set of external conditions, not just flourishing. Happiness requires some fit between a person's expectations and results, as well as an extended internal peace. While I resist the particular expectations Stoicism urges and question whether extended peace, however attained, is enough for everyone, Stoicism contains lessons for seekers of happiness.

- We often cause ourselves needless suffering by our unnecessary, self-undermining reactions to events outside our control.

- We bear primary responsibility for our attitudes, judgments, and evaluations.
- Do not whine, be accountable for what you can control, suck it up.
- Happiness requires a reasonable fit between our expectations and results.
- A worthwhile happiness must include a relatively enduring, positive psychological state.
- Whether a person is happy depends largely on that person's character.
- We are responsible for our own happiness.

Stoicism bested its rival Epicureanism in the Greco-Roman world because it was better suited for mass acceptance. Stoicism's egalitarianism, cosmopolitanism, monotheism, natural law, and rational universe embodied popular appeal. The reign of Stoicism as the dominant way of life ended when a new philosophy of life, Christianity, promised even more.

## 6. HAPPINESS AS WORLDLY TRANSCENDENCE

Plato understood well that human beings yearn for a connection to enduring value, a rational cosmos, and a final culmination. These aspirations fueled his philosophy. The transcendent world of Forms defined and grounded value as permanent, immutable, and absolute. The cosmos is rational insofar as it is ordered by natural laws and it provides opportunities for spiritual purification. Our final culmination is realized through the purification of our souls in this world and our continued existence in a better, nonmaterial world that defines Reality.

Why did Platonism not become a dominant worldview? Platonism was too abstract for mass appeal in two ways. First, Platonism was too abstract in an intellectual sense: It required rational capabilities far exceeding those of common people. The Socratic quest for deep theoretical understanding, so ably explained in Plato's dialogues, defines knowledge in terms of rational understanding of the Forms, a project perhaps beyond the capabilities of every human being. Socrates' wisdom was that he grasped his own limitations, he was aware of his ignorance of deep, theoretical understanding. The folly of the important men of Athens was that they thought they possessed knowledge when they did not. If Socrates did not possess deep, theoretical understanding and if he was correct in thinking that no one else did, what hope is there for the rest of us? We are condemned to glimpses, faint images, ersatz copies of Reality.

Second, Platonism was too abstract in an emotional sense: The world of Forms lacks anthropomorphic panache. The Forms themselves are the ultimate abstractions. Although they are the foundation of and define Value, Truth, Knowledge, and Reality, they are not beings in a way relevant to us. The Forms do not care about us, are not conscious of us, do not look out for us. They provide consolation to our yearnings for a connection to enduring value, rational order, and an ultimate culmination, but they are unlikely to inspire us in a personal way. Our relationship to the Forms lacks the emotional intensity of our worldly images of great love, grand causes, and monumental adventures.

Accordingly, Plato's unabashed intellectual elitism and abstract rendering of a transcendent world doomed his prospects of earning mass appeal. Winning the allegiance of the masses, though, was not Plato's objective.

Christianity eventually overtook Stoicism as the dominant philosophy of life in the West. By co-opting Plato's transcendent vision and remedying his penchant for abstractness, Christianity offered the masses ultimate hope and transformed the world.

I will sketch the development of the Christian view of happiness through four giants of theology: Plotinus (205–270), Augustine (354–430), Boethius (475–525), and Aquinas (1225–1274).

Plotinus articulated the classic version of the marriage of Platonism and Christianity. Human beings are defined by their immortal souls. Perfect happiness is achievable only in the other world and consists of the everlasting merging of the soul with God, the One. Through a mystical experience, achievable only through the special grace of God, we may temporarily glimpse perfect happiness. But everlasting perfect happiness is union with the One.

The goods of this world, such as wealth, honor, fame, and the gratification of desires, are unimportant. At worst, pursuing these goods distracts us from our primary mission. At best, these worldly pursuits can be instrumental goods if they help our souls move toward the One. Happiness, contra Aristotle, does not require good fortune, material success, felicitous personal relationships, or a well-ordered state. Most bodily pleasures typically interfere with the soul's movement toward the One. Instead, happiness requires the proper preparation of the soul for its highest destiny. We must live virtuously and practice fortitude, prudence, wisdom, and temperance. We must nurture our intellect through commitment to philosophy, math, science, and beauty. We must begin to go beyond multiplicity and individuation by understanding the unity of the cosmos and what it includes.

The One is pure, self-sufficient, and the source of all good. Through special dispensation of grace, the One facilitates an indescribable, mystical experience through which a human being briefly apprehends the soul's merging with the One.

All human beings have the potential to achieve perfect happiness. Happiness is a changeless moment in which no desire remains. To have a desire implies a lack: We seek what we do not have or more of what we already possess. Happiness extinguishes desire because our souls are completely and everlastingly fulfilled. As such, we cannot become happier. A brief moment of perfect happiness includes as much as a long period of perfect happiness. Perfect happiness, then, is an ever-present moment.

> If [happiness] is to be found in possession of the true good, why should we disregard this and omit to use it as a standard to which to look in judging [happiness], and look for other things which are not reckoned as part of [happiness]? If it was a collection of goods and necessities, or things as well which are not necessities but even so are called goods, we should have to try and see that these were there too. But if the end at which we aim must be one and not many . . . one must gain that alone which is of ultimate and highest value and which the soul seeks to clasp close within itself . . . the real drive of desire of our soul is toward that which is better than itself. When that is present within it, it is fulfilled and at rest, and this is the way of living it really wills.[27]

Plotinus's account takes a Platonic base—the celebration of immateriality, perfection, immutability, firm foundations, a higher Reality, and complete fulfillment—and remedies the problem of excessive abstraction. The One is a personal God and human beings achieve happiness only in relation to this highest being. The happiness we all potentially can realize is ultimate and incomparable to any earthly experience except for the few who experience a mystical vision.

Augustine argued that our desire for happiness was an instinct implanted by God to draw us toward God. All human beings desire happiness as the greatest good. Following Plotinus, Augustine defined happiness as the satisfaction of desire. The satisfaction of one desire, however, gives rise to other desires. Happiness cannot be a treadmill of following desires. We must fundamentally desire the satisfaction of all our desires and liberation from the cycle of desiring. The logic of happiness suggests that only freedom from need and want produces a condition in which nothing is lacking and all desires are fulfilled once and forever. We are drawn naturally to the extinction of desire itself. If happiness is the greatest good then it must be stable and superior to all other goods. Contingencies and misfortunes cannot destroy happiness.

Augustine recognizes that human beings cannot attain such happiness in this world. Nothing available to us in this world can produce freedom from all need and want. Desire is part of the human condition. Stoicism's prescription for internal peace is unsuccessful. Although it correctly identifies the self-defeating dimension of desiring things outside of our control, Stoicism fails to carry its logic to its full conclusion. Concerning ourselves only with things within our control cannot extinguish desire; desire implies lack; lack prohibits happiness. Aristotle's appeal to a measure of material success, intellectual capability, and cordial relations likewise fails. As Aristotle noted, most of these elements require good fortune or, at least, the absence of misfortune. For Augustine, the greatest good cannot be hostage to contingency and luck.

> The definers of all these defective conclusions [about happiness] should yield to those philosophers who taught that man is never fully blessed, in the enjoyment of either corporeal or spiritual good, but only by a fruition in God. This joy in God is not like any pleasure found in physical or intellectual satisfaction . . . the pursuer of wisdom, that is, the philosopher, will only be truly happy when he begins to rejoice in God. [28]

Accordingly, happiness is attainable only in the other world. Augustine, though, refines Plotinus's sketch of the unity of the immortal soul with the One. Augustine's notion is reminiscent of Plato's disembodied soul apprehending the Form of the Good. Augustine introduces the notion of beatific vision: the soul's apprehension of God's manifestations, the fulfillment of our deepest yearnings, our final destiny. Only beatific vision can extinguish all desire and saturate the soul forever.

Boethius and Aquinas refined early Christian notions of happiness. Boethius directly confronts the tragedy of life in this world. Suffering deprives us of finite goods, but offers us an opportunity to reaffirm our relationship with God. Our tragedies highlight what should matter most. Suffering and pain are not merely adversities unless we collaborate to make them so. Creative human beings turn adversity to practical advantage.

Aquinas adds that a modicum of suffering is part of a happy life. We define ourselves not merely by the amount of our pleasures, the percentage of fulfilled desires, and material and intellectual successes. We also measure ourselves by the amount of suffering we bear and the fashion in which we bear it. Pain and suffering are not evils as such. Instead, as the life of Christ exemplified, they are a necessary part of the virtuous and happy life. This insight is acute, extraordinary, and transformative.

Numerous philosophers had hitherto assumed that pain and suffering are inherently bad and should be avoided. The happy life was thought to be as free as possible from anxiety. Epicureanism was geared to avoiding suffering more than to experiencing pleasure. Stoicism championed indifference and low expectations as a solution to suffering. Boethius and Aquinas understand the connection between suffering and a meaningful life. The pain-free life is inhuman. We are not rocks nor islands. We suffer. We cry.

Our growth and suffering are often connected. The Italian proverb, which generously predates Nietzsche, is "Ciò che non mi distrugge mi rende più forte" ("What does not destroy me will make me stronger"). The loss of adolescent innocence as we gain worldly experience, of infinite possibilities as we make choices that narrow our imaginings, of boundless hope as we bury our loved ones, of transcendent power as we suffer debilitating diseases, of inflated self-esteem as love turns sour, can trigger growth and meaning. Or self-destruction. We must integrate the tragic, painful aspects of human experience into our reality. Evil, suffering, death, and the loss of what is closest to us are also part of life. Adversity can be refashioned to practical advantage where the will to do so is resolute. But we find no guarantees.

Getting what we want too easily, without struggle, induces boredom more predictably than simply accomplishing a goal. The classic, sometimes irritating, adages bear currency: "Only things that take great effort are worth having" and "Nothing worthwhile comes easily." Those of us who assiduously avoid all pain pay a stiff price. We never test ourselves with a grand cause, or flirt with high adventure, or expend ourselves extravagantly in intensely creative projects. Whether these ventures are successful or not, they include pain and suffering. Robust self-making, whether inspired by theistic or secular narratives, requires no less. Boethius and Aquinas understood.

Aquinas accepts the early Christian view that happiness is defined by the complete satisfaction of our desires. To argue, though, that all our desires must be satisfied is misleading. Not every desire is worthy of being fulfilled. Some of our desires conflict and cannot be simultaneously satisfied. Some of our desires may be logically or empirically impossible to fulfill. The relevant desires are those that facilitate our perfection, the full actualization of our higher potentials. We must become more God-like to attain happiness.

Aquinas, following the tradition, insists that perfect happiness can be found only in the other world through beatific vision. But imperfect happiness, which prefigures perfect happiness, can be attained in this world. The moral and intellectual virtues are necessary but not sufficient for imperfect happiness. Human beings also require divine grace, which is necessary to make appropriate choices, cultivate the right habits, and embrace the theological virtues of faith, hope, and charity. Only God can infuse the theological virtues in us. Aquinas oscillates between happiness acquired through human efforts and happiness requiring the grace of God.

> Ultimate and perfect happiness can only be in the vision of the divine essence . . . man is not perfectly happy as long as something remains for him to desire and seek . . . the intellect is perfected in the measure that it knows the essence of a thing . . . for perfect happiness, the intellect must reach the very essence of the first cause. Thus its perfection will be had by its union with God as an object.[29]

As the greatest good, happiness cannot be geared to a further end or objective. Whereas Augustine argued that earthly happiness was impossible and this world offered only hope for happiness in the next world, Aquinas claimed that perfect happiness in the next world is a continuation and refinement of imperfect happiness in this world. The happiest human beings must be the saints, those who best exemplify the moral, intellectual, and theological virtues. Imperfect happiness for Aquinas is more of a condition of the soul than an enduring, positive psychological state.

Bowing in the direction of Aristotle, Aquinas accepts that a measure of material and bodily pleasure is necessary for imperfect happiness. The Stoics were incorrect in thinking that pleasure was an evil. The Epicureans were incorrect in thinking that pleasure is the greatest good. Pleasures are good or bad according to the moral value of the actions that produce them. Aristotle valued friendships more than Aquinas. For Aquinas, friends are necessary for earthly happiness insofar as they help us produce good deeds.

Aquinas accepts a host of classical principles: Happiness is the greatest good; human beings should not try to fulfill all desires, only worthy desires; perfect happiness requires the satisfaction of all worthy desires; human beings desire something to the degree they think it is a good; happiness is not merely an enduring, positive state of mind—not merely joy, peace, or exuberance; how we attain a positive state of mind is crucial; and earthly happiness requires a measure of material and physical pleasure.

The great Christian theologians, then, defined perfect happiness as fulfillment of all worthy desires. Their recipe for happiness was attaining eternal salvation through virtuous thought and action, which may require divine grace. Christians explained how and why following this recipe makes us happy by appealing to our relationship with the Supreme Being and the grand design of the universe.

The Christian notion of happiness both invites and evades rigorous examination. At first blush, perfect happiness is inhuman. Imagine a fully satisfied soul: no desires, no projects, no changes, no activity, no opportunities for improvement. Perfection sounds numbingly boring. What would we experience? How would we kill time in eternity? Have the Christian philosophers been seduced by the Stoic happiness quotient into wrongly concluding that the presence of desires destroys the highest happiness?

Bertrand Russell (1872–1970) rightly questioned all utopian theorists who longed for a fixed condition where all desires were fulfilled:

> The men who make Utopias proceed upon a radically false assumption as to what constitutes a good life. They conceive that it is possible to imagine a certain state of society and a certain way of life which would be once and for all recognized as good, and should continue for ever and ever. They do not realize that much of the greater part of a man's happiness depends upon activity, and only a very small remnant consists in passive enjoyment . . . Every vigorous man needs some kind of context, some sense of resistance overcome, in order to feel he is exercising his faculties.[30]

At closer examination perfect happiness is still inhuman, but understandably so. On the Christian view, death separates our bodies from our souls. The everlasting afterlife is not a human temporal existence. The criticisms and questions I lodged against the Christian view evaluate a nontemporal, unified, immaterial condition of being from the perspective of a temporal, individual, material existence. That the everlasting afterlife of our souls is ineffable from a human vantage point is unsurprising.

Is the Christian view sound? If the existence of God and an afterlife are merely fables concocted by human beings to fulfill their deepest psychological desires, or to justify the power of certain interest groups, or to reinforce societal codes and norms, then Plotinus and Augustine have sketched a fantasy of perfect happiness unavailable to us. But if their metaphysical position reflects underlying Reality then they offer us hope for a better, everlasting future.

Where does this view leave nonbelievers in God? Doomed to wander the earth seeking a happiness they cannot find. From the Christian standpoint, our world is a vale of tears that is instrumentally valuable if we lead a virtuous life. Our earthly lives prepare the soul for its final, glorious destiny. If we live inappropriately we are twice disappointed, in this world and the next.

That Christianity surpassed Stoicism and Epicureanism as the dominant way of life is due mainly to its greater offer of reward—an afterlife of eternal bliss—and the vivid, inspiring narrative of the life of Christ. The story of a savior willing to pay the highest price to redeem the sins of human beings resonates with our yearnings for a personal connection to enduring value, a rational cosmos, and an ultimate culmination. Epicureanism's divine indifference and Stoicism's blander monotheism pale in comparison.

The Christian philosophers teach several important lessons about happiness:

- Happiness requires the proper internal condition.
- The presence of desires is incompatible with perfect happiness.
- Perfect happiness requires a nontemporal state of being.
- Perfect happiness is, thus, impossible in this world.
- Pain and suffering are not inherently evil.
- Pain and suffering provide rich opportunities to nurture meaningful and valuable lives.
- The way human beings confront pain and suffering is indispensable to the characters they forge.
- A measure of pain and suffering is necessary for imperfect, worldly happiness.

The Christian philosophers, as did almost all previous thinkers, were firmly convinced that happiness is the greatest good and that moral virtue, among other things, was necessary to attain the greatest good. They added explicitly a view, perhaps implicit in Plato, that perfect happiness requires the fulfillment of all worthy desires once and forever. The Christian philosophers, however, appreciated the role suffering could play in a meaningful, valuable, happy life.

That moral virtue is necessary for happiness I will call the virtue thesis. That happiness is the greatest good I will call the *summum bonum* thesis. That perfect happiness requires the fulfillment of all worthy desires once and forever I will call the saturation thesis. That pain and suffering can play a constructive role in a happy life I will call the no guts, no glory thesis.

Are the four theses persuasive? The virtue thesis and *summum bonum* thesis are persuasive only if we build them into the concept of happiness. The classical thinkers identified in various degrees happiness with virtue. They conceived happiness to be about enduring character and progress toward perfection. Under such conceptions, the virtue and *summum bonum* theses are true, but only as a matter of definition. "Happiness" means in part "possessor of virtuous character" and "pursuer of the greatest good."

Contemporary uses of "happiness" could deny both the virtue and *summum bonum* theses. If we take happiness as merely an enduring, positive psychological state such as joy, peace, or exuberance, then we might well argue that virtue is not necessary for happiness. Happy villains, miscreants, and scoundrels exist. Also, we could argue against the *summum bonum* thesis by insisting that other social values—moral, aesthetic, scientific, or cognitive—can be more important than an enduring, positive psychological state. More important, I will argue that happiness is not the greatest personal value; it is not the greatest good specifically valuable *for the individual.*

The saturation thesis does not warrant our allegiance. I have already argued that this thesis sets too high a standard for happiness and misconceives human life. The standard can be used too facilely to denigrate this world. It teaches that profound happiness is impossible, human beings are always unfulfilled, and this world is, at best, only an ersatz image of paradise. Even if an afterlife and eternal bliss are available to us, the happiness we can attain in this world deserves a more sophisticated hearing.

The no guts, no glory thesis is compelling. We manifest our greatest virtues in crisis. Courage, creativity, altruism, community, faith, hope, charity, and the like are best exemplified in trying contexts that test our resolve and our ability to confront pain and suffering meaningfully. One of the puzzles of heaven is whether robust virtue makes any sense in an everlasting state of bliss defined by the beatific vision that presents neither challenges nor hardships.

The modern era analyzed these four theses and enhanced our understanding of happiness. To that era I shall now turn.

**NOTES**

1. V. J. McGill, *The Idea of Happiness* (New York: Frederick A. Praeger Publishers, 1967), 5.

2. Rick Foster and Greg Hicks, *How We Choose to Be Happy* (New York: Penguin Putnam, Inc., 1999), 3.

3. Dr. David Lykken, *Happiness* (New York: St. Martin's Press, 1999), 7.

4. David G. Myers, *The Pursuit of Happiness* (New York: Avon Books, Inc., 1992), 23–24.

5. Lynne McFall, "Happiness, Rationality, and Individual Ideals," *Review of Metaphysics* 38 (March 1984): 596.

6. John Wilson, "Happiness," *Analysis* 29 (1968): 13.

7. *The American Heritage Dictionary of The English Language*, ed. William Morris (Boston: Houghton Mifflin Company, 1969), 599.

8. Mark Kingwell, *In Pursuit of Happiness* (New York: Crown Publishers, 1998), 11.

9. Ludwig Wittgenstein, *Notebooks 1914–1916*, 2d ed., eds. G. H. von Wright and G.E.M. Anscombe, trans. G.E.M. Anscombe (Chicago: University of Chicago Press, 1979), 8.7.16, 75.

10. Dr. Joyce Brothers, "You Can Lead A More Joyful Life," *Parade Magazine*, October 15, 2000, 6.

11. Richard Kraut, "Two Conceptions of Happiness," *The Philosophical Review* 88 (April 1979): 170.

12. Luo Lu, "Personal or Environmental Causes of Happiness," *The Journal of Social Psychology* 139:1 (1999): 79.

13. Roy F. Baumeister, *Meanings of Life* (New York: The Guilford Press, 1991), 214.

14. Bertrand Russell, *The Conquest of Happiness* (London: Horace Liveright Publishers, Inc., 1958), 143–144.

15. Plato, *The Dialogues of Plato*, 2 vols., trans. B. Jowett (New York: Random House, 1920).

16. Plato, *Phaedo*, trans. David Gallop (Oxford: Oxford University Press, 1993), 79d.

17. Aristotle, *Nicomachean Ethics*, trans. W. D. Ross, revised by J. L. Ackrill and J. O. Urmson (Oxford: Oxford University Press, 1980).

18. Ibid., Bk. I, sec. 2, 4.

19. Ibid., Bk. I, sec. 8.

20. Ibid., Bk. X, sec. 4–7.

21. Wallace I. Matson, *A New History of Philosophy*, vol. I (New York: Harcourt Brace Jovanovich, Inc., 1987), 153.

22. Ibid., 167.

23. Epicurus, "Letter to Menoeceus," in *The Stoic and Epicurean Philosophers*, ed. Whitney J. Oates, trans. C. Bailey (New York: The Modern Library, 1940), 31; Lucretius, "On the Nature of Things," in *The Stoic and Epicurean Philosophers*, ed. Whitney J. Oates, trans. H. A. J. Munro (New York: The Modern Library, 1940), 131.

24. Matson, *A New History of Philosophy*, 166.

25. See, e.g., Raymond Angelo Belliotti, *Seeking Identity* (Lawrence, Kansas: University Press of Kansas, 1995), 156–158, 191–193.

26. Epictetus, *Encheiridion*, trans. W. A. Oldfather (Cambridge, Mass.: Harvard University Press, 1928), 1.

27. Plotinus, *Enneads*, vol. I, trans. A. H. Armstrong (Cambridge, Mass.: Harvard University Press, 1966), sec. 6.

28. St. Augustine, "City of God," in *Fathers of the Church*, trans. Gerald G. Walsh, Daniel J. Honan, and Grace Monahan (Washington, DC: The Catholic University of America Press, 1952), Book VIII, ch. 8.

29. St. Thomas Aquinas, *Treatise on Happiness*, trans. John A. Oesterle (Notre Dame, Indiana: University of Notre Dame Press, 1983), 39.

30. Bertrand Russell, *Principles of Social Reconstruction* (London: Allen & Unwin Publishers, 1916), 93–94, 96.

# 2

# HAPPINESS RECONCEIVED

The modern era began to recognize happiness as merely an enduring, positive psychological state of mind. If such a state of mind can be attained in numerous ways, including some not characterized by virtuous living, then happiness could not be the greatest good. Some modern philosophers scrutinized, then rejected, the virtue and *summum bonum* theses.

## 1. HAPPINESS AS MORALLY EARNED

Immanuel Kant (1724–1804) denied all logical connection between virtue and happiness. Happiness is not the greatest good because we can easily identify happy villains and unhappy heroes. The classical Greco-Roman philosophers were mistaken in linking the two concepts. Performing moral duty is superior to attaining happiness.

Kant gave the most detailed classic expression to the inherent moral standing of human beings. The constitutive elements of Kantianism are well known: morality based on a categorical imperative reflecting a practical reason that finds benevolent motives unnecessary; morality identified as rationality imposed on human beings by the terms of their existence; the notion of duty exalted as the fundamental moral concept; and the universality of moral judgments founded on the impersonal equality of human beings.[1]

His standard for happiness was excruciatingly lofty: happiness is the satisfaction of all our desires.

Happiness is the satisfaction of all our desires: extensive, in regard to their multiplicity; intensive in regard to their degree; protensive, in regard to their duration.[2]

Kant, though, oscillates between defining happiness in terms of the fulfillment of all desires and describing happiness as the positive psychological state of uninterrupted pleasantness.

Now, a rational being's consciousness of the pleasantness of life uninterruptedly accompanying his whole existence is happiness.[3]

Kant sets the bar of happiness too high on both accounts. Requiring the fulfillment of all desires makes happiness unattainable. If we amend Kant's account to read "all worthy desires," happiness is still unattainable, and we wrongly unify happiness and moral virtue. Kant clearly insisted that while moral virtue is required to make a person worthy of happiness, happiness might be attained by someone of inadequate moral character. Perhaps it is most charitable to Kant to talk of degrees of happiness. While fulfilling all desires is impossible—and I argue that is good news—satisfying enough desires to enjoy a measure of happiness is not.

On Kant's other account of happiness as uninterrupted pleasantness, happiness is also unattainable. Who achieves uninterrupted pleasantness? Perhaps those in a contented, catatonic state, but not real human beings functioning in the world. Again, we should most charitably interpret Kant as pointing to the contemporary notion of happiness as a predominantly positive state of mind.

Alternately, we might interpret Kant to be defining happiness as uninterrupted pleasantness while the recipe for attaining happiness is the satisfaction of all desires. Then we can soften Kant's account by adding that achieving a predominantly positive state of mind, even if not uninterrupted pleasantness, describes a reasonable degree of happiness which is reached by satisfying enough of our most important desires.

The categorical imperative was grounded in the only conditional good, the good will: doing the morally proper act only because it is the morally proper act. For Kant, the pursuit of happiness and the desire to express love are unreliable motivations. They hold out the possibility that if doing the morally right thing did not involve a loved one or was not likely to produce happiness then the agent would not perform his or her duty. Contra Epicureanism, pleasure is not inherently good. Pleasure is a good only when it accompanies moral action. Happiness and moral duty are often incompatible. Duty has no regard for consequences.

All human beings naturally desire happiness. If their only reason for complying with moral duty is pursuit of happiness then they are doing only what comes naturally. Moral approbation, however, accompanies duty only when it is done for its own sake, not when a moral act is performed from the natural pursuit of happiness. What we do necessarily and naturally is not done from moral duty. The pursuit of happiness is an unreliable motive for another reason. Moral actions may bring happiness to some, but unhappiness to others. Duty, though, is universally binding, as it is grounded in reason. Through the categorical imperative, we can determine what logic requires of us. All immoral actions, it felicitously turns out, are self-contradictory. Immoral actions are both evil and logically deficient.

A virtuous life involves recurrent conflict between the natural allure of happiness and the moral requirements of duty. A limited reconciliation is possible. Moral action is the greatest good and firmly grounds claims of worthiness. Performing our moral duty makes us worthy of happiness and provides us a valid, objective claim to happiness. In a perfectly just world only those worthy of happiness would be happy, and all those unworthy of happiness would be sad. Our world is not perfectly just.

A detailed analysis of Kantian moral theory is beyond the scope of this work. In sum, Kant's categorical imperative has historically been chastised as form without content: an abstract formulation that cannot yield substantive moral conclusions without a specific, antecedent moral vision. Accordingly, Kant's categorical imperative is a device that cannot *justify* our basic moral judgments because to generate conclusions it must *presuppose* such judgments. Kant's moral theory tends to reinforce the dominant view of the moral order. Using the categorical imperative in a predominantly Christian community to reinforce what people already assumed was morally true made sense. Using the categorical imperative in a pluralistic setting to resolve highly contestable moral questions is either futile or an exercise in begging the question.

Kant's musings on happiness, though, are important. He explicitly rejects the virtue and *summum bonum* theses because he tacitly identifies happiness as merely an enduring, positive state of mind. Kant subscribes to the saturation thesis as he unfortunately equates happiness with the satisfaction of all desires. That Kant follows the Christian thinkers and is seduced into endorsing the saturation thesis is no accident. He was a devout Christian who, despite the claim that his moral theory is grounded only in reason and makes no appeal to the divine, is deeply influenced by theism.

Kant strikes several responsive chords. He understands acutely that once we identify happiness as merely an enduring, positive state of mind, happiness cannot be the greatest good. Once we analyze this concept of happiness, certainly the dominant contemporary understanding, we understand why happiness is overrated.

Kant provides the key when he talks about being worthy of happiness. Under the contemporary understanding of happiness, we can have the requisite state of mind even if we are morally unworthy. Or if the state of mind has been artificially induced by a master hypnotist. Or if we harbor massive delusions. Or if we live our lives throughout as a contented child.

While the possibilities of a thoroughly depraved, moral monster enjoying extended peace or exuberance are slim, morally unworthy people can attain the relatively enduring positive psychological state required for the contemporary understanding of happiness. Kant argued that the morally unworthy do not deserve happiness and that being morally worthy is a greater good than the happiness enjoyed by the unworthy villain. He was correct, at least insofar as the happiness of the villain is derived from unworthy deeds. We should not begrudge the happiness that the scoundrel gains from loving relationships, charitable acts, appreciation of nature, and other worthy activities. To the extent, though, that the scoundrel wrongly benefits from villainy, he or she does not deserve happiness. For Kant to say that the morally unworthy do not deserve to be happy, that justice would be better served if they were unhappy, makes sense. That he understood the possibility of someone becoming unrighteously happy, being gratified by attaining wrongful goals, undermines the virtue and the *summum bonum* theses.

Although Kant did not bring them to the forefront, his analysis suggests other ways that happiness would not be a great good. Suppose a master hypnotist charms a person into thinking he or she possesses a happy state of mind. The person thinks he or she is happy and, thus, is happy under the contemporary understanding of the term. This state of mind, though, is false. It is not causally connected to the life the person has led, the character the person embodies, the choices the person has made, or accurate self-appraisals. The happiness is artificial because it is based only on an externally induced illusion.

Consider another case. A person enjoys extended bliss and recurrent joy. He has attained the requisite psychological state that defines the contemporary notion of happiness. The person, however, suffers from deep delusion: He sincerely believes he is living in the early nineteenth century and is Napoleon. His happiness is based on savoring his imagined power, his string of military triumphs, and hatching grandiose plans for the future. How can such a condition be good at all, much less the greatest good? If our joyful state of mind is not connected to moral goodness, to valuable accomplishments, to continued intellectual growth, or even to reality, what is it worth?

If you were victimized by a horrible accident that rendered you incapable of any biographical life beyond that of a contented child, would we consider you fortunate because you were happy? If you were strongly socialized, even brainwashed, into responding joyfully to small pleasures and minor enterprises but were unable to show courage, self-sufficiency, and boldness, would we count you fortunate because you were happy? I do not think so. Ignorance, under certain circumstances, can be bliss. Such bliss is no more valuable than the ignorance that grounds it.

Consider the lives of the following: Ludwig van Beethoven, Joe DiMaggio, Emily Dickinson, Sören Kierkegaard, Queen Elizabeth I, Abraham Lincoln, Jesus, Michelangelo Buonarroti, Moses, Socrates, Emma Goldman, and Vincent van Gogh. These lives are paradigms of meaning and significance in religion, sports, literature, music, politics, philosophy, and art. In terms of relatively enduring accomplishments, influences, excellences, creations, and social effects these lives are among the best in their fields.

Yet these people were not strikingly happy. While each of them flourished in many respects, none realized the extended joy or peace characteristic of happiness. Perhaps they demanded too much of themselves, saw reality too clearly, were unable to harbor self-flattering illusions, could not savor their feelings of pleasure, lacked the necessary biochemistry, or were too heroic to be happy.

Meaningful lives, then, are not necessarily happy lives. But happy lives, at least those that are not artificially induced, are invariably meaningful. Happy people report that their lives are meaningful. To hear someone gush, "My life is meaningless. Isn't it grand? I am so happy about it!" would be peculiar.

Chalk one up for Kant: Under the contemporary understanding, happiness cannot be the greatest good, is often not a great good, and is sometimes not a good at all. To be a good, happiness must be earned, we must be worthy of happiness. Otherwise, happiness is overrated.

- How we attain happiness is crucial to its value.
- To be a great good, happiness must necessarily constitute or be connected to the higher values.
- The dominant modern and contemporary understanding of happiness is a relatively enduring positive psychological state: extended peace, joy, or exuberance.

- Such happiness cannot be the greatest good because it is not necessarily linked to the highest value: compliance with moral duty.
- A worthwhile happiness is more than merely a relatively enduring positive psychological state.
- Happiness is a good only when it is earned, only when the happy person is a worthy person.
- Attaining happiness should not be the immediate, direct motive for human action.

## 2. HAPPINESS AS COLLECTIVE ACHIEVEMENT

Georg W. F. Hegel (1770–1831) advanced a different version of human happiness, a version founded on a philosophical system.[4] Finite objects and beings are transitory manifestations of the Absolute, which is called at various stages and in different dimensions Mind, Reality, Reason, Idea. Unlike the Western God, Hegel's Absolute is not a transcendent reality that stands independent from the world and complete from the beginning. Instead, the Absolute develops through time, as the goal and result of an historical process. The Absolute comes to know itself through the movement of finite reality. Every concrete particular is a moment in the development of the Absolute. Thus, human beings make an historical contribution to the life of the Absolute and to Its awareness and freedom. We are necessary for the Absolute to become aware of Itself.

Unlike the Western God, the Absolute has no meaning apart from the cosmos. The Absolute in full development is the integrated unity of all that is real, conscious of everything, infinite, free, and self-conscious. The self-actualization process has three main stages. First, as Idea-In-Itself, or Absolute without the world, the Reality is abstract, has no particularity, and is aware only of being self-contained. Second, as Idea-Outside-Itself, or Absolute with the world, Reality exhibits order, pattern, and an evolving human consciousness. Third, as Idea-Conscious-of-Itself, or Spirit, the Absolute is self-conscious, concrete, aware, and free, and the world includes developed collective human consciousness. At this stage, human beings share recognition of their mutual interdependence and collective identity.

Hegel's Absolute is not grander and more powerful than the natural world; instead, It becomes manifested only in the world. The progress of history is necessary and inevitable, but not linear: We experience backings and turnings, not merely straightforward advances. The cosmos reflects a developing rational Mind, acting to make Itself more concrete, more self-aware, more free. Neither random nor absurd, the cosmos embodies high rationality and intelligibility. Contra Kant, our desires are not opposed to our reason. Each desire contains a quantum of reason. Desire is fueled by reason and is necessary to motivate action. We can attain both virtue and happiness. Happiness requires proper choices which require virtues such as prudence, self-control, and temperance. For Hegel, happiness is a collective accomplishment that requires the historical development of the state and other social institutions such as family, police, economic structures, and judicial bodies. The happiness of the whole is a precondition for the happiness of individuals.

> [Happiness] has no independent validity as the embodiment of a single particular will but only as a universal welfare and essentially as universal in principle, i.e., as according with freedom. [Happiness] without right is not a good.[5]

Hegel insists that freedom, moral goodness, and happiness are intertwined. The coming of Christianity and the modern nation–state heralds the era of higher freedom. An individual cannot consistently will his or her happiness if it conflicts with the collective happiness.

> There is formed a system of complete interdependence, wherein the livelihood, happiness, and legal status of one man is interwoven with the livelihood, happiness, and rights of all. On this system, individual happiness . . . depend, and only in this connected system is it actualized and secured.[6]

For Hegel, the meaning of human life and the attainment of happiness are clear. We can know and appreciate the ideal of Reason and the growth of the Absolute. We can advance those ideals through earthly struggle with good and evil. Our lives are in a sense the lives of the Absolute as the Absolute comes to know itself by creating more life and by exhibiting order and purpose. History is on a nonlinear march, advancing the freedom and self-activity of all, a movement toward maximizing justice, beauty, love, and happiness. Human beings, therefore, play important roles in the triumphant historical drama that is earthly life. Our final culmination is the complete self-actualization of the Absolute. Human beings are not only connected to enduring value, but play an indispensable part in developing that value. And the cosmos strides cheerfully through time toward increasing rationality, justice, beauty, and truth.

Hegel's scheme may fulfill an account of our deepest yearnings, but provides few consolations. The individual is a tool for grander purposes: I help the Absolute gain self-consciousness and full development, but what does the infinite do for me? Am I not a miniscule cog, one of trillions of drones, who labors in the cosmic hive only to evaporate into the void at death? The meaning of my life is purely instrumental and impersonal. The prospects of my happiness are hostage to collective action. In Hegel's scheme, the individual plays a role in the self-realization of the Absolute. But our lives are only means to another's good. Our fulfillment is only partaking of a Grand Fulfillment which we will not experience directly. Our meaning, value, fulfillment, and even happiness are external to us in important respects.

A Hegelian might argue that we enjoy the fruits of historical progress as earthly life storms along to higher forms. But history can be interpreted in numerous ways. Faith in inevitable progress is only one such way and not necessarily the most convincing. The nineteenth-century faith in progress, captured by Hegelian metaphysics and Darwinian evolution, may be less compelling today. While scientific and technological innovations are striking, the condition of the environment, the threat of nuclear annihilation, the disaggregation of confidence in fervent religious belief, the unsettling of a robust sense of community, and the explosion of accessible information distort the promise of Hegel's triumphant historical march.

Let us stipulate for the sake of argument that Hegel is correct: History skips joyfully along the path of nonlinear progress. Still, his notions of happiness and meaning of life require great collective identification. Individuals must be satisfied even though they may not realize the fruits of the final triumphant moments. We also find it more difficult to identify with the Absolute than to identify with the God of Western religions. Whether the possible abstract benefits to future people and to the Absolute Itself are sufficient to vivify a person's sense of purpose now is questionable.

Hegel's understanding of happiness is too collective for contemporary democratic sensibilities. Personal happiness is hostage to the well-being of the entire nation-state. Identifying individual happiness with the collective welfare forges a kinship with Plato and Aristotle, while it distances Hegel from Stoics, Epicureans, Christians, and Kantians. For Hegel, Stoicism is too self-contained, Epicureanism is wrongly minimalist, Christianity is preoccupied with another world, and Kantianism is dourly severe.

Hegel's idea of self-development through history, although overly sanguine in its acceptance of inevitable progress and falsely confident in its interpretation of the past, is insightful. Hegel understood that happiness depends on the actualization of valuable human potentials. He tacitly denied that happiness is merely an enduring, positive state of mind. Happiness, for Hegel, is a confluence of desire and duty, sensibilities and reasons, freedom and historical necessity, and internal development and external institutional life. Prefiguring the evolutionary theory of Charles Darwin in some respects, Hegel celebrates ultimate happiness as the exact correlation of individual adaptation to a wider environment.

- Worthwhile happiness is not a fixed state, but a process including an ongoing series of activities.
- Worthwhile happiness requires maximum development of the most valuable human attributes. This development requires extensive time.
- Pleasure should not be sought for its own end or as an end in itself. Instead, pleasure is an appropriate accompaniment to the development and exercise of our highest faculties.
- Worthwhile happiness and an appropriate social context are linked. Social contexts often define the possibilities for happiness.
- Worthwhile happiness is more than merely an enduring positive psychological state. It requires self-actualization and the requisite external social conditions.

Meanwhile, in England, a different conception of happiness was emerging, one that joined classical hedonism, egalitarianism, and community into a grand moral theory.

## 3. HAPPINESS AS THE GREATEST GOOD FOR THE GREATEST NUMBER

The British utilitarians, most notably Jeremy Bentham (1748–1832) and John Stuart Mill (1806–1873), endorsed the fundamental principle of ancient hedonism: Pleasure is inherently good and pain inherently bad. They rejected, though, the egoistic basis of ancient hedonism. The utilitarians embraced the goal of the greatest good for the greatest number. My personal pleasure will often have to take a backseat to the greater pleasure of the community. We can calculate, roughly, the amount of pleasure and pain various acts and policies will produce. We should choose the acts and policies that facilitate the greatest amount of pleasure over pain. Happiness is defined by a strongly positive balance of pleasure over pain.

When calculating the respective pleasures and pains of competing actions, we must consider each person affected by the actions: "Each [person who is affected] is to count for one, and no one for more than one."[7] Some utilitarians would go beyond egalitarianism only for human beings and consider all sentient beings—all beings capable of experiencing pleasure and pain who are affected by an action—in their hedonic calculations.

Utilitarians insist that the principle of utility defines morality. If we act only in ways that produce the greatest balance of pleasure over pain we will fulfill our moral duty. Accordingly, utilitarianism refines ancient hedonism by adding egalitarian and communal dimensions. Egalitarianism parts company with Aristotelian *eudaemonism*, while concern for the entire community distances utilitarianism from Epicurean hedonism. The result is the convergence of social happiness with morality.

Bentham argued that seven factors are relevant when we calculate pain and pleasure: Intensity, duration, certainty, propinquity, fecundity, purity, and scope. Our first focus is our own pleasure not because it is more valuable than the pleasure of others but only because we are better placed to advance it. Bentham does not recognize qualitative differences among pleasures: "Pushpin is as good as poetry if the quantity of pleasure is identical."[8]

Mill distanced himself from Bentham on the issue of qualitative pleasures. Pleasures differ not only quantitatively but qualitatively: "Better to be Socrates unsatisfied than a pig satisfied."[9] How do we determine which of two pleasures are qualitatively superior? We consult the source that has experienced or could experience both and discover which the source prefers. Unfortunately, that rules out the pig in almost all cases involving a conflict between human and porcine pleasures.

Bentham's belief that pleasures differed only quantitatively kept utilitarianism pure but violated common convictions. Mill's introduction of a qualitative dimension to pleasures ratified common convictions but introduced a troubling feature to the hedonic calculus: gradation of pleasure based on a non-utilitarian standard.

A thorough examination of utilitarianism is beyond the ambition of this book. Utilitarianism has been criticized on numerous grounds: The long-range effects of our actions are notoriously difficult to foresee, yet they are required for a view that marries overall pleasure to morality; Bentham's hedonic calculus requires us to consider seven factors for each pleasure and pain produced by an action—the calculus needs precision to determine moral action but is too complicated to secure it; conflicts between the greatest balance of pleasure over pain, the greatest good, and pleasure for the greatest number will sometimes occur; utilitarianism does not recognize the intrinsic value of certain actions such as truth-telling and promising; the hedonic calculus could sacrifice the interests of an individual or a minority group if in doing so greater pleasure results for the majority; and utilitarianism recognizes only forward-looking reasons, those related to present and future hedonic consequences. Yet backward-looking reasons, such as honoring promises and prior commitments, also are an important part of morality.

Utilitarians have responded to these and other objections. Although I remain skeptical about the marriage between utilitarianism and morality, the nature and success of specific utilitarian responses is not my present concern.

Utilitarians identify happiness with a highly favorable balance of pleasure over pain. Happiness is the greatest human goal. Utilitarian morality and happiness are linked. Even the hero, martyr, or saint—exemplars of self-sacrifice—seek happiness: perhaps not their own happiness but the happiness of others.

> Unquestionably it is possible to do without happiness; it is done involuntarily by nineteen-twentieths of mankind . . . and it often has to be done voluntarily by the hero or the martyr, for the sake of something which he prizes more than his individual happiness. But this something, what is it, unless the happiness of others, or some of the requisites of happiness? It is noble to be capable of resigning entirely one's own portion of happiness, or chances of it: but, after all, this self-sacrifice must be for some end . . . would the sacrifice be made if the hero or martyr did not believe that it would earn for others immunity from similar sacrifices?[10]

If happiness is construed only as pleasant feelings, which include sensuous pleasures as well as intellectual and spiritual pleasures, utilitarianism is unpersuasive. Imagine that the greatest balance of pleasure over pain could be produced by mass hypnosis or a congenial simulated environment or the manufacture of a pleasure pill that stunts creativity. Happiness, indeed utilitarian morality, would require these measures. Yet happiness, defined as a highly favorable balance of pleasure over pain, is worth little if disconnected from reality, creativity, and human achievements. Process values, how we attain a good, are often more important than the consequences embodied by that good.

If happiness is construed as objective well-being or human flourishing or a standard wider than maximizing the balance of pleasure over pain, my objections would fail. So much would be packed into "happiness" that any value I might advance would already be included. We could define happiness, whatever we take it to be, as the supreme good, but that is supremely redundant and thus supremely uninteresting. This strategy is ill-advised because it makes happiness the greatest good through trivialization: Any plausible human value, everything that benefited human beings, would antecedently be part of "happiness." Besides, this strategy is unavailable to utilitarians because it presupposes that the hedonic calculus is an insufficient guide to action: More than merely calculating the balance of pleasure over pain would be required to determine right actions.

The hero, martyr, and saint are typically concerned with more than producing a favorable balance of pleasure over pain. Their self-sacrifices serve their deepest values, their firmest commitments, their grandest causes. These projects presumably advance the human good. They benefit other people. Whether they invariably increase the balance of social pleasure over pain is an open question. The human good is wider than collective human pleasure. Friedrich Nietzsche (1844–1900) sarcastically expressed his disdain for the utilitarian conception of happiness as a positive balance of pleasure over pain: "Humanity does not strive for happiness; only the English do."[11] To be a great value, happiness must be more than collective human pleasure. The British utilitarians oscillate uneasily between identifying happiness with well-being widely construed and defining happiness as a highly favorable balance of pleasure over pain. Under the first understanding, happiness is overly determined and represents everything positive, while under the second understanding happiness is only collective hedonism. Neither understanding of happiness is persuasive.

Worthwhile happiness is typically an accompaniment to, not the direct goal of, a life lived well. The British utilitarians portray suffering and pain too crudely as evils. Interpreted strictly, the utilitarians would welcome the end of all pain, suffering, struggle, and anxiety. Perhaps, at first blush, many human beings would agree. We should reconsider.

Nietzsche understood that greatness necessarily involves suffering and the overcoming of grave obstacles. He evaluated peoples, individuals, and cultures by their ability to transform suffering and tragedy to spiritual advantage. We cannot eliminate suffering, but we can use it creatively. Suffering and resistance can stimulate and nourish our highest creative energies. By changing our attitude toward suffering from pity to affirmation, we open ourselves to greatness. For Nietzsche, joy and strength trump the "happiness" of the herd and their philosophical apologists, the utilitarians.

Every art, every philosophy may be viewed as a remedy and an aid in the service of growing and struggling life; they always presuppose suffering and sufferers.

But there are two kinds of sufferers: first, those who suffer from the *over-fullness* of life—they want a Dionysian art and likewise a tragic view of life, a tragic insight—and then those who suffer from the impoverishment of life and seek rest, stillness, calm seas, redemption from themselves through art and knowledge, or intoxication, convulsions, anesthesia, and madness.[12]

A life without suffering and pain is not a human life. Human beings are born to suffer and die. The best of us infuse our lives with meaning, value, and significance in part by how we confront tragedy and transform suffering to creative advantage. The utilitarians could benefit from a dose of Stoic wisdom and a dash of Nietzschean panache.

## 4. HAPPINESS AS ILLUSION

Arthur Schopenhauer's (1788–1860) outlook was pessimistic.[13] Human life is beset with universal, unavoidable suffering which prevents fulfillment of basic needs and wants. Life itself, not merely mortality and fear of death, renders human existence problematic. Although our world of appearance yields the illusion of individuation, Reality, as thing-in-itself, is a primal unity without individual parts. Our notions of space, time, and causality are functions of the way the human mind actively shapes and organizes sensory material: They have no independent existence as substances or categories of Reality. For Schopenhauer, individuality itself is a grand illusion. Life is a totality to which all creatures belong as expression of a oneness in flux.

We are aware of ourselves as self-moving and active, as direct expressors of wills. Schopenhauer took this inner consciousness to be basic and irreducible. What we will and what we do are one phenomenon viewed from the different vantage points of inner consciousness and body, respectively. He extended his notion of will, seeing it as definitive of the fundamental character of the universe, in order to undermine those who insisted on the underlying rationality and morality of the cosmos.

Schopenhauer tries to reorient philosophy away from the dominant rationalism of his day to greater emphasis on unconscious, biological forces. He denies the inevitability of human progress and the perfectibility of people. He insists that human beings are doomed to an eternal round of torment and misery.

Striving is the basic nature of the will, and no finished project can end striving. Because striving is incapable of final serenity, we alternate between the lack of fulfillment we feel when not achieving temporary goals and the sense of letdown and boredom we feel when we attain them. Schopenhauer concludes, along with the Buddhists, that we should minimize our attachments to and withdraw as much as possible from this life.

Nietzsche was concerned with the links between the conditions and fulfillment of culture and a tragic view of life. Nietzsche's tragic view of life was influenced significantly by Schopenhauer who was in turn influenced by Buddhist thought. Although Nietzsche tries to distance himself from Schopenhauer, his own views on suffering, the pervasiveness of will, the lack of final resolutions, the role of strife, and the contingency of individuation owe much to Schopenhauer's work. Nietzsche, however, is an active nihilist while Schopenhauer is a passive nihilist.

The difference between these two forms of nihilism can be illustrated by the ancient myth of Sisyphus.[14] Condemned by the gods to push a huge rock to the top of a hill from which it fell down the other side, to be pushed again to the top from which it fell again, and so on forever, Sisyphus was doomed to futile, pointless, unrewarded labor. His immortality was part of his punishment. His consciousness of the futility of his project was his tragedy. Sisyphus's life is supposedly representative of human life: repetitious, meaningless, pointless toil that adds up to nothing in the end. The myth portrays the eternal human struggle and indestructible human spirit. Although Sisyphus is not mortal, that deepens and does not redeem the absurdity of his life. While human life bears more variety than Sisyphus's life, the matter is only one of degree. While some human beings take solace in producing and raising children, that can be viewed as more of the same: adding zeros to zeros.

Schopenhauer would counsel Sisyphus to withdraw from his task of endlessly pushing the boulder up a hill, and, failing that possibility, to detach himself from the task as he performs it. Nietzsche would advise Sisyphus to affirm his fate, to desire nothing more than to do what he is fated to do eternally, to luxuriate in the immediate texture of what he does, to confer, through attitude and will, meaning on an inherently meaningless task.

Schopenhauer fails to see that value and meaning need not be permanent to be real; that process renders fulfillments independently of attaining goals; that the attainments of great effort and creation do not instantaneously produce emptiness; that suffering is not inherently negative but can be transfigured for creative advantage.

Schopenhauer claims human desire is unquenchable. Much like Plato's tyrannical man, we create new desires soon after we fulfill earlier desires. We always want more regardless of how many desires we fulfill. Thus we are frustrated either by failure to fulfill our desires, or we are bored once we fulfill them, or we are creating new desires that lead to the same self-defeating alternatives.

What is the state to which Schopenhauer aspires? Does he secretly yearn for a condition of never-ending bliss? Does freedom from suffering require that we want nothing more? Many would find such a life deadening. A life devoid of new projects, adventures, journeys, and goals lacks creativity: Bland contentment replaces vigorous thought and action. Perhaps suffering is produced not by the process of seeking fulfillment of new desires but by the taming of our desire-creating mechanism. Having unfulfilled desires need not be painful; it is often exhilarating. We imagine rewarding new situations and pursue them vigorously. We find fulfillments in the process and, often, in achieving the goal. Our insatiability ensures that we continue to imagine and pursue rewarding projects instead of being limited to contemplating earlier fulfillments. Whether the new desires we create produce suffering depends on what they are and how we pursue them, not solely on their presence.

A crude dualism infects Schopenhauer's analysis. He separates human experience into desires and results. Human beings desire what they lack or what they seek more of. This sense of deprivation itself is a type of suffering. When we act to attain our desires we either fail or we succeed. If we fail we deepen our suffering. If we succeed in attaining our goal we may experience temporary satisfaction. This satisfaction, however, is soon followed by boredom. Our striving, willful nature cannot find contentment. Final serenity is available only in the tomb or womb.

The crudeness of Schopenhauer's dualism lies in his categories. Human life is not experienced as a series of discrete pursuits of isolated goals. The process of striving itself yields satisfactions independently of attaining its goals. Upon being attained, goals propel us to new projects. Boredom results from inactivity, a loss of faith in life, and a lack of imagination. But human beings live in a continuous process of desires, finding appropriate means of satisfying those desires, and failing to achieve or attaining the ends we seek. In this continuous process, the categories of desires, means, and ends are fluid. What is called an end in relation to a particular means is itself a means to another end. What is an end with respect to a particular desire is itself a desire leading to pursuit of another end. The continuous process, at its best, energizes our spirit, manifests our faith in life, and reveals our imagination.

Schopenhauer talks of our incessant striving as if it were a disease to be eradicated through withdrawal. But human beings are not static characters trying to find a fixed point called "contentment." If contentment suggests inactivity, a final termination, or a mere savoring of the past, then it does conjure terminal boredom or retreat from the world. If we understand contentment more robustly we will underscore its compatibility with continuous activity and self-creation. Contentment is not a final resting point, but a positive self-appraisal: an acknowledgment that we are on the proper course, a savoring of the past seasoned with hope for the future, a satisfaction with the self we are creating. Schopenhauer failed to understand that if we create an endless supply of rewarding projects, our lack of final satisfaction bears joyous tidings.

Whereas Schopenhauer tacitly accepts the criteria of hedonism and permanence, Nietzsche embraces the criterion of power: Exertion, struggle and suffering are at the core of overcoming obstacles, and human beings experience and truly feel their power only through overcoming obstacles. Higher human types joyfully embrace the values of power, while "last men," Nietzsche's male-gendered notions of embodied banality, and utilitarian philosophers extol the values of hedonism.

The highest ambitions of last men are comfort and security. They are the extreme case of the herd mentality: habit, custom, indolence, egalitarianism, self-preservation, and muted will to power prevail. Last men embody none of the inner tensions and conflicts that spur transformative action. They take no risks, lack convictions, avoid experimentation, and seek only bland survival. Utilitarian philosophers, although not themselves last men, unwittingly fuel the herd mentality with their celebration of egalitarianism and happiness as collective pleasure.[15]

Nietzsche's tragic view of life understands fully the inevitability of human suffering, the flux that is the world, and the Sisyphus-like character of daily life. Yet it is in our response to tragedy that we manifest either a heroic or a herd mentality. We cannot rationalize or justify the inherent meaninglessness of our suffering. We cannot transcend our vulnerability and journey to fixed security. We are contingent, mortal beings and will remain so.

We are free, however, to create ourselves: We bear no antecedent duties to external authority; we are under the yoke of no preestablished goals. We need not recoil squeamishly from the horrors of existence; instead, we can rejoice in a passionate life of perpetual self-overcoming. Art can validate our creativity; laughter can ease our pain and soften our pretensions.

For Nietzsche, happiness based on pleasure or the avoidance of suffering or the quest for contentment is overrated. High creativity, robust meaning, the

attainment of great value, and the conquest of mighty obstacles are paramount.

From the insights and deficiencies of the utilitarians, Schopenhauer, and
Nietzsche we can derive the following lessons:

- Happiness as a merely positive psychological state, as enduring joy, exuberance, or contentment, is overrated.
- Such happiness is sometimes grounded in radical self-delusion; it can
  be unconnected to reality; it can be artificially produced; and it can
  occur without the exercise of the most valuable human capabilities.
- High creativity, robust meaning, the attainment of great value, and the
  conquest of mighty obstacles are more worthy than happiness defined as
  a relatively enduring psychological state.
- Value and meaning need not be permanent to be real.
- Process renders fulfillments independently of attaining goals.
- Suffering is not inherently negative but can be transfigured for creative
  advantage.
- In a continuous process, the categories of desires, means, and ends are
  fluid.

## 5. HAPPINESS AS POSITIVE PSYCHOLOGICAL STATE

Contemporary social scientists, such as Robert Lane, Ruut Veenhoven, David
Myers, and David Lykken, invariably define happiness as a predominantly
positive state of mind or psychological condition. Their recipe for happiness
includes the fulfillment of certain desires: a reasonable income, good health,
love, long-term romance, satisfying sex, a preferred job, and some success
and recognition.[16] Personal traits such as self-confidence, an articulated value
system, a belief that life generally has meaning, and a sense of empowerment
and control over our lives also have been found to contribute to happiness.
Those who are happiest in our culture are married, but without children
living at home, employed in a relatively prestigious and fulfilling job, well
educated, with high income.

Strong personal relationships reduce stress, improve health, and promote
self-esteem. Social support and a sense of controlling one's own fate are the
most important sources of well-being. Social support and a sense of control
are interchangeable. If people have a heightened sense of control over their

lives, social support adds little to their well-being, while if people have much social support, whether they have a sense of personal control matters little. Therefore, those who seek solitude may find well-being in work, creative activity, or choices that heighten their sense of control over their lives; while those who pursue intimate bonds, if successful, may find well-being in spite of a low sense of control over their lives.

Happiness is tied less to our objective situation and more to our inner judgments and perceptions, the way we feel about our objective situation. Score one for the Stoics against Aristotle! We will be happy when we compare our circumstances to our expectations and inner standards, and judge ourselves successful. Thus, our expectations and standards are at least as important as our actual situation in determining our level of happiness. Here happiness is taken to be a healthy psychological state or relatively enduring feeling of joy, contentment, or exuberance.

We might be tempted to apply for our membership card in the modern Stoics' club. We might conclude that the trick of the good life is to drastically lower our expectations and standards, thereby ensuring a favorable comparison with our actual situation. But life is not so simple. First, the suggested trick reeks of sour grapes: If we desire something but do not obtain it, we pretend we never wanted it to begin with or that it must be flawed. The fox wanted the grapes, could not reach them, and concluded they were sour anyway. Second, the trick requires too much explicit self-deception. By lowering our expectations as a recipe for happiness, we too often artificially and insincerely simulate desires rather than pursue real ones. "I wanted to marry Mr. Right, but I have not done it. So I will marry Mr. Not-So-Hot. He is not much but he does bathe regularly." Third, we cannot ignore Schopenhauer and Nietzsche. In different ways, they understood our tendency to raise, not lower, the bar of expectations upon meeting initial success. Part of a meaningful and significant life involves reimagining and re-creating our self and our projects, not resting on our laurels or merely contemplating past triumphs. Although the Stoic prescription is prudent under dire circumstances, it too easily surrenders the vast potential richness of human life for the fool's gold of an artificially induced sense of contentment.

Good news follows. The happiest and healthiest people have an internal solution to the problem of matching expectations to actual circumstances. They distort reality. They harbor illusions. The happiest and healthiest human beings have unrealistically positive views of themselves, exaggerate the amount of control they have over their lives, and are unrealistically optimistic. In sum, the traditional advice of academic philosophy, such as to distinguish rigorously between appearance and reality, know ourselves as thoroughly as possible, and eliminate illusions, may not be the most reliable path to happiness.

People can go overboard. Embracing delusions of grandeur is not a road to happiness. But neither is relentlessly viewing things as they really are. Happiness typically flows from a measure of success in meeting our expectations and internal standards plus slightly enhancing the fit between external circumstances and internal standards in our minds. The enhancement factor consists of self-flattering, optimistic illusions that overestimate our accomplishments in relation to the success of others. If we are below average in a certain respect, we perceive ourselves as average. If we are average, we perceive ourselves as above average, and so on. The self-flattering misperception cannot be wildly exaggerated lest it border on delusion, nor can it be consciously induced: "I understand that I am only average, but I will consider myself above average so I will be happier." The controversial self-esteem programs of self-help literature and education theory may be ways of learning how to innocently induce the enhancement factor.

Take a common example. Most motor vehicle operators gleefully recount the driving errors of their fellow operators. Others "drive like maniacs" or "dawdle along like little old ladies" or "fail to keep their attention on the road" or "think they are the only car on the highway." How many people admit that they are below-average drivers? I once asked an undergraduate class of 150 whether any of them considered themselves below-average drivers. Two students raised their hands. Clear evidence that the enhancement factor is alive and well. For the record: I am an above-average driver.

Some readers will recoil at the social-comparison aspect of happiness. Judging myself, whether realistically or optimistically, in relation to others, introduces an unseemly competitiveness into the happiness quotient reminiscent of the cruel slogan: "It is not enough to succeed. My friends must fail." The danger of desires based on social comparison is that we both depend on and fear others. We need others, particularly those who are "below average," to feed our self-esteem. Yet others threaten us, particularly those who are "above average," by potentially deflating our illusions.

Whether the social comparison aspect of happiness is universal or whether it is unique to competitive cultures such as the United States goes beyond the scope of my inquiry. Happiness, at least in this culture, is tied closely to a subjective judgment that the self is worthy and effective. This judgment involves the intersection of objective circumstances, internal expectations and standards, and the enhancement factor. These aspects involve social comparisons.

We can also select carefully the relevant social comparisons. I have taught at a state comprehensive college for over twenty years. Prior to that I was an attorney in New York City. If I compare my salary to those who started at the law firm with me and continued as attorneys, my salary is the lowest. If I compare my salary to other 1982 graduates of Harvard Law School, it is among the lowest, if not the lowest. If I compare my salary to other professors who have taught at my school over the same period, it is among the highest. If I compare my salary to all residents of the United States, it is high. Which comparison should I use? I do not advocate salary comparisons as the road to happiness, but illustrate only how any social comparison is malleable. Sociologists argue that once a person earns a livable salary, additional income is irrelevant to a person's sense of well-being.

The happiest among us follow a typical pattern: a gradual pattern of objective successes spiced with periods of celebration, slightly rising but achievable expectations, and a lowering of expectations with age. Healthy social relationships, a subjectively meaningful life, reasonable success in achieving goals, appropriate internal expectations and standards, and optimistic illusions are necessary. Happy people are not so much heroic as they are well suited for life in their social environment. They are typically sociable, vigorous, assertive, socially involved, active, humorous, warm, open to experience, have daydreams and fantasies, seek excitement, and embody positive sentiments, ideas, and values. Happiness depends on attitude toward life more than accomplishing specified goals. The pursuit of goals and the reasonable belief that one is progressing toward them is paramount. We are happiest when a great goal has been pursued and seems within reach.

Human beings are stunningly adaptable. Extreme disappointment and vivifying euphoria do not persist.

[H]umans have an enormous capacity to adapt to changed circumstance . . . the worst emotional consequences of bad events are usually temporary. With major setbacks or injuries, the emotional after-effects may linger a year or more. Yet within a matter of weeks, one's current mood is more affected by the day's events—an argument with one's spouse, a failure at work, a rewarding call or a gratifying letter from a dear friend or child—than by whether one is paralyzed or mobile, blind or sighted . . . What matters, then, is whether things have just changed . . . Better than a high income is a rising income. If we get a pay raise, receive an improved test grade, bring home a promotion, or get asked out, we feel an initial surge of pleasure. But if these new realities continue, we adapt . . . life could be an unending pleasure cruise only if happiness were continually rejuiced by upward surges . . . If you're headed for the top, the pleasure of going by stairway will outlast that of a fast elevator ride.[17]

The adaptability factor underscores a lesson implicitly taught by Schopenhauer and Nietzsche. We sometimes fantasize that achieving one great goal— whether it be meeting the person of our dreams, attaining material or occupational success or celebrity, or winning a coveted award—will transform our lives and stabilize happiness. We aspire to one big score that would allow us to become our idealized selves. This aspiration, though, is unadulterated delusion: "New levels of wealth and success bring but temporary pleasure. After adapting to the new circumstances, and raising one's standard of comparison, life settles back to its normal mix of emotions."[18]

Social scientists, following the Stoics, talk of happiness in terms of state of mind, feelings, and experiences. They wisely point out that our external circumstances are less important to happiness than our judgment of those circumstances and how they fit with our expectations and social comparisons. But philosophers recoil at the acceptance of salutary illusion and the enhancement factor into the happiness calculus.

Consider the following exchange of letters on the topic of happiness between a contemporary, analytic philosopher and a nonacademic hedonist:

Dear Good Time Sal:

If happiness is to be greatly valuable it must be more than attaining a positive state of mind. It requires an evaluation of our lives and a correct assessment of the conditions of happiness, whether they are seen as relevant social comparisons, the fit between internal standards and external success, or the amount of control we have over our lives. The distinction between healthy illusion and delusion of grandeur is unpersuasive. To be truly happy, we need the state of mind that is appropriate to an accurate judgment about the life we have lived and the value to which we have connected. Healthy illusion is no different from induced peace or joy. While it may well aid in bringing about a joyful or peaceful state of mind, illusion depends on inaccurate judgments about social comparisons and the other conditions of happiness. While we may be blameless for harboring such illusions, they produce only an unearned joyful or peaceful state of mind. Such illusions are no better than drugs injected into us while we sleep or the instructions of a master hypnotist. They may stimulate the feelings of happiness, but cannot achieve the real thing. Sal, stop pursuing happiness at any price and, instead, nurture a meaningful, valuable life that merits happiness.

All the best,
Philosopher Sophia

Dear Philosopher Sophia:
   I want only to be happy. I do not care about philosophical neatness. If healthy illusions are the road to happiness, I hope that I can produce them, although I understand I cannot do that self-consciously. If people feel happy, report that they are happy, then they are happy. That is all happiness is. Go preach elsewhere!

Don't tread on me,
Good Time Sal

Sal is incorrect about the value of happiness. A worthwhile happiness is much more than a felicitous, honest self-report. Numerous movies, television programs, and novels have been produced featuring characters who are drugged, hypnotized, or deceived into thinking they are happy. The message is that such people are the most pathetic, not the most fortunate, among us. Are illusions that lure us into thinking we are happy any different? One difference might be that these illusions are self-produced. But would the media message be different if the characters choose to drug, hypnotize, or deceive themselves? If they inadvertently did so? We might conclude that being an agent in our flight from reality makes us more, not less, pathetic. If happiness as a positive state of mind should be earned by living and correctly assessing certain types of lives, then illusions are obstacles to worthwhile happiness even when they can stimulate happy feelings.

Sal might still be unconvinced: "If those who see reality most clearly are less likely to be happy, what does that say? Give me a little self-induced illusion any day. Better to be John and Jane Doe, happy through the enhancement factor, than to be Socrates, dissatisfied because he sees the truth so clearly. Remember, Socrates, at least as described by Plato, had to invent another world of perfection and timelessness. The horror of reality led him to fantasy, too. Socrates' fantasy was much more extensive than slightly self-flattering illusions."

This rejoinder is powerful only if the feelings of happiness are always a great good. They are not. A life lived well, one connected robustly to meaning and value, that earns the feelings of happiness as a fitting response, is a greater good than feelings of happiness grounded on illusion or deception. I will later argue that such a life, even devoid of the extended feelings of happiness, is a greater good than the feelings of happiness.

Sal might press: "Look here, happiness is only a state of mind, an extended experience, an aggregate of feelings. We may attain that state of mind in better or worse ways, but that does not mean we are happy only when we attain the relevant feelings in the best way. I do not necessarily hold that happiness is always the greatest good, only that it is a good. And I would rather have that good, attained almost any way, than most other goods."

This generates two concessions. I concede that "happiness" is used in several ways, and that my insistence in connecting happiness with both the relevant state of mind and certain accurate judgments about our lives reflects my philosophical bias. That is why I call my preferred version worthwhile happiness—happiness tightly linked with value—not happiness as such. Sal, the nonacademic critic, though, concedes that happiness as only the relevant state of mind loses some of its panache and its claim to being the greatest good. The question then becomes whether Sal's happiness is a great good or necessarily a good at all.

Contemporary social science ably describes happiness understood as a relatively enduring positive state of mind:

- The fulfillment of certain desires is more likely than the fulfillment of other desires to produce such happiness.
- A reasonable income, good health, love, long-term romance, satisfying sex, a preferred job, and some success and recognition are among the happiness-producing desires.
- Happiness depends less on our objective situation and more on our inner judgments and perceptions, the way we feel about our objective situation.
- Temperament is also important. Personal traits such as self-confidence, an articulated value system, a belief that life generally has meaning, and a sense of empowerment and control over our lives contribute to happiness.
- The happiest human beings benefit from an enhancement factor. They subconsciously overestimate their situation. They have unrealistically positive views of themselves, exaggerate the amount of control they have over their lives, and are unrealistically optimistic.
- We facilitate happiness by rejecting unrealistic expectations, formulating short-term, achievable goals, and selecting social comparisons that nurture appreciation for our achievements and circumstances.
- A continually rising curve of circumstances is a better recipe for happiness than any specific attainment or any particular set of social circumstances.

I will now turn to contemporary philosophers who have grappled with the findings of social scientists and thereby refined classical and modern understandings of happiness.

# NOTES

1. Immanuel Kant, "Fundamental Principles of the Metaphysic of Morals" in *Kant's Critique of Practical Reason and Other Works on the Theory of Ethics*, trans. Thomas Kingsmill Abbott (London: Longmans, Green Publishers, 1879), sec. 1.

2. Immanuel Kant, "Transcendental Doctrine of Method," in *Critique of Pure Reason*, trans. J. M. D. Meiklejohn (New York: John Wiley, 1943), ch. 2, sec. 2.

3. Immanuel Kant, *Critique of Practical Reason and Other Works on the Theory of Ethics*, trans. Thomas Kingsmill Abbott (London: Longmans, Green, 1926), Part I, Book 1, ch. 3, 108.

4. Georg W. F. Hegel, *The Phenomenology of Mind*, trans. J. B. Bailie (London: George Allen & Unwin, 1949); and *The Philosophy of Right*, trans. T. M. Knox (Oxford: Clarendon Press, 1942).

5. Hegel, *Philosophy of Right*, 130.

6. Ibid., 183.

7. Jeremy Bentham, *A Fragment on Government and the Principles of Morals and Legislation* (Oxford: Basil Blackwell, 1948), ch. 1, 126.

8. Ibid., ch. 4, 151.

9. John Stuart Mill, "Utilitarianism," in *Utilitarianism, Liberty and Representative Government* (New York: E. P. Dutton, 1944), 32–33.

10. Ibid., 14–15.

11. Friedrich Nietzsche, "Epigrams and Arrows," sec. 12 in *Twilight of The Idols* in *The Portable Nietzsche*, trans. Walter Kaufmann (New York: Viking Press, 1954).

12. Friedrich Nietzsche, *The Gay Science*, trans. Walter Kaufmann (New York: Random House, 1967), sec. 370.

13. Arthur Schopenhauer, *The World as Will and Idea*, 3 vols., trans. R. B. Haldane and J. Kemp (London: Routledge & Kegan Paul, 1948).

14. Albert Camus, *The Myth of Sisyphus*, trans. Justin O'Brien (New York: Vintage Books, 1991).

15. Friedrich Nietzsche, "Zarathustra's Prologue," sec. 5 in *Thus Spoke Zarathustra*, in *The Portable Nietzsche*, trans. Walter Kaufmann.

16. Robert E. Lane, "The Road Not Taken: Friendship, Consumerism, and Happiness," *Critical Review* 8 (1994): 521–554; M. J. Stones, Thomas Hadjistavropoulos, Holly Tuuko, and Albert Kozma, "Happiness Has Traitlike and Statelike Properties," *Social Indicators Research* 36 (1995): 129–144; Roy F. Baumeister, *Meanings of Life* (New York: The Guilford Press, 1991); Ruut Veenhoven, *Conditions of Happiness* (Dordrecht, Holland: Reidel Publishers, 1984); Ruut Veenhoven, "Is Happiness a Trait?" *Social Indicators Research* 33 (1994): 101–160.

17. David G. Myers, *The Pursuit of Happiness* (New York: Avon Books, Inc., 1992), 48, 51–52, 53.

18. Ibid., 68.

# 3

# CONTEMPORARY PHILOSOPHICAL VIEWS

R ecent philosophical work can be classified into four categories: the marriage of philosophy and social science as happiness understood as a relatively enduring, positive psychological state; happiness as a positive self-
appraisal; happiness as an accurate, positive self-appraisal; and happiness as
connection to an objective, preexisting good.

## 1. PHILOSOPHY JOINS HANDS WITH SOCIAL SCIENCE

Some philosophers, such as G. H. von Wright and Robin Barrow, agree with
contemporary social scientists: Happiness is merely introspective and descriptive, an accurate self-report of a person's positive state of mind.[1] If I report
truthfully that I am happy—that I have a relatively enduring positive state of
mind such as joy, peace, or exuberance—then I am happy. Period. Happiness
does not include a necessary normative element. If I have attained my positive
state of mind through deeds that society labels inappropriate, I am still happy.
A person could argue that my happiness was parasitic on the unhappiness of
others or that my happiness is unworthy from the standpoint of conventional
morality, but he or she could not plausibly argue that I am not happy. My
self-conscious, good-faith recognition that I am pleased or satisfied with my
overall situation is sufficient for happiness. If I described myself as happy yet
exhibited significant estrangement, depression, low self-esteem, or pervasive
anxiety, that would call into question whether my description was in good
faith. I could describe myself as happy but be lying, self-deceived, joking, or
the like.

Advocates of this view argue that talk about flourishing, a degree of fit between a person's expectations and results, the enhancement factor, and the like, is inflated. All that is required for happiness is the desired conscious condition. Extended joy, peace, or exuberance is enough for happiness, however it is attained. The argument would spin like this: When we ask people whether they are happy, we are not looking for an extended discourse on whether they are flourishing, whether they have met their expectations, the specifics of their personal standards and norms, the details of their self-flattering illusions, or anything else. We are asking only about their conscious condition: Are they experiencing sustained joy or peace? If they, in good faith, answer yes and their actions confirm that answer, we conclude that they appear happy. And that is the entire matter. Perhaps flourishing, meeting personal expectations, adjusting standards, and the like are a recipe that leads many people to extended joy or peace, but the typical recipe is only one means to the desired general condition. To think otherwise is to confuse a means to happiness with the definition of happiness.

Under this view, Aristotle's list of requirements for living and faring well is only a recipe for, not a definition of, happiness. Aristotle offers only a version of how to attain the requisite psychological condition. Aristotle would object that happiness is a condition of the soul, not merely a positive state of mind. He would refuse to accept extended joy, peace, or exuberance as a definition of happiness. Only by doing so could Aristotle salvage the connection between happiness and the greatest good.

Advocates of the happiness-as-positive-state-of-mind position make the strong point that their understanding, not Aristotle's, best reflects the contemporary usage of the term "happiness." But their victory weakens the value of happiness. Suppose happiness is merely the experience of sustained joy or peace, and the means by which that experience is attained are irrelevant. Suppose the biochemistry of our brains can be manipulated to make us more likely to experience sustained joy. Perhaps a new pill, an enhanced form of Prozac or Lithium, can alter our brain biochemistry to simulate the desired conscious condition. Happiness is now within the reach of all. We take our medication, we are joyful and peaceful, all in the world seems right. Is this heaven? Not likely.

Savor the irony. Prozac and Lithium are typically prescribed for those who are unhappy or depressed. If a powerful version of these pills could heighten the joy of everyone, that might be because we were all depressed. Instead of saying, "Well, old Spike is doing better now that he is on Prozac," his friends could gush, "Old Spike is happy, just like the rest of us." Who Spike was, what values he embodied, what creativity he exhibited, and what he did would not matter. As long as Spike pounded down the pills, he would exude the conscious state that equals happiness. But Spike's happiness is not a great good. Instead, happiness through pharmaceuticals dehumanizes and trivializes us. Although legitimate, salutary uses of antidepressant medications abound, routine prescriptions to elevate the mood of everyone are unwise.

While it is true that happiness is plausibly defined as sustained joy or peace, that is small consolation to happiness-mongers. Aristotle understood perceptively that to be the greatest good happiness must embody the most important values. He overplayed his hand and paid too little attention to the conscious condition required for happiness. The happiness-as-positive-state-of-mind position inverts the mistake. By attending only to the conscious condition, it ignores the most important values. As a result, any gains in defining happiness accessibly set back claims that such happiness is the greatest good or necessarily a great good.

Typically, good-faith descriptions of happiness result from an individual's relatively harmonious relationship with his or her environment. A thoroughly depraved or hostilely criminal person is unlikely to attain such a state. The possibility of a less morally deficient person achieving happiness, though, remains. Likewise, people might be happy even though their felicitous psychological state rested on radically false, even delusional, beliefs.

I will not waste time and energy trying to argue against the view that a relatively enduring, positive state of mind can be legitimately understood as happiness. Contemporary literature, academic and otherwise, is replete with such references. Indeed, this understanding of happiness is dominant in popular culture. I assume that a relatively enduring, positive state of mind is necessary for happiness. Going further—taking that state of mind as necessary and sufficient for happiness—does not violate language nor usage. Such a rendering, though, undermines the value of happiness. Worse, we can demonstrate how happiness as a relatively enduring, positive state of mind is often not a good at all. Such happiness is overrated.

Recall past examples of seven happy lives. Imagine a middle-aged, deeply delusional man who is convinced he is Napoleon and who derives great joy from contemplating his past and conjuring his future military triumphs. Imagine a young adult hypnotized by a master magician into a relatively enduring serenity. Imagine a person injected with a powerful, infallible drug that produces a felicitous psychological state. Imagine someone connected to a mighty virtual reality machine that simulates a rich, deep, seemingly real variety of pleasurable experiences.[2] Imagine a person living an ordinary life who suffers a terrible brain injury. The person's new life reflects that of a contented infant. Imagine a normal person whose happiness is predicated on ignorance, radically false beliefs, or pathological denial of salient facts. Imagine a contemporary version of Nietzsche's last man: a seeker only of comfort, security, habit, custom, indolence, self-preservation, and conformity. Such a person lacks deep convictions, inspiring projects, or significant purposes.

With the proper imagination and appropriate details these examples can be more vividly and convincingly drawn. As it stands, I have sketched at least seven versions of happy people, in the sense of people enjoying a relatively enduring positive state of mind. None of these types exemplify an attractive lifestyle. Some deserve our pity, some our concern, others our contempt. Happiness so conceived is not the greatest good, nor a great good, and in several cases not a good at all.

Note that as unalluring as the seven hypothetical lives appear, they are not the worst imaginable existences. To say that we would never prefer to adopt these lifestyles would be a mistake. Everything depends on our point of comparison. I would not prefer any of the seven hypothetical lives given my present situation. The seven lives are deficient. Some lack appropriate connection to reality. Some provide only muted meaning, significance, and value. Some are animated by extravagant psychological deficiencies. Such lifestyles neither warrant our allegiance nor inspire our confidence. Nevertheless, we can imagine even worse circumstances. We might prefer, for example, the simulated joys of the virtual reality machine to a life filled with enduring misery, oppression, and ignorance. That the seven hypothetical lives are not the worst imaginable existences is, though, faint consolation.

Accordingly, I have no problem accepting happiness as a relatively enduring, positive state of mind. But much more is needed to link happiness with robust value.

## 2. HAPPINESS AS POSITIVE SELF-APPRAISAL

Some contemporary philosophers, such as Richard Kraut and Irwin Goldstein, argue that happiness is not merely an enduring positive state of mind. Happiness is not merely descriptive, but also normative. When we assert in good faith that we are happy we are not only reporting our psychological state but also positively evaluating our lives.[3] We are saying that we are joyful, peaceful, contented, or exuberant and that we deserve these feelings given the lives we are leading. Our happiness is not capricious or fortuitous. It is merited by a life well lived. Appeals to evaluation invite a question about standards: Whose standards supply the relevant criteria for appraisal? Conventional societal norms? Objective criteria embedded in the universe by nature or a Supreme Being? Objective standards discoverable by proper application of human reason?

The answer from this group of philosophers is none of the above. The relevant standards are purely subjective. I am living up to my personal preferences about how I should live. These preferences may or may not correlate to those of societal norms, alleged objective criteria embedded in the universe, or the imperatives of human reason. We may, though, be mistaken in our evaluation. We could err in thinking that we are living up to our personal preferences. Under such circumstances, we think we are happy but we are not. Because the happiness-as-positive-self-appraisal philosophers add a normative component to the meaning of happiness, they must admit the possibility of mistake in our appraisals.

The happiness-as-positive-state-of-mind sociologists and philosophers claim happiness is purely descriptive: If I report truthfully that I am happy, then I am happy. Period. The causal link between my positive state of mind and what brought it about is unimportant for accurate claims to happiness. Deluded Napoleon, the drugged young adult, the person in the virtual reality machine, the modern version of Nietzsche's last man, and the rest of my hypothetical frolickers are all happy. If I think in good faith that I am happy, then I am happy.

The happiness-as-positive-self-appraisal brigade disagrees. If I am deluded and merely think I am living up to my personal evaluative standards while I am not, then I wrongly think I am happy. So deluded Napoleon, assuming his personal evaluative standard is to conquer Europe, is not truly happy. He is not living up to his standards. He only thinks he is. Likewise with several of my other hypothetical cases. If the drugged young adult and the person on the virtual reality machine have standards different from the lives they are actually leading, then they are not happy, even though they appear and claim to be happy. The modern version of Nietzsche's last man, though, could still be happy under this view if and only if his major desires focus on leading precisely the indolent life he exemplifies.

The happiness-as-positive-self-appraisal view underscores that claims to happiness are evaluations: They require judgments, not merely sincere reports of feelings or psychological states. Judgments are sometimes mistaken. Therefore, our sincere reports of a positive, relatively enduring state of mind are not enough to establish that we are happy. We must also judge accurately that we are meeting our subjective standards about how our lives should be lived. Richard Kraut argues:

> When we say that someone is living happily, we imply that he has certain attitudes towards his life: he is very glad to be alive; he judges that on balance his deepest desires are being satisfied and that the circumstances of his life are turning out well.[4]

Kraut and his philosophical cohorts understand that the Stoic happiness quotient is woefully inadequate. Merely satisfying a high percentage of our desires is not enough. Some desires are more important than others. Also, some human beings, such as the hero, martyr, and saint, pursue desires that they know often conflict with personal happiness. And the passionate pursuit of our desires, even if some of them are never fulfilled, can itself bring deep satisfaction.

Our second-order desires that our most important first-order desires are being fulfilled are crucial. Our second-order desires reveal our self-identities and our fundamental projects, purposes, and interests. In order to be happy we must recognize correctly that our subjective standards are being met. That we might be even happier if we accepted different standards of self-evaluation is unimportant.

> A person is living happily only if he realizes that he is attaining the important things he values, or if he comes reasonably close to this high standard . . . One must also find that the things one values are genuinely rewarding and not merely the best of a bad range of alternatives . . . a person is happy only if he meets the standards he imposes on his life. Even if many others consider his standards too low, and would never switch places with him, he can still have a happy life.[5]

Why, though, are the standards of evaluation subjective? Several reasons. First, objective standards are notoriously difficult to establish. Are they grounded in the dictates of a Supreme Being or embedded in Nature or in the proper application of Reason? All such claims are metaphysically dubious. And even if we could establish the existence of these metaphysical linchpins, we face the daunting problem of discerning which of our conclusions correspond to the imperatives of the Supreme Being, Nature, or Reason. That is, even if we know that an objective standard exists, how do we know when our judgments comply with that standard? Second, an objective standard might suggest implausibly that one ideal lifestyle and series of preferences exists for all of us. Third, if the alleged objective standard is more earthbound, grounded only in our traditions and societal ideals, then it is accessible. But accessibility brings a stiff price. The objective standard is merely intersubjective agreement, perhaps over time. Such a standard urges us to conform to prevalent norms and dominant ideas. These invitations are redolent with the stench of mere conventionalism.

Kraut, though, understands the limits of his position:

> For subjectivism says so little about how we should lead our lives: it tells us that if we want to be happy we should make up our minds about what we value most, and this is of little help to those who are uncertain about what kind of life to lead.[6]

The happiness-as-positive-self-appraisal view connects happiness to reality and to normative judgment. The position denies legitimacy to those whose claims to happiness are grounded in deep delusion, artificial inducement, or external imposition. The position forces us to evaluate, not merely describe, our psychological state. The position admits degrees of happiness and does not impose a particular ideal on everyone.

By reconnecting reality with normative judgment, this view makes happiness more valuable than it sometimes is under the happiness-as-positive-state-of-mind position. Still, happiness can be attained by meeting subjective standards that are uninspiring and effete. Nietzsche's last man, steadfastly pursuing only comfort, security, conformity, and indolence, could easily be happy. A young adult who suffers a serious, irreversible brain injury and endures as a contented child thereafter could easily be happy. Such happiness, although not the worst alternative available, is not necessarily a great good. Nietzsche sneers contemptuously at the happiness of the last man. We would not cheer the brain injury of the young adult even if it made her "happier" than she was prior to the injury.

Again, I am not arguing that the happiness-as-positive-self-appraisal position fails to understand the real meaning of "happiness." Such arguments are not my concern. I argue only that happiness attained on these grounds cannot be the greatest good, nor necessarily a great good, and is sometimes not a good at all. Such happiness is often overrated.

## 3. HAPPINESS AS ACCURATE, POSITIVE SELF-APPRAISAL

Disturbed by the subjectivism of the two previous views, some philosophers, such as John Kekes and Lynn McFall, argue that a reasonable objectivism is required.[7] Such an objectivism demands an appeal to both subjective standards internal to a life and to objective standards grounded in shared community life.

The motivation of this view flows from a conviction that the happiness-as-positive-self-evaluation position does not go far enough in connecting happiness and value. Although advocates do not insist on one final good or a particular ideal lifestyle applicable to everyone, they resist the invitation of subjectivists to accept claims to happiness based on the satisfaction of immoral or unworthy desires. Opponents of subjectivism argue that someone who fulfills internal standards that are immoral or unworthy does not merit happiness. Accordingly, merely fulfilling our subjective standard is insufficient for happiness. Our positive self-evaluation must be accurate; it must be based on a standard that is valuable, not merely a standard that happens to be ours.

John Kekes, for example, does not subscribe to metaphysically objective standards of evaluation, but also rejects simple subjectivism.

> A man's judgment about his own happiness can be mistaken and the mistake can be pointed out to him by others. What makes this possible is not the existence of objective standards of happiness, but the rational appraisal of subjective standards . . . a man's commitments are made by him, but nevertheless they can be justified and criticized independently of what he thinks or does.[8]

Under this view, people may assert sincerely that they enjoy a relatively enduring positive psychological state and that they are meeting their subjective standards for living, but be mistaken that they are happy. Happiness also requires standards that are rationally justified. Some subjective standards will fail this test. This can happen for numerous reasons. A set of subjective standards might not fulfill the needs and basic wants of physical, emotional, and social life: A person might set standards that are dismally low. A set of subjective standards might be radically at odds with dominant, justified social morality: A person might have immoral standards. A set of subjective standards might not lead us to a good life, one embodying sufficient exercise of the best human capabilities: A person might set standards that dishonor uniquely human attributes, or that insufficiently animate robust self-creation. Although no single ideal or particular lifestyle must be fulfilled, not all subjective standards will foster a happy life. Kekes rejects the Aristotelian claim that a determinant human nature militates what constitutes a happy life. He nevertheless insists that we can deduce from a broad sketch of human nature what lives cannot be happy. Human lives have no preordained *telos*, but some lives are rationally indefensible.

A man's sincere judgment that his first-order wants are satisfied in accordance with his life-plan, and that he is happy, is open to rational evaluation. And the evaluation may be adverse. This is the reason why a man's sincere judgment that he is happy is only necessary and not sufficient for his happiness. If, however, his judgment is supported by independent rational evaluation, then, I claim, both necessary and sufficient conditions of his happiness are met.[9]

The independent rational evaluation to which Kekes appeals provides external justification for happiness claims without resort to Platonic-Christian metaphysics or an Aristotelian greatest good. He assumes we are living in a morally acceptable society.

What, then, are these grounds? The first one is that [paramount] wants created by physiological, psychological, and social conditions . . . must be minimally satisfied . . . The second ground is that we must observe the required conventions of the moral tradition of our society . . . The third ground . . . is that we must sincerely believe that we are satisfied with [our lives]. But such beliefs must be held on the ground that our important specific wants are being satisfied . . . The fourth ground of evaluation concerns the appropriateness of our ideals . . . The fifth ground is the possession of the virtues of self-direction . . . The sixth ground . . . that we adopt ideals from our moral tradition and make such adjustments to them as necessary to fit our own context and characters.[10]

In a similar vein, Lynn McFall advances minimal, independent conditions for happiness:

Seven minimal conditions are considered necessary for the happiness of rational affirmation: logical consistency, conformity of behavior with value, motivation by reason, conscious awareness of values, absence of regret, belief in justified values, and affirmation of one's whole life. Beliefs do not have to be true for happiness, but they must be well-grounded. Truth sets too high a standard of justification and knowledge . . . rational affirmation requires that one must be able to overcome the experience of learning that one's beliefs were false without sliding into dissatisfaction.[11]

Happiness-as-accurate-positive-self-appraisal has its roots in Aristotelian and self-realization theory. Under this view, people whose dominant life goals are to collect bobby pins, to become a famous gangster, to luxuriate in a simulated, favorable environment, to derive contentment from deep delusion, and the like cannot be happy. Regardless of their extended joy, serenity, or exuberance, and their correct judgment that they are fulfilling their internal standards, such people lead rationally or morally indefensible lives. As leading a rationally and morally justified life is also necessary for happiness under this view, this collection of fun-seekers falls short.

Beginning with sound intentions, this view strikes an imperialistic chord. The good intentions center on reconnecting happiness with value. Possessing a relatively enduring, positive psychological state grounded in adequately satisfying our subjective standards is not enough. Such a happiness can be overrated, even dishonorable, irrational, or pathetic. Only reconnecting happiness with value, rationality, and higher human capabilities can reestablish its necessary worth.

The imperialistic chord resounds when we understand that this view dismisses sincere, accurate claims to happiness through semantic fiat. The advocate of happiness-as-positive-state-of-mind could object: "Why cannot happiness be grounded on simple pursuits, based on the exercise of limited capabilities, or correlated to our subjective expectations? Why say that the adult who suffers a terrible brain injury and who can live only the life of a contented child cannot be happy? Granted, such a life is less worthy than the lives to which we aspire, but sometimes we must play the cards we are dealt. Better, in the circumstances described, to live the life of a contented child than numerous other horrible imaginable lives. Why not say that the injured adult is happy, while recognizing that but for the injury he or she would have probably lived a much better life? As long as we do not insist that happiness is the greatest good no problem arises. Sure, some happy lives are better lives overall than others on a host of dimensions, but that does not rule out the former from being happy lives."

Again, we confront the tension in conceptions of happiness. Kekes, McFall, and their ilk are correct: Achieving happiness understood as a positive psychological state does not necessarily translate into a valuable life. Worthwhile happiness presupposes a connection to value, grounded either in metaphysically objective standards or in rational human appraisal. Why, though, must happiness be understood as only accompanying valuable lives?

Nietzsche disparaged the happiness of last men as unworthy of emulation, but he never denied that they were happy. Their happiness manifested acutely that a positive psychological state is not necessarily the highest value or even valuable. Nietzsche's highest value, captured by the slogan *amor fati*, was a maximally affirmative attitude toward life. Such an attitude exemplified and was reinforced by great creative projects; sharp understanding of the tragic dimensions of life; acceptance of the world as it is; enthusiastic engagement in the recurring process of self-evaluation, self-deconstruction, reimagination, and re-creation; the ongoing transformation of values; and willingness to live our lives innumerable times over and over in the same sequence and without editing out disturbing events. Nietzsche would agree with Kekes and McFall that a worthy happiness must be grounded in valuable attitudes and activities—although he would excoriate the conventionalism and appeal to societal norms upon which their rational and moral appraisals often depend. Nietzsche would also agree that self-direction was crucial and that a relatively enduring, positive psychological state is merited by those who live well. Happiness, though, for Nietzsche was not the greatest good. The greatest good is the maximally affirmative attitude toward life, the values it exudes, the creative projects it undertakes, and the obstacles it vanquishes. A worthwhile happiness is often, but not invariably, an accompanying benefit.

In sum, the happiness-as-accurate-positive-self-appraisal position does fine work in reconnecting happiness with value in the most plausible manner available to us. By going beyond happiness-as-positive-self-appraisal and requiring independent rational evaluation or minimal conditions of rational affirmation, the happiness-as-accurate-positive-self-appraisal position ensures that happiness is always a good, often a great good. Yet it does not appeal to highly contestable metaphysical entities such as the dictates of a Supreme Being, the natural order built into the universe, or the imperatives of a fixed human nature. As a result, the position defines *worthwhile happiness* well. My only misgiving is its aspiration to define happiness as such. I have argued that some forms of happiness are overrated, other forms are not even valuable, and still other forms are worthwhile. I prefer this broad understanding of happiness to views that demand through definitional fiat that happiness must be valuable, even a great good.

## 4. HAPPINESS AS CONNECTION TO OBJECTIVE, PREEXISTING GOOD

The strongest version of objectivism connects happiness to a preexisting good that human beings can only discover, not create.[12] Grounded by a metaphysical linchpin—a Supreme Being, Nature, or the imperatives of a fixed human nature—happiness is the greatest good. We sincerely report a relatively enduring, positive psychological state; we adequately satisfy our internal standards of living; and our internal standards are rational, moral, and focused in reality. Our lives must be in accord with our *telos*. Our final end is fixed by our shared human nature and the nature of the cosmos. Happiness must be grounded in eternal, unchanging, universal normative imperatives.

Subjective views of happiness and views that rely only on community moral standards are insufficient. Both positions must ultimately appeal to unreliable individual or collective preferences. Happiness is the greatest good only if it includes the highest value. Only an understanding that requires a tight link between happiness and the highest human end can silence those who clamor that happiness is overrated. The highest human end cannot merely be what an individual or community chooses, but what all human beings must seek in order to be moral and rational. The happiness-as-accurate-positive-self-appraisal theorists do not go far enough. In their zeal to recognize a range of lives that can legitimately be praised as happy, they fail to connect adequately happiness and normativity. Their depiction of normativity is too fragile because it reduces to particular or collective preferences. Only a link to a normativity external to human choices can reestablish happiness as an unvarnished good.

> An objectivist theory of happiness can embrace the content but not the rationale of other theories. It can acknowledge the necessity of subjective satisfaction without regarding it as the only content of happiness. An objectivist can affirm the importance of freely choosing personal goals and of being committed to personal values without a relativist accent on the personal. An objectivist could no doubt stress the importance of employing a rational approach to weighing and measuring important choices within the context of an overall lifeplan that embraces what are regarded consensually as the basic goods of life—as long as the weighing and measuring is done with a universal and determinate goal in mind.[13]

Following aspects of Platonic, Aristotelian, and Thomist thinking, strong objectivists, such as John Finnis, Josef Pieper, and Stephen Theron, conclude that happiness is attained only by those who rationally apprehend and obey the imperatives of an external, metaphysical normative order. If successful, they can show how happiness is not overrated, but instead is invariably the greatest good. Although some contemporary objectivists, following Plato and the Christian theologians, argue that perfect happiness can be attained only in a transcendental world, all concede that happiness is possible in this world.

The main problem with strong objectivism lies with its alleged metaphysical linchpins. Many thinkers regard the existence of a Supreme Being or fixed human nature or moral imperatives embedded in the universe as unworthy of belief. Moreover, even if such a normative order exists, our ability to access it is problematic. Without an accessible, preordained normative order, the persuasiveness of the happiness-as-connection-to-preexisting-good view vanishes. Strong objectivists invariably are convinced that self-evident moral principles or privileged intuitions—immediate apprehensions of the essence of humans and the human good—are like scientific observations which indicate independent natural moral facts. Alternately, they may espouse a literal rendering of the moral truths revealed by a Supreme Being. Happiness, under this model, is, or should be, linked with absolute, transcendent principles of morality which human beings can discover but not create.

Critics disparage these metaphysical assumptions. Based on faith and wish more than demonstrable proof, such beliefs appear to critics as the anachronistic psychological vestiges of primitive human beings desperate in the face of unexplained powers. Influenced by the accounts of Marx, Nietzsche, and Freud, critics point to a variety of possible explanations of widespread belief—none of which confirm the existence of a pre-established normative order—in the strong objectivists' metaphysical beliefs.

Critics claim that the only broad areas of cross-cultural, normative agreement concern highly general, abstract principles which lack the specification required for consensus over concrete issues. Truisms such as "do good, avoid evil," "honor the dead," and "respect families" admit of too many contestable interpretations when specific policies are at stake to support the thesis that there is a normative order embedded in nature. They ask rhetorically, "Given the available evidence and the fact that we seemingly cannot prove the existence or nonexistence of such entities conclusively through rational demonstrations, which is more likely—that a supernatural being or other source confers a natural normative order upon our world, or that any perceived order is in fact a human invention subject to reimagination and re-creation?"

We need not begin our normative quest with aspirations for an ideal vantage point or an abstracted universal human chooser. Instead, we start with the values we presently embody and the social world that is our context: our traditions and conventions have currency because they partly constitute who we are. This does not counsel an arid conventionalism because social transformation is necessary, among other reasons, to close the gap between our moral expectations and our institutional outcomes. Once we self-consciously abrogate the search for certainty and fixed foundations, our normative inquiries can attend to the social contexts in which we participate in the process of acquiring understanding and knowledge. We need not believe in a unique best moral vision to retain our conviction that we have better and worse visions.

Although I am not drawn to the strong objectivist position because of the reasons cited, I cannot disprove its metaphysical assumptions. Nor can strong objectivists prove them. I will explain in the final chapter why such assumptions will always be attractive to human beings, despite their highly speculative nature.

Strong objectivists might moderate their position by claiming that our lives are happier only due to certain goods, such as good health and friendships, regardless of our attitudes toward them. This position does not require lavish metaphysical assumptions. This moderate objectivism is reminiscent of but not identical to the happiness-as-accurate-self-appraisal view.

Although I am attracted to the moderate objectivism of the happiness-as-accurate-self-appraisal view as the best description of worthwhile happiness, I must reject the reformulated position of the strong objectivists. If a predominantly positive state of mind is required for happiness, then we cannot neatly separate goods from our attitudes toward them. Some goods may make our life better in certain respects regardless of our attitude toward them, but not necessarily make us happier. Having good health makes our life better regardless of our attitude toward it—we probably take it for granted—but it does not necessarily make our life happier. The proper subjective response to a good is required for that good to make us happier. What makes our life better in certain measurable ways does not always make our life happier.

## 5. WHAT WE LEARN FROM CONTEMPORARY PHILOSOPHERS

If happiness is understood only as a relatively enduring, positive psychological state, then it can be attained, at least occasionally, by people lacking a firm connection to reality, or leading a relatively immoral life, or pursuing trivial tasks, or incapable of exercising the higher human attributes, or suffering from psychological maladies, or impaired by uncommon ignorance, or victimized by artificial inducements or drugs. Contrary to the imperialism of philosophers who would deny that this conception captures "happiness," its advocates do not violate language or historical practice. Happiness attained in these uninspiring ways is not the worst evil and can often be a significant good when contrasted to the practical alternatives. Better to be deluded Napoleon pleased by his imaginary lot than to be deluded Stalin dissatisfied by his imaginary life. After suffering a serious brain injury, better to be an adult leading the life of a contented child than to be leading the life of a miserable brat. Such lives, however, neither mirror our aspirations nor highlight our ideals. We do not yearn for a relatively enduring positive psychological state as such—at least not from the outset, not as our first choice.

Other things being equal, a typical fully human life, whether happy or not, is preferable and more valuable than a happy life flowing from delusion, immorality, psychological maladies, and the like. Identifying happiness only with a relatively enduring, positive state of mind illustrates sharply how happiness is overrated.

Viewing happiness as a positive self-appraisal reconnects happiness with reality and normative judgment. Only if we accurately judge that our lives are meeting our own internal standards is our claim to happiness sound. Its reconnection with reality and normative judgment makes happiness more valuable than it sometimes is under the happiness-as-positive-state-of-mind view. Still, happiness can be attained under this conception by meeting any subjective standards that happen to be ours. Nietzsche has no problem declaring his last men happy. So much the worse for happiness. Many greater values should be pursued instead of the banal, uninspiring contentment of the last man. Happiness-as-a-positive-self-appraisal is still overrated and, sometimes, not even a good.

Understanding happiness as an accurate, positive self-appraisal revives the value of happiness. Under this conception, happiness requires a sincere self-report of a positive psychological state, an accurate evaluation that our lives are meeting our internal standards, and validation of those standards by objective criteria grounded in social life. Our internal standards are not justified merely because they are ours. These standards must be rationally justified. This position, in my judgment, best describes worthwhile happiness, but should not define happiness as such.

The usual rhetorical questions raised against appeals to objective criteria grounded in social life are the following: Are not such criteria founded only on conventionalism, the historical judgments of particular people at a particular time? Are not such criteria, at worst, devised by powerful groups to advance their class interests? Are not such criteria, at best, grounded merely in intersubjective agreement instead of truly objective considerations? Are not such criteria imperialistic in rejecting some claims to happiness on elitist grounds?

Such objections are not fatal to this view, but they underscore the limitations and illustrate distorting features of normative discourse. To conclude that normative discourse is a sham, though, would be unsound. Brush aside these objections for the sake of argument. Even though this conception reconnects happiness to reality and value, and describes a worthwhile happiness, it underscores why even worthwhile happiness is overrated. Happiness so grounded is still not the most important human goal, nor the greatest personal good.

Consider the following analysis of human lives. A life is *minimally meaning-ful* if it embodies enough freely chosen interests, projects, purposes, and commitments to engage the bearer and animate his or her faith in life. Even a minimally meaningful life has a narrative structure as a person organizes her energies and resources around her interests and projects. A minimally meaningful life is *minimally worthwhile*. A minimally worthwhile life is one worth living, a life such that one would not be better off dead or never having been born. The activities that bring minimal meaning must be appropriate to the experience, they must be real not simulated, not induced through external agency, nor merely hallucinations. The bar of a meaningful life is quite low. Minimal meaning produces enough satisfaction of desires and interests to block suicide or voluntary euthanasia. Lives are worth continuing and minimally meaningful where great achievement is lacking.

Some lives are more meaningful than other lives. *Robustly meaningful* lives, the ones to which we aspire, embody interests, projects, purposes, and commitments that produce *significance*. A robustly meaningful life is significant, sometimes important, occasionally even exemplary. We, typically, hope not merely to maintain our lives, but to strive for our vision of a good life. To be *significant*, a life must influence the lives of others in uncommon ways. A significant life leaves historical footprints. To be *important*, a life must be significant enough to make a relatively enduring difference in the world. These historical footprints express, thereby making more public, the importance of the life. To be *exemplary*, a life must be meaningful, significant, important, and valuable enough to serve as a model or ideal.

The distinction between minimally meaningful and robustly meaningful lives allows us to include, as we should, both a disabled, slightly retarded person and Leonardo da Vinci into the pantheon of lives worth living. Thus, meaningful lives need not be significant, important, or valuable lives.

Most of us do not have stunningly significant and important lives, although almost all of us do affect the lives of others. Most of our lives fall somewhere between minimally meaningful and robustly meaningful lives. The degree and manner of influence is crucial. To be *valuable*, lives must be linked to and support value. Some of the more important types of value are moral, cognitive, aesthetic, and religious. Hitler had a meaningful, significant, and important life. He did not have a valuable life nor an exemplary life. A valuable life is always meaningful, but a meaningful life may not be valuable. Hitler's life was meaningful but it is reasonable to view it as valueless in the sense that his collective deeds were stunningly immoral.

If our actions fit into a reasonably coherent scheme, are not futile in that we can in principle achieve our goals or at least make valuable progress toward them, and have purposes within our life scheme, we have no good reason to think our lives are meaningless or that they are absurd. Even if life as a whole lacks inherent meaning, particular lives can range from minimally to robustly meaningful. Some lives, however, fail even to fulfill the criteria of minimal meaningfulness. Such lives are literally not worth living.

Consider, again, the lives of Beethoven, Joe DiMaggio, Emily Dickinson, Kierkegaard, Queen Elizabeth I, Abraham Lincoln, Jesus, Michelangelo, Moses, Socrates, Emma Goldman, and van Gogh. These lives are paradigms of meaning and significance in religion, sports, literature, music, politics, philosophy, and art. In terms of relatively enduring accomplishments, influences, excellences, creations, and social effects these lives are among the best in their fields.

Yet these people were not strikingly happy. While each of them flourished in many respects, none realized the extended joy or peace characteristic of happiness. Perhaps they demanded too much of themselves, saw reality too clearly, were unable to harbor self-flattering illusions, could not savor their feelings of pleasure, lacked the necessary biochemistry, or were too heroic to be happy. Meaningful lives, then, are not necessarily happy lives. But happy lives, at least those that are not artificially induced, are invariably meaningful.

We might be led to conclude Aristotle was correct. Happiness must be the greatest good because if my life is happy then it will also be meaningful, but if it is meaningful it may not be happy. If all other goods aim at happiness, then Aristotle is on firm ground in arguing that happiness is the greatest good. And the homespun wisdom of parents, "I want only that my children be happy," is upheld.

Such a conclusion would be hasty. First, to call two lives meaningful does not suggest they are equally so. If the standard of meaningfulness is minimal—having goals, projects, interests, relationships that engage and energize one's life—most of our lives on the whole meet it. But that is not saying much. Few have lives as meaningful as Beethoven, Joe DiMaggio, Dickinson, Kierkegaard, Elizabeth I, Abraham Lincoln, Jesus, Michelangelo, Moses, Socrates, Emma Goldman, and van Gogh. Is it better to live Michelangelo's life and not be particularly happy or to live an obscure, minimally meaningful life, and be happier? If living a happy life was a greater good than living a robustly meaningful, significant, valuable life, then we should prefer the former. Yet we reasonably value a life replete with enduring accomplishment, high creativity, powerful social effects, and unparalleled excellence more than a minimally meaningful, happy life. While minimal meaningfulness is surely not a great good, a robustly meaningful and valuable life is at least a candidate for the greatest personal good.

Second, the relationship between happiness and the intellectual and moral virtues is less clear than Aristotle supposed. The intellectual and moral virtues can sometimes conflict with happiness. High intelligence may make it more difficult to sustain the self-flattering illusions sometimes required for feelings of happiness. The pursuit of truth is sometimes accompanied by hardship, frustration, even persecution. Following the morally correct path may bring a decrease in one's personal happiness. The righteous path did not lighten Lincoln's load. At times, pursuing a moral path results not in Aristotle's fortuitous convergence of leisure and a congenial home life, but in more labor and domestic conflict. In sum, happiness must be sometimes sacrificed for higher concerns: intellectual or moral values, or enriched meaningfulness.

One could argue that I have not demonstrated that happiness is not a great personal good. Even if someone would prefer the life of Michelangelo to the life of an obscure, happy person with a minimally meaningful life, that may show only that having numerous lesser goods in high quantity and quality is preferable to having a single, great good. So on a personal level, high creativity, enduring accomplishment, artistic excellence, and the like, when combined may be preferable to obscurity and basic happiness. Still, one could argue that happiness is the greatest good because the other goods aim at it. What is the point of high creativity, enduring accomplishment, and artistic excellence other than their contribution to someone's happiness? Even if artists lead unhappy lives, they bring much happiness to others through their creations. Likewise, even if the moral and intellectual virtues do not always lead to happiness for their practitioners, their point is to contribute to the general happiness. Perhaps Michelangelo was a tortured soul, but his art continues to bring joy to others. Perhaps Lincoln was personally tormented by taking the moral path, but doing so increased the overall happiness of future generations. So happiness is the greatest good, despite the considerations raised earlier.

This argument is unsound. Aristotle was not describing the greatest happiness for the greatest number, nor was his a conception of general happiness. He outlined the requirements for personal happiness for those few males able to live and fare well. But truth, art, creativity, and meaning do not necessarily lead to personal happiness. Often we must choose between having more truth, creativity, and meaning, or having more happiness. We do not invariably choose happiness. If happiness was the greatest good toward which all other goods aimed we would expect a different result. To aim directly at happiness may be self-defeating. At best, happiness is a by-product of a well-lived life, salutary biochemistry, a measure of success in meeting expectations and internal standards, and evaluating life positively.

Although robustly meaningful lives do not necessarily include extended joy or peace, they almost always include the ecstasy joined to great accomplishments and pursuits. But heroism and greatness often lack extended joy or peace because periods of savoring and contentment are more fleeting than in nonheroic meaningful lives. The hero confronts greater obstacles, expends his or her energies more extravagantly, and is less likely to survive than the nonhero.

Better to be Beethoven, DiMaggio, or Michelangelo unhappy than to be happy by minimally fulfilling the criteria of the happiness-as-accurate-positive-self-appraisal conception. John Kekes, one of the most perceptive advocates of that conception of happiness, admits that happiness is not the most important human aspiration:

> Reasonable people want to be as happy as possible. But this does not mean that all reasonable people want the same thing, nor that whatever they want is wanted by them unconditionally . . . we may come to believe that our important specific wants are incompatible, harmful, or injurious to those we love; or that the requirements of our family, country, or profession take precedence over the satisfaction of our wants. So, while it is reasonable to want to be happy, this does not mean that happiness is the only or the most important aim reasonable people can have.[14]

Happiness is not everything, but it is something. Beethoven's life would have been better if he could have been happy, as well as being one of the world's greatest creators, but his life was still great and eminently worth living. DiMaggio's life would have been better if he could have been happy, as well as being one of the world's greatest athletes, but his life was still great and eminently worth living. (A complicating factor: Is there a connection between unhappiness and exceptional creativity? Did Beethoven's and DiMaggio's perfectionist tendencies, psychological conflicts, and profound dissatisfactions contribute to their high creativity? Could they have been happy and still have produced what they did?)

Only the happiness-as-connected-to-a-preexisting-good conception can salvage happiness as the greatest good. By grounding happiness in eternal, unchanging, universal normative imperatives, this conception cements happiness to the highest values. The good news: Under this view, happiness is not overrated. The bad news: Salvaging happiness as the greatest good is costly. The main problem with this conception lies with its alleged metaphysical linchpins. Reliance upon the existence of a Supreme Being or fixed human nature or moral imperatives embedded in the universe invites grave suspicions. Even if such a normative order exists, how can we know when we have discovered it or met its standards? Without an accessible, preordained normative order, the persuasiveness of the happiness-as-connection-to-preexisting-good view evaporates.

Under the other contemporary understandings, happiness falls short of the greatest good. Happiness remains valuable in most cases, but it is not the most important human aspiration. Instead of mouthing the platitude "I want only that they are happy," parents would better serve their children by helping them appreciate and lead robustly meaningful, valuable lives. Such lives bring satisfaction and typically bestow happiness. Even if they cannot guarantee happiness, such lives are more valuable than happy, minimally meaningful lives. We should not overrate happiness.

## 6. CAN EVERYONE BE HAPPY?

Although Aristotle incorrectly restricts potential happiness to a small subset of males, he is correct in thinking not everyone can be happy. Some people, perhaps because of the biochemistry of their brain, uncongenial temperament, unsuitable personality, or obsessively perfectionist tendencies, will always deny themselves a positive self-appraisal regardless of their objective social circumstances or achievements. Jake LaMotta—a ferocious prize fighter of the 1940s and 1950s—even after becoming the middleweight champion of the world, was tormented because he would never weigh enough to fight heavyweight champion Joe Louis. His inability to establish himself as the greatest professional fighter as such, and his lack of control over the circumstances that prevented it, were two of many factors that undermined his happiness despite his enormous professional success.

Bertrand Russell understood how the appropriate temperament and attitude were indispensable for the subjective experience of happiness:

> The happy man is the man . . . whose personality is neither divided against itself nor pitted against the world. Such a man feels himself a citizen of the universe, enjoying freely the spectacle that it offers and the joys that it affords, untroubled by the thought of death because he feels himself not really separate from those who will come after him. It is in such profound instinctive union with the stream of life that the greatest joy is to be found.[15]

You could argue that I have cited only a contingent factor preventing people from being happy. At least in principle or in theory, you might protest, we can all be happy. I am not so sure. For all of us to be happy we would all need the psychological prerequisites for happiness, and all have to experience the blessed intersection of objective circumstances, internal expectations and standards, and accurate evaluation. Perhaps if we were all inclined temperamentally toward optimism, enjoyed congenial brain biochemistry, chose our social comparisons carefully, and were educated toward self-esteem and nurturing our self-images, we could all be happy. That is a long shot in principle, and impossible in practice.


## 7. SHOULD EVERYONE BE HAPPY?

The Stoics placed their faith entirely in nurturing salutary human attitudes. Regardless of what we confront and endure, our evaluations and judgments should remain steadfast. By refusing to accept and label events as evil, we can transform their effects. Contemporary positive thinkers refine the Stoic analysis. We should not merely be indifferent to those events not totally within our control. We should, instead, accentuate the positive and celebrate the kernel of value within even the worst human tragedies. Beyond moderating our expectations, refusing to add to our travails by wallowing in self-pity, and avoiding dwelling on matters that we cannot change, we should proactively ferret out the valuable aspects of every disappointing outcome. Happiness, then, is more a function of our outlook than of the inherent nature of external events. Happiness, properly understood, is within our control just as our evaluations and judgments are within our control. Whereas the Stoics' aspiration was minimal—an internal peace grounded on indifference to pleasure and pain—contemporary positive thinkers raise the bar: We need not be indifferent to pleasure and can alter painful experiences by appreciating that every tragic cloud has a silver lining.

Positive thinkers express important truths. Our attitudes, judgments, and evaluations are crucial to psychological health. Tragedies should not defeat us. We can transform adversity to practical advantage. If taken as the complete story on happiness, however, positive thinking degenerates into absurdity.

A positive attitude toward certain kinds of lives—those that are minimally meaningful, not closely connected to value, insignificant, and unimportant—is inappropriate. Positive attitudes may facilitate relatively enduring, positive psychological states. They may bring happiness understood as subjective feelings of pleasure. But I have previously argued such happiness is not always a great good and, depending on its ground, sometimes not a good at all. If Jones whistles a happy tune in the face of her minimally meaningful life, her biography is less, not more, appealing. A worthwhile happiness must flow from an accurate appraisal of our characters, actions, and connection to value. Happiness is not the end we seek so much as the rational and emotional satisfaction we experience when we judge accurately that our lives have been lived well. Lowering our expectations radically and cultivating a cheerful outlook regardless of worldly outcomes are insufficient for worthwhile happiness. We must earn worthwhile happiness through meritorious development of our characters, real achievements, and connection to value. While it may be possible for most people to be happy in the sense of subjective well-feeling, most people may not deserve worthwhile happiness because an accurate appraisal of the lives they have led concludes they do not merit it.

People should be unhappy about their wrongful actions, despicable characters, and lack of achievements. Regrets and recriminations are often appropriate as they express our sense of value. Worthwhile happiness demands deserved self-approval, not merely accommodation to world outcomes. Imagine approaching someone and asking him whether he is happy. He answers, "Sure, I enjoy a relatively enduring, positive psychological state." You rejoin, "Well, you shouldn't be happy. Given the life you lead, you do not deserve to be happy. You have inaccurately evaluated your character, achievements, and connection to value." Putting aside the stilted nature of the conversation, Kant was correct: Worthwhile happiness must be earned and only those who have accurately evaluated their lives as meaningful and valuable deserve it.

## 8. HOW MUCH SUFFERING IS COMPATIBLE WITH HAPPINESS?

The most rigid versions of Stoicism and Epicureanism defined pain and suffering as evils. Aristotle designed his optimistic *eudaemonism* to minimize misery. Augustine observed that earthly happiness is never complete because it is always tainted by suffering. He concluded that perfect happiness was attainable only in heaven through the beatific vision. That the literature is rich with theories that contrast happiness with suffering is indisputable. The dominant classical view is that the most rewarding happiness is self-sufficient and must exclude pain and suffering. Common sense, also, endorses the classical view. Imagine asking someone if she was happy and having her reply, "No. Things are going well, but I simply do not have enough pain and suffering in my life for me to be happy." Such a response, once we eliminate the possibility that the speaker is mentally ill or deficient, is difficult to comprehend.

Nietzsche, again, provides an antidote to conventional wisdom. His desiderata for higher human types include the ability to marginalize but not eliminate negative and destructive impulses within oneself, and to transfigure them into joyous affirmation of all aspects of life; to understand and celebrate the radical contingency, finitude, and fragility of ourselves, our institutions, and the cosmos itself; to regard life itself as fully and merely natural, as embodying no transcendent meaning or value; to harbor little or no resentment toward others or toward the human condition; to confront the world in immediacy and with a sense of vital connection; to refuse to avert one's gaze from a tragic worldview and, instead, to find value not in happiness conceived as complete pleasure uncontaminated by pain and suffering, but in the inherent activities and processes themselves; to refuse to supplicate oneself before great people of the past but, instead, to accept their implicit challenge to go beyond them; to give style to one's character by transforming our conflicting internal passions into a disciplined and dynamic unity; to facilitate high culture by sustaining a favorable environment for the rise of great individuals; to strive for excellence through self-overcoming that honors the recurrent flux of the cosmos by refusing to accept a "finished" self as dispositive of personal identity; and to recognize the Sisyphus-like dimension to human existence—release from the tasks described is found only in death. Given the human condition, high energy is more important than a final, fixed goal. The mantra of "challenge, struggle, overcoming, and growth," animating and transfiguring perpetual internal conflict, replaces prayers for redemption to supernatural powers.

Suffering is necessary for greatness and true fellow-feeling should not degrade, condescend, or exhibit contempt. Instead, mastery of our impulses demands that we concentrate our efforts internally: "My humanity does not consist in feeling with men how they are, but in *enduring* that I feel with them. My humanity is a constant self-overcoming."[16]

Nietzsche's work admits several interpretations. We might argue that Nietzsche had no appreciation of happiness and that his celebration of suffering as necessary for the creation of robust human power and meaning signals a higher value. This interpretation has limited merit. We must understand the particular kind of happiness that Nietzsche disparages: the comfortable, risk-adverse, uncreative, unstrenuous life of the conformist to mass values. For Nietzsche the presence of a relatively enduring positive psychological state is insufficient. We should interrogate contented, peaceful, harmonious, and joyful people. Their positive mental states may have been purchased at an unacceptable price.

We should interpret Nietzsche differently. A happiness worth pursuing is based on experiencing and expressing human creative power. Instead of taking refuge in an easy, secure, comfortable life, the best among us will achieve creative greatness through confrontation with and overcoming of formidable suffering. Under this view, suffering is not inherently evil, but provides opportunities for the only happiness worth pursuing. Imagination and effort provide pain and suffering with an important role in a happy life. While a life of overwhelming misery precludes happiness and prevents the robust creativity Nietzsche prizes, a worthwhile happiness resides in passionate response to an appropriate amount and range of suffering.

We are tempted to fantasize a painless life devoid of suffering and loss. Such a life is more easily stated than fully imagined. A life without pain, suffering, and tragedy is not human. Completeness, self-sufficiency, and the absence of suffering are unreliable criteria for human happiness. No single accomplishment or event is capable of saturating our spirits once and forever. And that is good news. Human life requires continuous activity, self-transformation, and exertion, not a perfection that ends the journey. A worthy happiness must be earned through choices, actions, and direct confrontation with suffering. The sense of having earned our satisfactions elevates our spirits and partially defines the only happiness worth pursuing.

Human beings are valuing creatures. We create, perhaps discover, value in our world. When we lose value—because of the departure or death of friends, family, and lovers; or because of the frustration of our grandest projects, purposes, interests, and commitments; or because of illness or physical debility; or numerous other reasons—pain and suffering are appropriate responses. Against the Stoics, our suffering confirms our evaluation. The trick of creative living, however, is to use this temporary suffering for practical advantage, to use it as a springboard for our pursuit of robust meaning and grand purpose.

Pain and suffering, then, should not be considered inherently bad. Through our responses to the reasonable amount of pain and suffering characteristic of human life, we can transform our selves and strive for the only worthy form of happiness, based on exemplary human character, robust meaning, high creativity, and resplendent value.

## 9. WHY HAPPINESS IS OVERRATED

Moral, aesthetic, and cognitive values embody wider social dimensions, but happiness is a *personal value*. Happiness is a good that is distinct in being specifically valuable *for me*. That happiness, understood as a personal value, is not the greatest good as such may be unsurprising. Surely, moral, aesthetic, and cognitive values will sometimes provide reasons for action that override those grounded in considerations of happiness.

My argument goes further. Happiness is not the greatest personal good, nor always a great personal good, and is sometimes not a personal good at all. Living a valuable, significant, robustly meaningful life is of greater personal value than attaining happiness. Although happiness will often flow from such lives, the connection is not ensured. Happiness is overrated in the sense that despite all the sound and fury it inspires, happiness is not the primary goal to which we should aspire.

A critic might respond as follows: The mantra that happiness is overrated rests on two mismatched claims. The first claim is that happiness is the greatest personal good. The second claim is that happiness is formally defined as merely a relatively enduring, positive state of mind. But few philosophers, aside from a few misguided hedonists, accept both claims. Aristotle, for example, took happiness to be the greatest good, but he emphatically rejects the second claim. Aristotle's recipe for happiness shows vividly that he did not formally define happiness as merely a relatively enduring, positive state of mind. While some contemporary philosophers, social scientists, and interested laypeople do accept the second claim—they formally define happiness as merely a relatively enduring, positive state of mind—it is not clear that they also subscribe to the first claim. If no one actually holds both claims, then whose position is being assailed? Is much of my attack directed only at straw persons?

The critic forces me to clarify my thesis, but does not render it moot. As I said, Aristotle's discussion of *eudaemonia* goes far beyond what contemporary thinkers take happiness to be. His is a theory of human flourishing or well-being that does not necessarily include a relatively enduring, positive state of mind. If such a state of mind is necessary for an accurate formal definition of happiness, then Aristotle is taking human flourishing, not happiness, to be the greatest good. I have questioned whether Aristotle's version of human flourishing is the greatest good, but that is a peripheral concern. Discussing Aristotle places us on the right track because it leads us to the view that more than a positive state of mind is required for the good life.

Whether contemporary social scientists and interested laypeople take happiness to be the greatest personal good is an interesting matter. Surely talk of "I want my children only to be happy" suggests that position, as does the effusive praise of happiness in the social science literature. The matter is complicated, though, by the lack of specific *summum bonum* claims. Unlike the ancients, contemporary writers do not use the locution. A charitable reading, one that favors the critic's position, is that contemporary social scientists, interested laypeople, and some philosophers—those who formally define happiness as merely a relatively enduring, positive state of mind—do not necessarily take happiness to be the greatest good, but "only" a great personal good. Thus, the critic's charge seemingly remains intact: No one, save for a few confused hedonists, clearly holds the two claims required to form a suitable target for my charge that happiness is overrated.

My thesis that happiness is overrated, though, does not depend on the claim that happiness is the greatest good—personal or social. I accept that happiness is generally, but not always, a personal good. But I argue not merely that happiness is not the greatest personal good, but that it is not always a great personal good, and sometimes is not a good at all. The targets of my thesis are those who formally define happiness as a relatively enduring, positive state of mind and who take happiness to be (at least) a great good. Such targets are not in short supply. Moreover, I advance several other subtheses about happiness along the way: Human happiness is not the complete satisfaction of all our desires; worthwhile happiness requires an accurate, positive self-appraisal; a measure of suffering is useful for worthwhile happiness, and the like.

The term "happiness" appears in the literature with different meanings. Socrates and Plato fashioned happiness as moral and intellectual virtue. But neither moral nor intellectual virtue is necessary or sufficient for a relatively enduring, positive psychological state. As is the case with all classical condition views of happiness—those arguing that happiness is defined by attaining certain objective conditions, whether internal conditions of the soul or external requirements of worldly success—we could fulfill all conditions, but nevertheless feel predominantly sad, distraught, even depressed. If moral and intellectual virtues are the greatest good, calling their attainment "happiness" adds nothing.

Aristotle offers the most comprehensive condition view of happiness, as he joins moral and intellectual virtues to worldly success. His account of human flourishing depends heavily on a specific notion of the human *telos*. Still, a person could fulfill all his conditions and be plagued by feelings of meaninglessness and sadness. Those who are happy surely cannot be predominantly sad. Happiness may be more than, but must include, a relatively enduring, positive psychological state. If Aristotle has described the greatest good, calling it happiness adds nothing.

The radical asceticism of the Cynics tightens the screws on Socratic virtue, extinguishes passion, denies society and civilization, and offers rugged individualism. Advancing a theory and practice that large numbers could not embrace even in principle, the Cynics' program degenerates into alienation and estrangement.

The long history of happiness as hedonism—stretching from Aristippus, Epicurus, Lucretius, and the British utilitarians to contemporary versions—identifies pleasure with happiness. Ignoring the role that pain, suffering, and overcoming obstacles can play in the good life, hedonists overemphasize sensations and underplay the highest human capabilities. While a life of pleasure can conceivably result in happiness, the product may be unworthy of the good life. Accumulating personal or collective pleasure is not necessarily a great good.

Stoic versions of happiness as tranquility try to mute, even filter out, human passions. Although Stoicism contains much wisdom, it fails to distinguish earned from simulated tranquility, obscures our role as evaluators, and exchanges the richness of human experience for smaller consolations and accommodations. Stoic expectations are pitched to those struggling for survival under adverse circumstances, and are too faint for general use.

Christians' notions of happiness as worldly transcendence depend on a questionable metaphysics, have difficulty articulating the nature of happiness in the other world, and perceive happiness as a final, fixed condition. As a transcendent vision, Christian happiness has limited applicability to this world. On this view, even imperfect worldly happiness requires divine grace.

Kant rejected the logical connection between virtue and happiness; tacitly accepted that happiness is a relatively enduring, positive psychological state; and wrongly identified happiness as the satisfaction of all desires. He wisely demonstrated that happiness so conceived cannot be the greatest good. Kant pointed in the direction of a worthwhile happiness that we must earn and thus deserve.

Hegel grounds happiness in a philosophical system. Sanguine about collective human progress and convinced of the continuing development of the Absolute, Hegel concludes that freedom, moral goodness, and happiness are linked. Beyond the speculative nature of Hegel's thought, he holds personal happiness hostage to the well-being of the nation-state.

Contemporary social scientists, such as Lane, Myers, and Veenhoven, identify happiness with a relatively enduring, positive psychological state. Their usage mirrors most closely our contemporary understanding. They understand that condition views of happiness falter because we could fulfill all objective requirements yet be predominantly sad. In making the requisite psychological state definitive of happiness, though, social scientists underscore how such happiness is overrated. Once details are supplied, we see that happiness can be attained through wrongful activities, by being disconnected from reality, in spite of diminished human capabilities, from trivial pursuits, through external inducements, or even from deep delusions. Such happiness is not necessarily a great good and is sometimes not a good at all. Worthwhile happiness must be more than merely the satisfactions, regardless of how they are attained, leading to a positive state of mind.

The best contemporary philosophical view is happiness-as-accurate-positive-self-appraisal. Worthwhile happiness involves an accurate, positive evaluation about the ways we have developed and employed our characters. Such happiness is defined by the deserved gratification that accompanies the process and result of this examination. Even worthwhile happiness, though, is not the greatest personal good. A life lived well is a greater good than the deserved gratification that typically accompanies it: Better to live extraordinarily well and not be particularly happy, than to live less well and be deservedly happy.

Only the happiness-as-connected-to-a-preexisting-good conception, whose advocates depend heavily on Platonic and Christian metaphysics, can connect happiness to the greatest good. By grounding happiness in eternal, unchanging, universal normative imperatives, this conception cements happiness to the highest values. Under this view, happiness is not overrated. But without an accessible, preordained normative order, the persuasiveness of the happiness-as-connection-to-preexisting-good view evaporates. Such an order is notoriously contestable. And even if such an order exists, the greatest good is the connection of human lives to the highest values, not the resulting positive state of mind we experience. So even if we are deservedly happy because we accurately conclude that our lives are connected to the highest values, the connection is a greater good than our earned positive state of mind. Moreover, those whose lives are joined to the highest values might not even experience their deserved happiness. They might not be aware that their lives have united with the highest values, or they might be aware of it but be incapable of reacting appropriately to the achievement. If happiness requires a predominantly positive state of mind, then even a connection to the highest values may not bring us the requisite peace or joy.

Happiness remains valuable, but it is not the most important human aspiration. We should teach our children how to lead robustly meaningful, valuable lives. If they do, they will deserve worthwhile happiness and often realize it. But even if they are not predominantly happy, they will have fought the good fight, fashioned a worthwhile biography, and added value to the world. We should all be so fortunate.

## NOTES

1. G. H. von Wright, *The Varieties of Goodness* (London: Routledge & Kegan Paul, 1963); Robin Barrow, *Happiness and Schooling* (New York: St. Martin's Press, 1980).

2. See, e.g., Robert Nozick, *Anarchy, State, and Utopia* (New York: Basic Books, 1974), 42–45.

3. Irwin Goldstein, "Happiness," *International Philosophical Quarterly* 13 (1973), 523–534; Richard Kraut, "Two Conceptions of Happiness," *The Philosophical Review* 138 (April 1979): 167–197.

4. Kraut, 170.

5. Ibid., 180.

6. Ibid., 192.

7. Lynne McFall, "Happiness, Rationality, and Individual Ideals," *The Review of Metaphysics* 37 (March 1984): 595–613; and *Happiness* (New York: Peter Lang, 1989); John Kekes, "Happiness," *Mind* 91 (July 1982): 358–376; and *The Examined Life* (University Park, Penn.: The Pennsylvania State University Press, 1992); James Griffin, *Well-Being* (Oxford: Clarendon Press, 1986).

8. Kekes, "Happiness," 369.

9. Ibid., 370.

10. Kekes, *The Examined Life*, 177–182.

11. Deal W. Hudson, *Happiness and the Limits of Satisfaction* (Lanham, Maryland: Rowman & Littlefield Publishers, Inc., 1996), 119.

12. John Finnis, "Practical Reasoning, Human Goods, and the End of Man," *Proceedings of the American Catholic Philosophical Association* 58 (1985): 23–36; Etienne Gilson, *The Christian Philosophy of St. Thomas Aquinas*, trans. L. K. Shook (New York: Random House, 1956); Jacques Maritain, *Moral Philosophy* (London: Geoffrey Bles, 1964); Josef Pieper, *Happiness and Contemplation*, trans. Richard and Clara Winston (New York: Pantheon Press, 1958); Stephen Theron, "Happiness and Transcendent Happiness," *Religious Studies* 21 (September 1985): 349–367.

13. Hudson, *Happiness*, 122.

14. Kekes, *The Examined Life*, 166.

15. Bertrand Russell, *The Conquest of Happiness*, quoted in *The Good Life*, ed. Charles Guignon (Indianapolis, Ind.: Hackett Publishing Co., Inc., 1999), 182.

16. Nietzsche, "Why I Am So Wise," sec. 8 in *Ecce Homo*, trans. Walter Kaufmann and R. J. Hollingdale (New York: Random House, 1967).

# 4

# THE PATHS TO
# HAPPINESS

Happiness understood as relatively enduring joy, peace, or exuberance is
not the greatest good, not always a great good, and sometimes is not a
good at all. Typically, though, it is a good. Social scientists, such as David
Lykken, David Myers, and Martin Seligman, have compiled and studied data
that strongly support the conclusion that certain strategies increase the likelihood of achieving a relatively enduring, positive state of mind. Philosophers
should include these findings as a way of connecting theory with practice.
Accordingly, the advice offered by social scientists who have analyzed the data
follows.[1] Throughout this presentation, unless otherwise noted, I use the term
"happiness" defined as a relatively enduring, positive state of mind such as
joy, peace, or exuberance. Social scientists advance a recipe with ten ingredients for such happiness: Adjust expectations; nurture relationships; be optimistic and appreciative; have faith; make peace, not war; be goal-oriented;
prioritize; use leisure wisely, energize the senses, eat and exercise properly; go
with flow; and be lucky.

## 1. ADJUST EXPECTATIONS

Being intensely competitive and a perfectionist is a poor strategy for happiness. Human beings will always fall short of perfection. Intensely competitive
people suffer more with losses than they enjoy with victories. Perfectionists
dwell on shortcomings more than they savor accomplishments. Happy people
find ways to rationalize their apparent failures as isolated events that do not
define their identities. Unhappy people obsess over failures, assume they will
continue, and define themselves through their disappointments.

By adjusting our expectations, we increase the likelihood of happiness. If we judge today in relation to the greatest days of our lives we court frustration. If we judge today in relation to tragic events in our lives we nurture appreciation. The difference between happy and unhappy people is less a function of the cumulative balance of objectively positive over negative moments they respectively experience and more a function of what standards they use to define experiences as positive and negative. If I judge my basketball talents in relation to those of Michael Jordan and Larry Bird in their prime, I am inviting humiliation. If I judge my athletic talents in relation to those closer to my age and occupational categories—56-year-old men who labor at sedentary careers—I am encouraging pride of accomplishment.

How we perceive and interpret the causes and consequences of the events in our lives is more crucial to our happiness than the apparent objective description and value of those events. The enhancement factor of self-flattering illusion energizes human happiness. A kernel of Stoic wisdom resonates: How we label events is crucial to our self-understanding and psychological condition.

Not only are our expectations important for happiness, but memories are also. We may choose to ruminate about past events that upset us such as injustices at the office, people who have insulted us, inequities in the world, hierarchical abuses, and family and friends who have betrayed our trust. If so, we foster unhappiness by the subjects we dwell upon. By concentrating on current and past events that we enjoy, we increase our prospects for happiness.

The nature of human life is that we can always imagine more and better. We lack a clear, antecedent notion of lifetime entitlements. If we are preoccupied with what we lack—after all, complete satisfaction is impossible and, perhaps, not even a coherent notion—we will be unhappy. If we appreciate the progress we are making toward our most important goals, understand that we will achieve some but not all of them, seek satisfaction from numerous aspects of our lives, and interpret the impossibility of complete satisfaction as a blessing not a curse, we nurture happiness. The Stoic happiness formula of dividing our satisfactions by our desires was misguided, but examining the reasons why it was unsound yields a deeper moral: Human happiness is more a function of sensing progress, improvement, and development than it is of achieving a fixed number of desires and goals.

David Myers ably explains the relationships among desires, goals, and serenity:

Recognizing that ever-rising desires mean never-ending dissatisfaction, we can also strive to *make our goals short-term and sensible*. Life's greatest disappoint-

ments, as well as its greatest attainments, are born of the hig
. . . We need visionary dreams. But to constrain the frustrat
what you want and what you have, work toward them in realisti
seek greater serenity, we can strive to restrain our unrealistic expectations, to go
out of our way to experience reminders of our blessings, to make our goals short-
term and sensible, to choose comparisons that will breed gratitude rather than
envy.[2]

In *The Republic*, Plato portrayed the tyrannical person who was consumed
by desire.[3] Every satisfied desire was followed by another desire, more difficult
to fulfill. Plato argued that once reason was no longer in control, human
beings were nothing more than insatiable desirers, sponges without limits of
absorption, doomed to frustration. We can draw a more acute message from
Plato's illustration: Human beings are inclined to want more, but we are better served by appreciating our accomplishments and the opportunity to continually reimagine and re-create ourselves through renewed efforts in service
of meaningful projects.

Appreciating what we have, instead of bemoaning what we do not have or
what we failed to obtain, increases the likelihood of happiness. The quantity
of social goods we have objectively accumulated is not as great a predictor of
our happiness levels as is our attitude about what we have accumulated. Our
happiness is better predicted by the extent to which what we have meets our
standards and expectations.

Our expectations of others are also a key ingredient of our happiness. If we
are rigid, uncompromising, and expect others to conform to our prescribed
ways of being in the world, we are begging for disappointment. Instead, if we
seek happiness we should recognize that change, alternate perspectives, and
conflicting approaches to life mark the diversity of human life and vivify the
human condition.

Again, Stoic wisdom glows: Even if we cannot markedly change our abilities, our social situation, our history, our objective accomplishments, and our
future prospects, we can alter to some degree our expectations and standards
for self-approval. Those who do so take a sizable step on the journey toward
happiness.

## 2. NURTURE RELATIONSHIPS

Aristotle insisted that human beings are social animals. If living for extended
periods in isolation, we are either gods or beasts, but not human beings.

Although we need, especially in Western cultures, a keen sense of our individuality, uniqueness, specialness, and autonomy, we also require a measure of community. We seek bonds, connections, and extended subjectivity through family, friends, and lovers. We need to transcend ourselves and to feel part of something larger. We need to enlarge our sphere of concern from ourselves to others and sense that others have enlarged their sphere of concern to include us. Intimacy, sharing, and social belonging are paramount ingredients for happiness.

A popular self-help book of recent vintage advised us to imagine what we might regret on our deathbed as we were evaluating the life we led.[4] It is unlikely we would regret not spending more time at the office, not viewing yet another episode of *Friends*, not having met Donald Trump, or not owning a Rolls Royce automobile. Instead, we are most likely to regret not having been a better parent, spouse, child, sibling, or friend. If this observation is correct, then the health of our relationships is more important than we commonly think and act.

Social scientists estimate that around 70 percent of our happiness hinges on the number and quality of our friendships, the closeness of our families, and the health of our relationships with neighbors and coworkers.[5] Social support, a sense of mutual appreciation, and the ability to share are crucial to happiness. These depend upon and are nurtured by communication. Telling others who are important to us that they are, deepens our mutual bond. In adverse times, sharing our problems with those closest to us softens the sting of tragedies.

Extending ourselves through volunteer and charitable work also increases the likelihood of happiness because we alleviate boredom, heighten our sense of purpose, and foster feelings of mutual appreciation. Developing and pursuing common projects and interests deepen our social connections. Extroversion is part of the process. People who are introverts are less likely to share themselves, to forge salutary communities, and to be happy.

A colleague once asked me for my preferred definition of friendship. I did not offer a definition, but responded with a Sicilian test of friendship: To be a friend a person must sometimes jeopardize his or her own interests for the sake of the other. My colleague was too polite to express explicitly the shock at my answer she registered involuntarily. I am sure she was expecting the usual pabulum about sharing interests or sincerely desiring the best for the other or providing aid in times of adversity or mutual support for healthy self-development. While the typical litany bears much currency and helps to define a range of friendships, my standard is even higher: At times, friends must put the interests and well-being of the other ahead of their own. Am I asking too much? That depends on how deeply our friendships constitute our identities and how closely our social bonds are forged.

In *An Instance of the Fingerpost*, Iain Pears captures my strenuous test for friendship through the main character, Marco:

> When a Venetian calls a man his friend, he does so after long thought, as to accept such a person is all but to make him a member of the family, owed much loyalty and forbearance. We die for our friends as for our family . . . The English are very different; they have friends at all stages of their lives, and maintain a distinction between the obligations of amity and those of blood. By taking [an Englishman named Lower] to my heart as I did . . . I made the mistake of assuming he did the same with me, and acknowledged the same obligations. But it was not the case. The English can lose their friends.[6]

Beyond friendships, offering small courtesies to strangers and altruistic behavior in general spreads human warmth and contributes to happiness. Undergraduates sometimes argue that if altruistic behavior makes the doer feel good then the action was really selfish. After all, the motivation for the action was the pleasure of the actor. This argument, though, widely misses the mark. That I would take pleasure in supporting the interests of others cannot plausibly count against the action. Instead, it counts in favor of the action and the actor. Should I not take pleasure that another's interests have been benefited? Should I, instead, shrug indifferently in a fatuous effort to preserve a bizarre notion of altruistic purity? Selfishness is ignoring the interests of others when we should not. The pleasure I garner from acting altruistically enhances my self-interest, but cannot count against the quality of my acts. That altruistic behavior increases my likelihood of happiness suggests that I gain self-satisfaction from acting virtuously. This is as it should be.

Not stridently criticizing those closest to you is a neglected part of nurturing community. Too often, we judge others by harsh standards and set ourselves up for recurring disappointments. Worse, we imperialistically impose our way of being upon others and then blame them for not adhering to our unstated models of living. Otis Redding was correct: Try a little tenderness.

Beyond human community, lies our relationships with animals. Those who care for pets increase their prospects for happiness. Dogs may not be our best friends, but they facilitate our sense of care, our need to be needed, and inspire our joy.

Our salaries and income, educational levels, social and marital status, gender, and race are less important for happiness than commonly assumed.

People who go to work in their overalls and on the bus are just as happy, on the average, as those in suits who drive to work in their own Mercedes. Although men still retain a perilous grip on most of the reins of power in our society, they are not happier than are women. In spite of racism and relative poverty, African Americans enjoy on average the same feelings of subjective well-being as do white Americans.[7]

In sum, spending more time and effort fostering healthy relationships is the most important ingredient for attaining happiness.

## 3. BE OPTIMISTIC AND APPRECIATIVE

Laughter is important for happiness and health. Instead of judging the quality of a joke to decide whether it merits a laugh, happy people just laugh. By laughing even when we are not antecedently in a positive mood, we can often trigger that mood. Laughing and smiling also encourage those around us to do the same. Positive moods reinforce others to remain or become upbeat. Laughter facilitates health by energizing the body's self-healing powers.

Happy people typically have positive feelings about those around them. Do they have positive feelings about others because they are already happy? Or do they have positive feelings because the people around them objectively merit such a response? Even if the people around them do not objectively merit a praiseworthy evaluation, rendering such judgments increases the happiness of the evaluator and has a positive effect on those judged.

Once again, our memories are important. Being able to reminisce about wonderful past events animates our happiness in the present. Even if retrospective falsification is at play, even if our memories are dim and do not accurately reflect the past, or even if we subconsciously alter the past to make it more glorious than it was, our distorted reminiscences brighten our present outlook.

Being able to adapt, to change our expectations and patterns, and being actively engaged in the world also increase the likelihood of happiness. Existential philosophers, such as Martin Heidegger (1889–1976), argue that the closest experience of nothingness, of our extinction, on earth is boredom.[8] To be bored connotes a weariness, detachment, and dullness that underscore a lack of imagination. To be bored for long periods speaks volumes about the decrepit condition of the self, but little about the state of the world. Activity, engagement in the world, is less stressful than prolonged boredom during which we feel the hot breath of nothingness on our necks.

Nietzsche claimed that the psychological test of human greatness is captured in his fable of eternal recurrence. If we can sincerely desire that our lives would be lived an infinite number of times in the same details, we manifest *amor fati*, our love of fate. To desire to edit out the tragedies, embarrassments, shortcomings, and sufferings of our life is to reveal the dwarf within us. Because Nietzsche was convinced of the interconnectedness of events, he claimed that complete acceptance of ourselves and our lives requires joyfully embracing the sour and the sweet as constitutive of who we are. Contemporary social scientists provide evidence for part of his thesis: Dwelling on how we might have altered the past for the better, what we might have done differently ("woulda', coulda', shoulda'" talk), decreases our happiness.

Contemporary philosopher Robert Solomon, influenced by Nietzsche, recommends gratitude as the wisest response to the tragic nature of life:

> Gratitude, I want to suggest, is perhaps the best answer to the tragedies of life. It is odd and unfortunate that we take special offense at the bad things in life, as if we could not possibly deserve those. The proper recognition of tragedy and the tragic sense of life is not [as Camus writes] shaking one's fist at the gods or the universe 'in scorn and defiance,' but rather, as Kierkegaard writes in a religious context, 'going down on one's knees' and giving thanks . . . It is the importance and significance of being thankful, to whomever or whatever, for life itself.[9]

Gratitude is crucial for realizing the value of our activities. Even if our activities are intrinsically valuable, we must appreciate that value for it to resonate within us. Our attitudes and emotions are indispensable for our vision of the world. We perceive and understand value through our emotions.

We may not be able to change the world in dramatic ways, but we can change the way we interpret the world. Jean-Paul Sartre (1905–1980) talks about the emotions as magical transformations of our world, as ways of changing our perceptions of the world without objectively changing the world.[10] Through anger we judge an imbalance in the condition of justice in the world. Our anger is intended to restore equilibrium, not necessarily in the world but in our interpretation of it. Through love we render a gloriously positive judgment upon the other as we perceive her actual characteristics, ideal possibilities, and her unique manner of embodying those qualities as worthy of our commitment and expanded identity. Our perceptions and interpretations may be inaccurate, but they nevertheless alter our vision of the world. Again, Stoic wisdom looms: Our happiness depends more on how we interpret and evaluate the world than on the objective condition of the world.

On Sartre's view, the emotions are not solely or mainly involuntary physiological responses. They are not merely transient, external intrusions into our lives for which we are not responsible. Solomon expands on Sartre's vision:

> An emotion is first of all an ongoing practice in which one is actively and interpersonally engaged . . . It is not merely personal but also interpersonal, socially constructed, and learned . . . an emotion *is not a feeling . . . cannot be reduced to a physiological occurrence . . . cannot be understood in terms of mere individual behavior* . . . the emotions are intentional and strategic ways of coping with 'difficult' situations. We 'choose' them . . . for a purpose.[11]

Existentialists, such as Sartre and Solomon, suspect that we too often use the emotions to evade personal accountability. We excuse our inappropriate behavior by appealing to the emotions as demons beyond our control that cloud our judgment and produce aberrant action. Our typical posture portrays us as victims not responsible for our deeds. As comedian Flip Wilson was fond of intoning, "The devil made me do it." The existentialist response is that our emotions are mainly chosen strategies of coping with a trying world. We are responsible for our emotions and the actions flowing from them. This refrain is sweet music to the Stoics' ears.

In that vein, positive beliefs, attitudes, and a general optimistic approach to life are far better predictors of our happiness than the objective quality of the events we have experienced. The Stoic conclusion that indifference was the road to peace, though, is incorrect. Because our interpretation of events is crucial, indifference refuses to evaluate and judge, suffocates our emotions, and can easily lead to disengagement. Instead, a better recipe for happiness counsels us to evaluate our life experiences from an optimistic, positive perspective.

Self-recriminations dull our prospects for happiness. Unhappy people tend to draw broad, negative conclusions about themselves when events in their lives fall short of their expectations. Better to focus on producing a bright future than to blame and psychologically scourge ourselves for an unsatisfactory past or present. The ability to reinforce ourselves and retain a strong belief in our success is essential. Self-confidence is not only sexier but also happier.

The enhancement factor, the self-flattering illusions we subconsciously promote, nurtures a positive outlook:

Depressed people are accurate judges of how much skill they have, whereas happy people think they are much more skillful than others judge them. Eighty percent of American men think they are in the top half of social skills; the majority of workers rate their job performance as above average; and the majority of motorists (even those who have been involved in accidents) rate their driving as safer than average. Happy people remember more good events than actually happened, and they forget more of the bad events. Depressed people, in contrast, are accurate about both. Happy people are lopsided in their beliefs about success and failure. If it was a success, they did it, it's going to last, and they're good at everything; if it was a failure, you did it to them, it's going away quickly, and it was just this one little thing.[12]

The conclusion to draw is not that happy people are dimwitted or less intelligent than depressed people. Instead, they subconsciously employ the enhancement factor more artfully. Happy people go beyond optimism. The cliché of optimism is viewing the glass as half-full, while that of pessimism is viewing the same glass as half-empty. The cliché is accurate because both descriptions of the volume of the glass are true. The optimist chooses to accentuate the positive, while the pessimist dwells on the negative.

But happy people strikingly change the world and their mood by altering their perceptions of the world. Their felicitous asymmetry when confronting successes and failures, their retrospective falsifications of the past, and their proclivity to inflate their skills and capabilities are not merely accentuating the positive. Happy people to a significant degree alter their perceptions of the world in ways that do not correspond to objective truth. While their flights from reality fall far short of grand delusion, they leap beyond optimism.

This invites the question: Which is better—to be unhappy with a firm grasp of reality and truth, or to be happy largely through the subconscious artful use of the enhancement factor? Is it better to be Socrates unhappy or Evelyn Enhancement happy?

These are not the only alternatives. We would aspire to be happy with a firm grasp of reality and truth. We would prefer both good cheer and profound knowledge. Achieving both values, though, is much harder than realizing one.

## 4. HAVE FAITH

People with strong spiritual beliefs are happier than those who lack such beliefs. Religious convictions, and the narratives, myths, and rituals that sustain them, offer meaning, a sense of order, and answers to the fundamental questions of life: Who am I? What is my destiny? Why am I here? How should I live? What does it all mean?

Fervent believers have answers to the seemingly unanswerable questions that plague nonbelievers. Leo Tolstoy (1828–1910), during his period of personal crisis, was stunned that peasants with lives far less pleasurable than his own had a far greater consciousness of life than he had. He concluded that their simple, strong religious beliefs connected them tightly to the life force. Contemporary social scientists confirm Tolstoy's observation: Faith nourishes us and soothes our doubts in times good and bad.

But religious faith cannot be simulated; we cannot simply adopt it as a strategy after analyzing the findings of the latest survey on happiness. True religious belief is founded on a spiritual commitment, not on prudential maneuvers. Readers who are already theists will probably nod appreciatively that their commitments bring an ancillary benefit. Few readers who are nonbelievers will immediately rush to a church, synagogue, mosque, or temple to declare their undying faith in a desperate attempt to become happier.

Kierkegaard celebrated the knight of faith, the person who renounced universal norms in the service of a higher calling. He understood the danger in doing so, and the lack of guarantees the leap of faith required to abrogate the general demands of reason and the moral law. These risks, though, promised greater rewards of those willing to take them in service to the religious life.

Not all faith, though, is religious. Believing in ourselves, accepting ourselves unconditionally, and being deeply committed to projects transcending our own concerns all nurture happiness. Nietzsche's highest value, *amor fati*, a maximally affirmative attitude toward life, required faith. Neither he nor anyone else can prove, deductively, that such an attitude is the greatest objective value. On Nietzsche's own standards, this is impossible. His highest value requires, instead, an act of faith defined as conviction, choice, and action in the face of epistemological uncertainty.

Living a robust life requires faith of some sort. Even the most pious worshipers at the shrine of reason must admit that reason cannot prove its own standards noncircularly; reason cannot prove itself. So even the idolators of reason require faith. Part of the human condition is the lack of certain answers to our most pressing questions about life. Religious believers accept a series of answers, but faith is at the core of their acceptance. Nonbelievers in the religious answers must develop other values, principles, and narratives that can sustain their connection to the life force. A maximally affirmative attitude toward life also has faith at its core.

That faith is required for happiness, then, is not earth-shattering news. For without faith in something we lose the ballast for living. Where there is no hope there can be no happiness.

## 5. MAKE PEACE, NOT WAR

Being cooperative instead of ultracompetitive, being collaborative rather than adversarial, and being a reconciler, not an instigator, increase the likelihood of happiness. The ancient Greeks and Romans were correct: Happy people tend to be harmonious, contented, and peaceful. Those who are adversarial, competitive, and militant are less happy because their victories are often achieved at the high cost of strained social relations. As communal bonds are the best predictor of happiness, those whose actions develop, maintain, and sustain those bonds will be more likely to be happy than those whose sense of personal accomplishment takes priority. Often, we cannot satisfy both our desire for triumphs in zero-sum contexts and our yearning for salutary personal relationships. Happy is the peacemaker.

## 6. BE GOAL-ORIENTED

Our primary aspirations focus on family, education, occupation, and locale. More than seventy-five percent of our life satisfactions revolve around this quartet. Happy are people who are doing what they want to do, with whom they want to be doing it, with the formal and informal training required to do it, where they want to do it.

Routines, habits, and plans foster order, decrease anxiety, and reaffirm our course toward paramount goals. Happy people do not permit one aspect of their life to determine its value. Multiple dimensions of our life must be assessed. The sense that we are making progress toward our important goals vivifies our positive attitude toward life and engages us in the world. The cliché that the journey is more crucial than the destination bears currency. We are happiest when our most valuable goals are just beyond our grasp, close enough that we are relatively sure we will achieve them but still far enough away that renewed effort is required.

If we view our jobs as merely necessary means to our ends we will be less likely to be happy than if we enjoy our labors for their own sake. When we choose a job we are not just selecting a method of materially surviving or flourishing. The activities and processes of our careers greatly influence the people we become. Our work is partly constitutive of our identities. After asking prospective employers about the salary, fringe benefits, prospects for promotion, and locale of jobs, we should ask ourselves what kind of people we would like to become and whether this or that job will facilitate our quest.

The mainstay of any happiness diet is productive effort, developing and exercising skills, doing something that needs doing—that is worth doing—and especially doing it well . . . the satisfaction of even the most spectacular achievement fades after a while . . . We moderns cultivate individualism, self-striving, competition, and self-indulgence. Many young people, even some with special talents, never learn that doing the job and doing it right is the sine qua non of human happiness . . . the best performance on complex or creative tasks, whether in academics or the workplace, is produced by people motivated by intrinsic interest in the task rather than by contingent rewards.[13]

The dominant goals of happiness vary with cultures. In Asian cultures, family responsibilities, family lineage, respect from and within society, and being at ease with life are paramount. Western notions of happiness focus more on internal evaluation and contentment, whereas Asian ideals stress societal contributions and evaluations, and nonhedonistic satisfactions.[14]

## 7. PRIORITIZE

The difference between happy and unhappy people is not their respective life experiences. Happy people have better strategies for creating and sustaining positive moods. These strategies are not always self-conscious. Dwelling on unpleasant experiences, insisting on perfection, seeing the glass as only half-full, and wallowing in self-pity ensure our unhappiness. Happy people consciously or subconsciously savor pleasant experiences, accept their fallibility and limitations, focus on the portion of the glass that is half-filled, and are deeply grateful.

Our goals should be in concert with our desired self-image. That means we must first have a clear image of the person we would like to become, then concentrate on significant projects that will facilitate that image.

Yet many of us are constantly in competitions where we don't really want the prize. We find someone to be in a secret economic competition with—a friend, a neighbor, a loved one . . . But is this really your goal? Were you born into this world to get promoted before one of your co-workers? Were you born into this world to get a better car than your neighbors? Let your real goals guide you, not meaningless competitions you don't really benefit by winning.[15]

Existential philosophers, such as Sartre, begin from an assumption of radical freedom: Human beings cannot choose not to choose.[16] Freedom is the basis of our actions; we have the power to change. The anxiety often accompanying our choices flows from the lack of ultimate justifications for our decisions. We live in a thoroughly contingent world, and we are thoroughly contingent beings. Lacking absolute grounds for our decisions, we must take recurrent leaps of faith. A robust sense of freedom is empowering and distinguishes happy people. But existentialists insist that freedom is not an unambiguous blessing. The lack of enduring foundations to guide human choice makes us completely responsible for the people we are becoming. No excuses are available to us.

I cannot prove that human beings are totally free. Existentialists cannot do so either. Typically, they appeal to moods or emotions, such as anxiety, angst, and dread, that allegedly accompany our choices and reflect our felt responsibility in the face of radically contingent decisions. Such strategies, though, are thoroughly indeterminate: Explanations other than our total freedom can account for our moods and experiences, while plausible philosophical and psychological evidence abounds suggesting that we are much less free than existentialists have supposed. Assuming that we are free, however, is a better way to live. People embodying a robust notion of freedom gain vivid feelings of autonomy and control over their lives that increase their happiness. Setting goals, prioritizing values, and developing and pursuing a self-conception require a strong sense of freedom.

## 8. USE LEISURE WISELY, ENERGIZE THE SENSES, EAT AND EXERCISE PROPERLY

On our deathbeds, as we evaluate our lives, we will not regret not having seen the complete television saga of *Xena, Warrior Princess* or the season finale of *Joe Millionaire*. The lack of sufficient television viewing is not an American problem. Most of us watch too much television to the detriment of active engagement in the world. Being glued to our television tubes is our way of killing time, of submitting to passive distraction. Social scientists conclude that watching television decreases our prospects for happiness while increasing our lust for material goods. Heidegger would disparage our addiction to television as another example of being sunk in everydayness: somnambulating through a life of habit and routine punctuated by diversion. Active engagement, experiences crucial for self-making, and luxuriating in the immediacy of life are better ingredients for a happy, meaningful existence.

Boredom is the closest experience to extinction we have in our lives. Better to be overscheduled than to have too much time on our hands and no interests to engage it. Nietzsche's dreary depiction of the last man, leading a risk-free, passive life of comfort, leisure, and social conformity, illustrates boredom writ large. Last men are sunk in an everydayness that is worse than hell on earth. Even in hell we feel and, perhaps, can reflect, while last men can only simulate nothingness. Contrary to the popular image of stressed-out, overworked Americans pointlessly engaged in a rat race with no winners, those of us with demanding schedules and challenging commitments are happier than those with too much time and too little to do.

A Puritan work ethic and nose-to-the-grindstone approach, though, is also self-defeating. We need to laugh, smile, be silly, even occasionally play the fool. Nietzsche's last men lacked the emotional range for such moods and emotions. Play requires exertion, brio, even a bit of chaos in our souls. Last men are barren. My mother's harshest evaluation of others was to call them *pasta asciutta* (dried-up macaroni). She never read Nietzsche, but her Sicilian instincts distrusted emotionless, robotic, stiff people.

Listening to music is one way of energizing our senses and stimulating our talents. Happy people are music lovers. Often, listening to music invigorates other pursuits such as dance, romance, athletics, and personal achievement. Prior to taking my first major exam in law school, I listened repeatedly to the theme song from the then-popular movie, *Rocky*. I later heard from a good friend that he had done the same thing. We had never discussed the movie nor music prior to that time. After law school, I began running marathons. As preparation for these grueling events, I would usually listen to some stirring Italian arias, peppered by selections from Jimmy Rosselli, Bob Dylan, and Bruce Springsteen. The research supports my conviction that listening to music facilitated my best performances.

Pleasant aromas also foster our happiness by triggering appropriate moods. Aromatherapy is used in numerous hospitals under the theory that pleasing smells facilitate recovery from illness. Certain smells are person-specific and dependent on our individual histories because they remind us of wonderful past times or glorious events. My father was a barber, and my family lived in an apartment over the barbershop during my early years. The aromas of witch hazel, bay rum, and Clubman aftershave still brighten my day because they remind me of my childhood. Others might well find them an annoying intrusion.

Clichés such as "smell the roses" and "count your blessings" embody salutary truths. The ordinary things we do every day can bring us great joy if we attend to them appropriately. We do not need an extraordinary triumph or special occasion to give ourselves permission to be exuberant. By focusing more on the immediacy of what we do, the present textures of experience, we will increase our happiness.

Physical exercise and proper nutrition also foster happiness. Proper conditioning increases our energy and animates our spirit. We should exercise not as a way to cheat the grim reaper. That is impossible. But we should exercise and eat properly as a way to enjoy our time on earth more thoroughly, improve our self-image, facilitate our self-confidence, and increase our opportunities for enjoyment.

## 9. GO WITH FLOW

The experiences that best exemplify Nietzsche's highest value, a maximally affirmative attitude toward life, completely engage us. To luxuriate in the immediacy of life is to be so totally involved that one loses track of time, the self, and everything external to the task at hand. We feel so transfixed in what we are doing that nothing else is important. We experience textures of our environment and sensual stimuli more acutely. We feel at one with our nature without attending to the vanities of the self.

Marx argued that the only fixed aspect of our species' being is our need for unalienated labor. He claimed that we are most truly ourselves when we are creatively engaged in projects that allow us to exert ourselves and realize our highest human capabilities. To be unalienated, labor must be freely chosen. We must have control over what we do, how we do it, what we produce, and what happens to our product. The image of an artist, fully absorbed by what she is doing, who gains enormous satisfaction from the process of creation, with full control over what she is creating, captures Marx's message. Under such conditions, we do not seek more leisure time nor more passive distractions. Instead, we deeply desire more strenuous activity that fills our souls with gratification as we profoundly experience our powers. To labor for its own sake from passionate commitment is to experience unalienated work.

When we view our work as serving values, purposes, and having effects that transcend ourselves, we are blessed.

Under such conditions, our labors are not merely undertaken for material reasons, recognitions, and status. Instead, we work as a means of self-expression and self-creation. Again, Nietzsche's last man is our counterpoint. The last man is unattractive because he has lost the desire to be deeply engaged in life. Sunk in everydayness, addicted to a life of habit and diversion punctuated by passive distractions, the last man has lost the yearning to create a dancing star. The last man is *pasta asciutta* writ small.

Psychologist Mihaly Csikszentmihalyi describes these periods of total engagement in life as flow experiences: "the state in which people are so involved in an activity that nothing else seems to matter; the experience itself is so enjoyable that people will do it even at great cost, for the sheer sake of doing it."[17] The wisest way to animate our lives, then, is to increase the amount and type of flow experiences. Nietzsche's intuitions about a maximally affirmative attitude toward life and Marx's celebration of unalienated labor were correct. The way to nourish our maximally affirmative attitude toward life and to realize unalienated labor is through increasing our experiences of flow.

Although flow experiences are immeasurably valuable for their own sake, they also bear great instrumental value. Such experiences not only express our creativity in salutary ways, but are also for our greatest existential projects: making a worthy self, leading a life worth examining, and constructing a valuable narrative.

[Every flow experience] provided a sense of discovery, a creative feeling of transporting the person into a new reality. It pushed the person to higher levels of performance, and led to previously undreamed-of states of consciousness. In short, it transformed the self by making it more complex . . . in the long run optimal experiences add up to a sense of mastery—or perhaps better, a sense of participation in determining the content of life.[18]

Existential philosophers, such as Kierkegaard, Sartre, and Heidegger, argued that social obsequiousness and abject conformity are the greatest obstacles to leading an authentic life. By subconsciously trying to abrogate much of our freedom and fixing our characters through the perceptions of others, we renege on the task of authentic self-creation. We fail to recognize our total freedom, make self-conscious choices upon which we act, and embrace responsibility for the person we are becoming. Flow experiences invigorate our robust sense of freedom by focusing on gratifications stemming from our own creative powers: "If a person learns to enjoy and find meaning in the ongoing stream of experience, in the process of living itself, the burden of social controls automatically falls from one's shoulders."[19]

Existentialists who believe that the cosmos is inherently meaningless, that no preordained value or meaning is built into the world, claim that our attitudes and creative powers can construct meaning and value. Much like we can create meaning and value upon a blank canvas through our creative endeavors, we can endow the universe. But the benign indifference of the cosmos is initially frustrating. We yearn for a connection to enduring value, an ultimate culmination for our lives, and a rational and just universe. The universe cannot answer our entreaties. We cannot take solace in societal conventions or popular opinions because such standards pander to mediocrity. Flow experiences distance us from the crowd and revitalize our sense of freedom and autonomy.

> To overcome the anxieties and depressions of contemporary life, individuals must become independent of the social environment to the degree that they no longer respond exclusively in terms of its rewards and punishments. To achieve such autonomy, a person has to learn to provide rewards to herself. She has to develop the ability to find enjoyment and purpose regardless of external circumstances.[20]

Flow experiences that foster enjoyment have eight dimensions: a project that we think we have a possibility of completing, that demands our focus, that is defined by specific goals, that furnishes immediate feedback, that requires profound involvement that pushes aside our mundane anxieties and frustrations, that affords us a sense of control over our activities, that temporarily allows us to transcend our self-absorption but later energizes our sense of self, and that permits us to lose track of time as we are unaware of the pace at which moments pass by.[21] Flow experiences are so enjoyable that we are willing to expend great effort, much time, and forego numerous other opportunities to pursue them. They are the best antidote to boredom and repel the hot breath of nothingness.

> The justification of climbing is climbing, like the justification of poetry is writing; you don't conquer anything except things in yourself . . . The purpose of the flow is to keep on flowing, not looking for a peak or utopia but staying in the flow . . . In normal life, we keep interrupting what we do with doubts and questions . . . But in flow there is no need to reflect, because the action carries

us forward as if by magic . . . people become so involved in what they are doing that the activity becomes spontaneous . . . they stop being aware of themselves as separate from the actions they are performing.[22]

Athletes often speak of being in the zone, a condition in which they perform to their highest capability with no apparent increase in effort. Their concentration, loss of self-awareness, and oneness with their activity constitutes the experience of flow. Nietzsche, a master psychologist prior to the invention of psychology, understood that the paramount experiences in life transform the self. His image of the grand transcender, the person deeply and self-consciously engaged in the project of deconstructing, reimagining, and re-creating the self, who recognized that the project was ongoing, admitted no final goals, and ended only at death or loss of fundamental human capabilities, anticipated contemporary research on flow. The activities of last men—personal comfort, social conformity, passive distractions, mild exertions, convenient pleasures, and minimal risks—do little to transform the self. These activities constitute the "happiness" that Nietzsche disdained and a life barely worth living.

Most of the strategies for happiness sketched above strive either to correlate external conditions with our goals, alter our experiences of external conditions to match our goals, or change our perceptions of the world to foster a serendipitous union of our goals and external conditions. But the underlying purpose to these strategies is to improve the quality of our daily experiences, to energize our maximally affirmative attitude toward life, and to nourish a positive, deserved self-evaluation.

Activities that fulfill the main strategies for happiness positively transform the self. This is one reason why identifying happiness and pleasure is unsuccessful. Numerous pleasures fail to positively transform the self. The pleasures of last men tend to retard the positive transformation of the self. Many Americans gain pleasure by passively viewing *Sabrina, Teenage Witch* and pounding down burgers at fast-food franchises. Few people are positively transformed and re-created by doing so.

Pleasure is an important component of the quality of life, but by itself it does not bring happiness . . . [many pleasures] do not produce psychological growth. They do not add complexity to the self. Pleasure helps to maintain order, but by itself cannot create new order in consciousness . . . Enjoyment is characterized by forward movement: by a sense of novelty, of accomplishment . . . we can experience pleasure without any investment of psychic energy, whereas enjoyment happens only as a result of unusual investments of attention . . . Complexity requires investing psychic energy in goals that are new, that are relatively challenging.[23]

I should not, though, oversell flow experiences. Flow experiences share a logical feature with existential authenticity: while both are necessary for the good life, they are not sufficient. For example, we can conjure an infinite number of activities that meet the standards of existential authenticity— activities that flow from our robust sense of freedom, that do not conform servilely to conventional norms, that reflect our anxiety-ridden, excuse-free autonomous choices for which we assume full responsibility under radically contingent circumstances without ultimate grounds—yet are immoral or socially undesirable. So, too, with flow experiences. Even those flow experiences that refine the complexity of the self must be morally evaluated.

The Greco-Roman philosophical tradition, based mainly on condition views that identified happiness with health, assumed an invulnerable marriage between virtue and happiness. Moral virtue was viewed as a necessary condition for happiness or a necessary and sufficient condition for happiness. To evaluate a person as lacking moral virtue was to conclude that he or she could not be happy. Regardless of the person's good-faith reports of a positive psychological state, he or she could not be happy simply because moral virtue was lacking. Contemporary social science research, though, supports the conclusion that the two most important factors for happiness—understood as a predominantly positive state of mind—are our relations with other people and our satisfaction with our work. While having an admirable amount of moral virtue typically facilitates satisfying personal relations and often invigorates our labors, moral virtue is not a necessary condition of happiness understood as a relatively enduring, positive state of mind. Altruism fosters positive emotions, strengthens relationships, and nurtures good health. Those of us who are on the whole morally deficient still practice occasional altruism. Typically, the altruism of the morally deficient is limited to a smaller group and is less frequent than the optimal altruism that defines the morally righteous. Thieves may not exude much honor among themselves, but they sometimes benefit their kind or their immediate family. Being thoroughly depraved and corrupt makes enduring joy and peace highly unlikely, but we can fall short of adequate moral virtue and still achieve happiness.

The connection between existential authenticity and moral virtue is even weaker. Leading an authentic life is an entirely formal requirement that instructs us how to make our choices and the conditions under which we should act, but says nothing about the substance of those choices and actions. Being a committed Nazi, a corrupt businessperson, or hit man for organized crime are possibilities not excluded by the formal requirements of existential authenticity. Likewise, the connection between flow experiences that transform the self and moral virtue is weak. The hypothetical Nazi, corrupt businessperson, and hit man could luxuriate in the immediacy of life and revel in the eight dimensions of enjoyment characterizing flow experiences. Accordingly, the good life requires more than an abundance of flow experiences, existential authenticity, and happiness understood as a relatively enduring positive state of mind.

## 10. BE LUCKY

Happy people have genetic advantages: brain chemistry conducive to and biological parents with a predisposition for happiness. Almost 50 percent of our personality traits flow from the genetic legacy of our ancestors. This does not mean that whether we are happy is simply a matter of destiny. Our genetic inheritance is more a range than it is a set point. Strategies for happiness, our choices, and actions pursuant to those choices are still crucial in determining whether we reside at the high end or low end of our happiness potential.

> Roughly half of your score on happiness tests is accounted for by the score your biological parents would have gotten had they taken the test. This may mean that we inherit a 'steersman' who urges us toward a specific level of happiness or sadness . . . we each have a personal set range for our level of positive (and negative) emotion, and this range may represent the inherited aspect of overall happiness.[24]

That our happiness potential is greatly influenced by biology should not surprise. The adage of the old Kentucky farmer who dryly observed that he could work his donkey from sunup until sundown but it still could not win the Kentucky Derby is instructive. I could have worked feverishly on my basketball skills during my prime years from sunup until sundown but I would still never have been Michael Jordan or Larry Bird, or even as proficient as the twelfth man on a major college team. Like everyone else, I had a range of athletic talent. To be the best that we can be means playing at the highest range of our talent. The set range of that talent, though, has a strong biological component: "Nearly every psychological trait or tendency that we can measure reliably owes part of its variation from person to person to genetic differences between people."[25] Intellectual ability may admit the same analysis. Instead of conjuring an abstract standard of academic accomplishment for all students, the most we should demand is that students do all that they can to operate at the highest range of their respective talents: You can work Jordan or Bird from sunup until sundown but Leonardo da Vinci and Albert Einstein will remain unchallenged.

What social scientists call the "hedonic treadmill" also supports the set range of happiness. We have a strong inclination to adapt to both grand accomplishments and significant setbacks. After a few months of either high achievement or serious misfortune, we revert back to our previous happiness levels.

> The 'hedonic treadmill' causes you to rapidly and inevitably adapt to good things by taking them for granted. As you accumulate more material possessions and accomplishments, your expectations rise. The deeds and things you worked so hard for no longer make you happy; you need to get something even better to boost your level of happiness into the upper reaches of its set range . . . Good things and high accomplishments . . . have astonishingly little power to raise happiness more than transiently.[26]

The good news, however, is that the hedonic treadmill is symmetrical. With the exceptions of certain horrors—the tragic, untimely death of a child or spouse, longtime caring for family members suffering from Alzheimer's disease, extreme poverty—we adapt to most tragedies.

> Depression is almost always episodic, with recovery occurring within a few months of onset. Even individuals who become paraplegic as a result of spinal cord accidents quickly begin to adapt to their greatly limited capacities, and within eight weeks they report more net positive emotion than negative emotion.[27]

Just as we cannot change our date of birth, our biological parents, and our country of origin, we cannot alter our set range of happiness, which is what some existential philosophers call a "facticity"—a givenness beyond our control. We can, though, use the strategies for happiness sketched above to live predominantly at the higher levels of our set range. We are just as responsible for our happiness as we are for other aspects of our lives. We can choose to pursue happiness in the same way we can choose intellectual or athletic success as a goal. We work within biological limitations and capabilities, but we are free to pay the price, to exert our energies into the world, in pursuit of our goals. During the process of our strivings, our characters are forged and revealed. All we can ask of ourselves is to live predominantly at the higher levels of our set ranges of abilities. Success, as always, is not automatic. Nothing worthwhile ever is.

Those of us longing for one big score—winning the lottery, earning a Pulitzer Prize, achieving our most desired goal—as the recipe for happiness are misguided. No single event, achievement, gift, or serendipitous blessing will result in a fixed increase of our joy, peace, or exuberance. Our search for happiness, like life itself, is a journey that ends only at death or when we lose the human capabilities to undertake it. What nurtures happiness, unsurprisingly, changes as we age. The happiest among us view their lives on an upward trajectory as the achievement of one goal leads to the pursuit of another, not as an endless series of doomed pursuits oscillating between boredom and frustration, but as a felicitous intermeshing of means and ends that continually energizes our zest for life. While we savor the past and earn gratification from reflecting on the characters we have forged, we must continue the saga and renew our engagement with the processes of life. The efforts we expend, the exertions we project, and the tasks we undertake are good for their own sake and as a means of developing and refining our characters. No single attainment or stroke of good luck can mark our happiness once and forever.

## 11. FORMS OF HAPPINESS

Those who overrate happiness most extravagantly prize it as a great personal good and identify it with relatively enduring joy, peace, or exuberance. I have argued that such happiness is often rightfully sacrificed for other values; that it is not necessary to a valuable, significant, or important life; that it often conflicts with the pursuit of truth; that it can be simulated and be divorced from reality; and that we sometimes fail to attain it because of perfectionism, singlemindedness, competitiveness, an uncommonly keen grasp of reality, or incompatible brain chemistry.

A relatively enduring, positive state of mind is usually a good, but not the greatest good, and often not a great good. The requisite psychological state is part of, but cannot define, a worthwhile happiness. To pursue happiness directly is often self-defeating. If happiness occurs it does so as a by-product of a life lived well, one filled with meaning. The main concern of human life is not merely to gain pleasure and avoid pain, but to capture meaning and to connect to value. The best human lives pursue adequate reason to be happy, instead of seeking only the feelings of extended joy or peace regardless of how they are induced. Creative activity, robust relationships, turning personal tragedy into triumph, and confronting difficult situations with courage and verve are but a few ways of embracing the meaning and value that is the adequate reason for extended joy or peace. Finding meaning in life, then, opens the possibility of achieving the only happiness worth possessing. But discovering or creating meaning and connecting to value cannot guarantee happiness will follow.

Happiness requires a measure of good luck. First, flourishing often requires some good fortune, or at least the absence of debilitating calamities. Second, the feelings of extended joy or peace are partially a function of a person's biochemistry in the brain. So a person must not have the bad luck of unusual, unhealthy biochemistry. But happiness is never only a matter of luck. Our attitudes, efforts, expectations, and deeds are crucial to happiness. Much is within our control. If we live robustly meaningful, valuable lives we, hopefully, increase our probability of attaining happiness. But happiness is the by-product, not the determinant, of a life lived well. Happiness as an experience, pleasant sensations, or enduring psychological state differs from happiness as a condition, state of affairs, or fulfillment of criteria. People are aware of whether they have the required psychological state, but they can be mistaken about whether they fulfill the rest. Do we want the experience of happiness? Or do we want the condition of happiness?

We want both. We want to experience happiness because we have the appropriate condition. But suppose we could have only one or the other. Advocates of the experience models could argue that the condition of happiness is worthless unless we experience happiness. They would be mistaken. The condition of happiness could bring great meaning and value in our lives even if we remained downbeat, even if we did not experience enduring peace of mind or pleasure. Advocates of condition models could argue that the experience of happiness can be simulated, fraudulent, or based on deep delusion: better to be a somber Michelangelo than a giddy Howard Stern. The happiness-as-positive-accurate-self-appraisal position fails as a formal definition of happiness as such, but points us to a deeper notion of worthwhile happiness. The persuasiveness of that position flows from taking meaning and value to be more important than the experience of happiness.

This analysis provides another reason why happiness is overrated. The minimally meaningful, but happy, life is less worthwhile than the robustly meaningful and valuable, but somewhat unhappy life. Robustly meaningful and valuable, but somewhat unhappy lives embody higher quality of activities, greater social effects, enduring legacies, manifested excellences, and greater values. Admitting this does not dismiss the allure of happiness. The best lives are robustly meaningful, valuable, and happy.

Lives lived well are connected to a rich network of interests, projects, and purposes that flow from ourselves; that fuel our commitment to, zest for, and faith in life; that are connected to reality, not based on radically false beliefs; that block claims that our lives are not worth living; that make our lives significant as they affect the lives of others and leave historical footprints; and that are valuable in that they are connected deeply with moral, cognitive, aesthetic, and spiritual values.

Happiness, understood as a relatively enduring, positive state of mind, often follows such lives, but not invariably. A worthwhile happiness—my preferred form of happiness—is the relatively enduring gratification that accompanies our accurate, positive evaluation that we are leading meaningful and valuable lives. Such happiness requires the development of a worthy character, the pursuit of meritorious activities, and a connection to important projects beyond the self. We would ordinarily decline an invitation to exist in a virtual reality machine because we yearn to deserve happiness, not merely experience the simulated sensations of happiness. While in the virtual reality machine, we lose numerous intrinsic goods—having relationships, reading books, playing sports—that are good for their own sake, not merely as means to other goods. In the virtual reality machine we gain the simulated pleasures of these activities, but only the illusion of doing them. To deserve happiness requires the development and refinement of praiseworthy human character. In the machine, we deserve nothing because we do nothing. We are reduced to a vacuous blob of sensations.

Identifying happiness with positive sensations too easily leads to sterile hedonism. Pleasure does not usually require deep reflection, only transient, desirable feelings. The feelings of happiness are often taken, particularly by social scientists, to define happiness. But worthwhile happiness goes beyond the popular conception. Under this notion, the feelings of happiness are, at best, evidence of our positive assessment of how our lives are faring.

> Gratification, the ground of worthwhile happiness, involves activities we very much like doing, but [which] are not necessarily accompanied by any raw feelings . . . [they] engage us fully, we become immersed and absorbed in them, and we lose self-consciousness . . . the gratifications last longer than the pleasures, they involve quite a lot of thinking and interpretation, they do not habituate easily, and they are undergirded by our [character] strengths and virtues.[28]

Worthwhile happiness involves an accurate, positive evaluation about the ways we have developed and employed our characters. Such happiness is defined by the deserved gratification that accompanies the process and result of this examination. This is the sense in which Aristotle was correct that genuine happiness arrives only at the end of our lives. Given that our characters are not fixed, we cannot be certain that today's accurate, positive assessment of our lives will be matched by tomorrow's performance. We can, nevertheless, continually assess our lives as we live them and, hopefully, derive the deserved gratification that defines worthwhile happiness.

Worthwhile happiness, then, is the feather in the fedora, but still not the greatest personal good. A life lived well is a greater good than the deserved gratification that typically accompanies it.


## NOTES

1. Rick Foster and Greg Hicks, *How We Choose to Be Happy* (New York: Penguin Putnam, Inc., 1999); Dr. David Lykken, *Happiness* (New York: St. Martin's Press, 1999); David G. Myers, *The Pursuit of Happiness* (New York: Avon Books, Inc., 1992); Roy F. Baumeister, *Meanings of Life* (New York: The Guilford Press, 1991); Martin E. P. Seligman, *Authentic Happiness* (New York: The Free Press, 2002); Mihaly Csikszentmihalyi, *Flow* (New York: Harper & Row Publishers, 1990); David Niven, *The 100 Simple Secrets of Happy People* (New York: HarperCollins Publishers, 2000).

2. Myers, *Pursuit of Happiness*, 65, 67.

3. Plato, *The Republic* in *The Dialogues of Plato*, 2 vols., trans. B. Jowett (New York: Random House, 1920).

4. Stephen R. Covey, A. Roger Merrill, and Rebecca R. Merrill, *First Things First* (New York: Simon & Schuster, 1992), 17–31.

5. Niven, *Happy People*, 22.

6. Iain Pears, *An Instance of the Fingerpost* (New York: Riverhead Books, 1998), 38–39.

7. Lykken, *Happiness*, 17.

8. Martin Heidegger, *Being and Time*, trans. John Macquarrie and Edward Robinson (New York: Harper & Row, 1962).

9. Robert C. Solomon, *The Joy of Philosophy* (New York: Oxford University Press, 1999), 142.

10. Jean-Paul Sartre, *Being and Nothingness*, trans. Hazel Barnes (New York: Philosophical Library, 1956).

11. Solomon, *Joy of Philosophy*, 43, 44, 53.

12. Seligman, *Authentic Happiness*, 37–38.

13. Lykken, *Happiness*, 63, 101, 105.
14. Luo Lu and Jian Bin Shih, "Sources of Happiness," *The Journal of Social Psychology* 137:2 (1997): 181–187.
15. Niven, *Happy People*, 167–168.
16. Sartre, *Being and Nothingness*.
17. Csikszentmihalyi, *Flow*, 4.
18. Ibid., 74, 4.
19. Ibid., 19.
20. Ibid., 16.
21. Ibid., 49.
22. Ibid., 53, 54.
23. Ibid., 46, 47.
24. Seligman, *Authentic Happiness*, 47, 48.
25. Lykken, *Happiness*, 3.
26. Seligman, *Authentic Happiness*, 49.
27. Ibid., 48.
28. Ibid., 102.

# 5

# THE MEANING OF LIFE

S tart laughing, run out some bad puns, polish up the sarcasm. What else could an author of a book chapter on the meaning of life expect? The topic invites ridicule.

Writing about the meaning of life invites two equally offensive responses. The first: "The question itself is confusing and meaningless. You are foolish for pursuing a Holy Grail without the right question, much less the right tools." The second: "You are a pretentious fool or an unintended comedian for taking on such a question. The answer is beyond our comprehension. Wasn't that the point of Monty Python's film, *The Meaning of Life*?"

Everyone seems firmly convinced that nothing startling will result from an inquiry into the meaning of life. The question is too daunting for human understanding. If people had something stunning to say about the meaning of life, they would be busy giving press conferences or promoting their own cult or at least selling a product to enhance meaning for $19.95 (plus $9.95 postage and handling) on television.

An earnest seeker of Truth journeys to a mountaintop in a faraway land. She hopes to learn the answer to the most fundamental question troubling human beings: What is the meaning of life? She has heard of a venerable sage who lives on the mountaintop, a modern-day Delphic oracle who embodies the greatest human wisdom. After an arduous trek, she is brought before the great man and with great anticipation asks her question. The sage casts his eyes skyward, shifts his body uncomfortably, and mumbles, "A lily pad."

Astonished, the seeker of Truth repeats, "The meaning of life is a lily pad!" The sage responds, "Yes, a lily pad." As she is escorted back down the mountain, she wonders, "Why a lily pad? Why not a turnip, an oak tree, a bumblebee, or a pepperoni stick?" She ponders whether the sage is a fraud, too insecure to admit he did not know the correct answer, or whether a lily pad has profound, metaphorical meaning. Is a lily pad just a placemarker, a vacuous phrase demanding that the questioner supply her own answer to a question unanswerable in general terms? Or did the sage intend to chastise her for asking such an impertinent question?

This tale is a common fable told when questions of ultimate meaning arise.[1] It provides no answers, only more questions. We dread questions about the meaning of life. They seem overwhelming, obviously beyond human comprehension, so we are repulsed by such questions. We often ridicule those who seriously ask them and naively expect substantive answers. We are, however, simultaneously attracted to questions about the meaning of life. We recognize that part of the human condition is that the questions most important to us—Why am I born to suffer and die? What, if anything, is my destiny? How did it all begin? How will it end?—evade incontestable answers and, instead, underscore the limitations of human reason. Seriously confronting such questions threatens our mundane lives of responsibilities and routines, punctuated by diversions and entertainments. Yet, to avoid questions of ultimate meaning strikes us as cowardly and inauthentic. Part of living a fully human life involves struggling with such fundamental questions while understanding that incontestable answers must elude us.

Some people claim that happiness is the meaning of life. This is wildly incorrect if we understand happiness merely as a relatively enduring, positive state of mind. Moreover, the claim assumes that life has meaning. We must, instead, examine what it means to say life has meaning, determine whether human life has meaning, and what sort of meaning that might be.

## 1. WHAT DOES IT MEAN TO SAY LIFE HAS MEANING?

The question is difficult to understand because it is so complex. Our answers could focus on the origins of the universe, the purposes of all life, the point of human life, the significance of an individual life, or how to understand any of these. Answers to such questions do more than examine why there is something rather than nothing. A scientific account of the origins of the universe cannot tell us whether a plan for the universe, an embedded meaning that human beings can discover but not create, is in place. Even if we cannot explain why there is something rather than nothing it may be possible to construct a purely human meaning in our lives, or not.

If asked for the meaning of a natural phenomenon we might respond by citing its genesis, how it came about, its likely consequences, or what it will probably produce. The question "What is the meaning of life?" is better understood as asking for the purpose or value of human life, or perhaps life in general. The notions of meaning and purpose, however, are distinguishable. "Meaning" can stand for how we understand or make sense of our lives in an ongoing way. "Purpose" can stand for the goals or ends, or the highest or final end, toward which we strive. Meaning, then, would be process-oriented, while purpose is goal-oriented. Nevertheless, purpose and value are linked with making sense of and understanding our lives, or life in general.

The complexity of the question, along with the different meanings of "meaning," leads some thinkers to conclude that the question itself is ill-formed or even meaningless. Some philosophers would argue that actions within a life have a meaning, but life itself does not. We can ask for the meaning of a word in a language and make ourselves understood. But we cannot ask for the meaning of the whole language: "What is the meaning of Latin?" is unanswerable because we neither understand the question nor can we conceive of what an acceptable answer would amount to. We can, however, answer: "What is the purpose of Latin?" One of the purposes of Latin is or was to permit communication. To ask for the meaning of life is best understood as an inquiry about the point, purpose, significance or sense of particular lives, or of life in general.

But the question, even if difficult to form and understand clearly, is not easily dismissed. Because they touch our deepest fears and hopes, inquiries into the meaning of life cannot be dissolved by semantic fiat.

Understanding the issues surrounding the meaning of life focuses attention on a nest of questions: Is a purpose, plan, or destination embedded in the universe? If not, does that mean human life is ultimately pointless or absurd? What ideals, norms, actions should inform human life? How can I understand and make sense of my life in an ongoing way? Is human life in general and my life in particular justified by the objective conditions in the universe? Must a life be infinite to be worthwhile? Is permanence a condition of meaning? Is the universe indifferent to the deepest human yearnings? Is life merely "sound and fury, signifying nothing"? Can human beings experience a final culmination, enduring value, and a rational and just universe? What is my destiny, if any? Do I really matter?

I do not claim that the question "Does life have meaning?" is logically equivalent to any of the other questions, or to all of them taken together. I am not making a logical or semantic claim. Instead, I claim only that the question of life's meaning rivets our concern on a host of issues, the most important of which are listed above. I will focus on the meaning of human lives, not on the general meaning of life itself.


## 2. THE EXISTENTIAL PROBLEM

In the 1960s and 1970s, an endearing actor, Peter Falk, played a detective named "Columbo" on a television show of the same name. The drama was unique in its genre because it revealed the identity of the murderer in the opening segment. The mystery was how Columbo was going to amass enough evidence to arrest the murderers, who were uncommonly clever and calculating. Happily, Columbo always nailed his target.

If you have read the first parts of this book attentively, you already know that I conclude that human life has meaning. The mystery is how I am going to argue for that conclusion. Although I am not as imaginative a scriptwriter as those who orchestrated Peter Falk's television triumphs, I will begin at the logical point: a historical example of a psychological crisis that triggered the quest for meaning.

Enter Leo Tolstoy, the embodiment of existential crisis. The great Russian novelist, the master wordsmith of *War and Peace*, *Anna Karenina*, and much more, was seemingly blessed. He had a good family, uncommon intelligence, stunning professional success, material well-being, good health, and most of any reasonable catalog of meaningfulness. Yet he was, around the age of fifty, tormented by the thought and psychological experience that life was meaningless. Tolstoy was plagued by the four horsemen of self-doubt: awareness of human mortality, lack of control of the things he most valued, absence of ultimate justifications for his actions, and an acute sense that his life might in the end add up to nothing. Tolstoy was threatened by his inevitable death, the fragility of the things and people he valued, and the apparent lack of foundational justification for his actions. Finitude, contingency, and arbitrariness haunted him.

> Sooner or later there would come diseases and death (they had come already) to my dear ones and to me, and there would be nothing left but stench and worms. All my affairs . . . would sooner or later be forgotten, and I myself should not exist. . . . How could a man fail to see that and live. . . . A person could live only so long as he was drunk; but the moment he sobered up, he could not help seeing that all that was only a deception, and a stupid deception at that![2]

Tolstoy saw no way out of this human predicament. He entertained four possibilities. First, if we remain ignorant of the facts, then the meaninglessness of human life would not affect our enjoyment of our existence. But ignorance was not an option for Tolstoy or any other educated or intelligent person. Once we are aware of the facts we cannot retreat to the safety of ignorance no matter how hard we try. Second, we might find consolation in enhancing our power and privilege. By focusing narrowly on personal and professional successes, through immersion in material pleasure, and by reveling in our relative advantages over others, we might avoid the pain of meaninglessness. But the road of invidious social comparison is only a diversion from the inevitable truth. We are all born to suffer, die, and be forgotten. Power and privilege do not alter the facts; they only divert our gaze. Third, suicide is always an option. Although Tolstoy sometimes called this the choice of "strength and energy," it is difficult to see this as a solution. Suicide evades the problem of a life by ending it. It does not, typically, create meaning as much as it capitulates to the felt absence of meaning. Fourth, the choice of endurance or "weakness": continuing to push on, hoping against hope that the meaning of life would make a surprise appearance in the future.

Tolstoy solved his distress by appreciating the lives of simple, uneducated people. Peasants, wanderers, monks, and social dissenters were his models. They had difficult, beast-of-burden lives, yet their religious faith gave them a "consciousness of life" that connected them to meaning. Only religious faith, not reason, can make life meaningful. Tolstoy vowed to link his being with spiritual conviction and action. He espoused humility, vegetarianism, and the value of manual labor, while rejecting luxuries, violence, coercion, and material accumulation. He also advanced the ideal of chastity, while recognizing that the nature and circumstances of people would not permit widespread compliance. Love of fellow human beings was a more important value than the ambition, vanity, and lust for individual success or the insulating consolations of an honorable family life. Sentimentalizing the life of peasants and glorifying faith in God permitted Tolstoy to celebrate personal immortality and a grand design, and to reinstate foundational justification for human action.

Critics see Tolstoy as evading the tragedy of life through flight to an imaginary, transcendental afterlife. Putting that issue aside, Tolstoy's crisis is significant. First, his life illustrates vividly that a meaningful life does not automatically result from the fulfillment of typical human desires. More is required. Second, his solution to the problem of the meaning of life demands a "consciousness of life" or a "faith" that cannot be rationally supported all the way down. Third, his life demonstrates a trinity of the deepest human aspirations: the yearning for a final culmination, a connection to enduring value, and a rational and just universe ("Tolstoy's trinity"). Fourth, Tolstoy accepts the theistic assumption: Either God exists as the creator of meaning embedded in the universe or there is only chaos and meaninglessness.

Tolstoy concluded that the meaning of life is to discover a way to live such that the question of life's meaning no longer arises. Find a better way to live and the ultimate questions wither away. Tolstoy was incorrect. He did not take his own counsel about ignorance seriously enough: Once we are conscious of the questions, we cannot suppress them, we cannot forget forever. The only solution is to find a way that permits us to ask the ultimate questions, struggle with tentative solutions, yet continue to live energetically. The path of denial through continually distracting engagement dehumanizes us.

The question, "What is the meaning of life?" is about the cosmos and about ourselves. To find out about the cosmos we must distinguish the world from ourselves. The answer to the question deeply influences how we should live. Therefore, the question itself arises from the human condition, from psychological curiosity, often from crisis. The question is not merely an abstraction fueling intellectual reflection.

One answer, The Religious Solution, is that a Supreme Being or Nature builds a human teleology, or overriding purpose, into the cosmos. If so, the further question is whether an external purpose that supposedly applies to everyone should issue any persuasive existential imperatives for me. Is the individual submerged by universal demands?

Another answer somberly resigns us to Cosmic Meaninglessness: The cosmos is inherently meaningless and, thus, human life is meaningless regardless of our best efforts to delude ourselves with frantic activity and joyful amusements.

A third answer advises The Creation of Contingent Meaning: The cosmos is inherently meaningless, but the meaning of human life is the search for and construction of meaning itself. If so, the further question is whether all meaning is equal or, if not equal, how does meaning relate to value.

## 3. THE RELIGIOUS SOLUTION

Religions prescribe ways of life and usually include formal organizations, elaborate rituals, discrete ceremonies, and, sometimes, methods of conversion and political goals. Buddhism, Hinduism, Judaism, Christianity, and Islam are examples of widely influential religions.

## A. Eastern Religion

Eastern religion begins with the Four Noble Truths: life in this world is predominantly suffering and dissatisfaction; the source of suffering is the craving or desire connected with ego-attachment; suffering can be overcome through the cessation of craving and ego-attachment; and the way to overcome suffering is contained in the Eightfold Path.[3]

Suffering predominates in this world and is most keenly experienced in death, illness and disease, old age, separation from loved ones, the presence of others who are malicious, unfulfilled desires, and frustrated cravings. The source of such suffering lies in misunderstanding the nature of worldly phenomena and, especially, in misconceiving personal identity.

The Eightfold Path has three stages. The first stage is the proper frame of mind (right views, right aspirations). The second stage is ethical action (right speech, right conduct, right livelihood). The third stage is proper meditation needed for transcendent experience (right effort, right mindfulness, right contemplation).

Buddhism, because of the Four Noble Truths, undermines our attachment to the self and to strong notions of individuality. Our belief in a substantial, persisting self is false, but this is good news because the belief in such a self fuels our ego-attachment and relentless cravings. We are only a shifting set of physical features, feelings, attitudes, emotions, moods, and so on. No permanent, unchanging substratum supports and unites human features. Nor is the self a pure consciousness distinct from bodily and psychological processes. Conscious experience depends on our perceptual equipment. The self plays no explanatory role in human activity. Nor is the notion of an abiding self required by other Buddhist beliefs.

The doctrine of karma contends that we reap what we sow. If something bad happens to me that I seemingly do not deserve, the law of karma insists that I am responsible because of what I have done in this or an earlier life. Buddhists can explain the notions of rebirth, moral desert, liberation, and the afterlife without resorting to the existence of an enduring self. Rebirth is merely a continuation, with a different body, of that shifting set of features and dispositions comprising human beings. Since only our physical packaging has changed we are still morally responsible for past deeds. When we are purified, by discharging our karmic debts, we are liberated from the round of rebirth.

Our reward is the cessation of craving and ignorance, and transcendence to Nirvana.

All worldly pursuits are temporal and cause suffering. True well-being lies in the midst of everyday life only when we observe the existence and phenomena of this world as they are. Renouncing social comparisons and the undignified scramble for privilege and social power, Buddhists insist that happiness is possible even under the worst conditions. The Buddhist goal, then, is the escape from suffering, ignorance, and desire and the attainment of enlightenment. The state in which we attain enlightenment is Nirvana, perfect tranquility devoid of all suffering. Abandoning all worldly desires and attachments through the realization of the impermanence and nonsubstantiality of this world, the enlightened Buddhist glimpses on earth what can be fully realized after death. Nirvana is understood in several different ways: as the negation or cessation of familiar worldly existence; as total extinction; as peace and tranquility as such; as part of everyday existence once the Noble Truths are understood and the Eightfold Path is embraced.

Lacking eternal souls and without an anthropomorphic creator, human beings can hope only to attain a transcendent, permanent state wherein their sense of individuality vanishes. In some versions of Buddhism, the (noncraving) quest for the eternal, universal, and transcendent replaces craving for the impermanent, individual, and earthly. In other versions, liberation is not a matter of escaping from this world to another, purer one, but of embracing a proper perspective on this world fueled by a sense of the insubstantiality of things and selves, and the futility of recurrent striving.

The central claims of one expression of Hinduism, Advaita Vedanta, have much in common with Buddhism: Human beings are enslaved in a horrifying cycle of rebirth through the karmic deserts of our actions fueled by desires. Liberation from this cycle can occur only when we are enlightened as to how we and the world really are. Nothing is real except *Brahman*, a unitary, seamless, ineffable being. Things we ordinarily take to be real belong to the world of appearance and illusion. Individual selves are also appearances, reflections of a single, pure consciousness, *atman*. Since reality is one, Brahman and atman must be identical. Belief in the existence of the apparent world is due to ignorance as we superimpose on Brahman/atman what does not belong to it. Because we are enslaved by the cycle of rebirth through desires that depend on our false belief in the physical world and individual selves, liberation is attained through experiencing the identity of Brahman and atman, thereby overcoming the delusion that there is a world. Thus, nothing is real except a single, ineffable mode of being, pure consciousness, which is experienced in a self-luminous flash that is itself liberation.

Without getting bogged down in the complexities of Asian religion, six common ideas form its framework: The mundane world is predominantly suffering and illusion; there is a comprehensive account of ourselves and wider reality that will dispel the ignorance in our everyday beliefs and exhibit the unsatisfactoriness of existence founded on those beliefs; human beings are trapped in a cycle of rebirth or transmigration; the doctrine of karma, a universal law of nature that embodies ultimate justice based on moral desert, rules; everything in the mundane world has an explicable place in an intelligible whole; and liberation from the cycle of rebirth to a timeless, unchanging, unconditioned state is possible through enlightenment and discharging karmic debts.

## B. Western Religion

Christianity worships an anthropomorphic divinity who embodies all positive human qualities amplified to their highest degree.[4] Understanding divinity in male-gendered terms, Christians believe that God is all-powerful, all-good, all-knowing, and creates the cosmos as an expression of His love. The first human beings inhabited a paradise, but, upon disobeying God's prohibition to eat fruit from the tree of knowledge, fell from grace and were relegated to the world as we know it. Human beings have free will to choose rightly or wrongly and they will eventually be judged in accordance with their earthly deeds. Thus, this world is a proving ground, and its trials and sufferings are opportunities to demonstrate moral worth. We are responsible for our actions, and God will evaluate us according to our moral desert. We will earn eternal bliss or eternal suffering. Many of those earning eternal bliss will first spend time in purgatory where they will, through suffering, cleanse themselves of sin. Our souls are immortal, and our souls define who we are, so we enjoy personal immortality.

Although specific, detailed descriptions are lacking, heaven is the state of eternal happiness that brings full, lasting satisfaction to the whole of our being through our union with Christ together with all members of His mystical body. Those who earn redemption will have their bodies restored in glorified form. But the essential part of heavenly bliss does not involve bodily activity; thus neither senses nor imagination are required. The beatific vision, the intuitive apprehension of God as He is in Himself, and love are the activities of the nobler, spiritual human aspects. In the beatific vision God Himself replaces ideas and sense impressions so that He is in direct contact with the human soul. A secondary feature of beatific vision is that we retain our past histories, cleansed of imperfection and sinfulness. Thus, we retain our affections for our backgrounds and contacts; we have continuing knowledge and love of the created beings with whom we had relationships in our earthly lives. Our restless, desirous spirits attain eternal serenity as our potentialities are fully realized so that no unfulfilled element remains.

The meaning of human life is to understand and embrace God's plan: to attain a personal relationship with God, to choose wisely, and through one's deeds to merit eternal salvation. Earthly life embodies Tolstoy's trinity of hopes: Our final culmination is judgment day, when we will be evaluated in accord with our moral deserts; our connection to enduring value is our immortality and opportunity for eternal bliss in the presence of a divinity who is all-good; and our universe is rational and just because, ultimately, the perfect judge with complete knowledge will assess our lives and reward or punish us according to our own free choices.

Judaism and Islam, the other great Western religions, cling to similar narratives. Judaism and Islam do not recognize Christ as the son of God, and many other details distinguish the Western religions: which scriptures or holy books are taken as sacred; which figures are identified as prophets; what type of political association, if any, follows from religious commitment; what imperatives the divinity has set forth; whether the divinity anoints a chosen people; and so on. But the Western religions share a common framework: monotheism, belief in personal immortality, an account of Tolstoy's trinity, the prize of salvation and eternal bliss, a preordained design (including a human purpose) built into the cosmos, and a clear understanding of the purpose of human life on earth.

## C. Assessment of Religion

Eastern religions are less successful in the West because, among other reasons, they undermine robust individualism. Most Eastern religions insist our notions of individuality are illusory, self-defeating, or both. The quest of life is to soften, even eliminate, ego-attachment as preparation for a higher, better unity. Doctrines such as rebirth and karma explain certain problems, such as the problem of evil, by contending that the universe responds to our choices with perfect justice: In this life or another we will all face the consequences of our actions. Tolstoy's trinity of yearnings is satisfied as Eastern religions begin from the perspective that the cosmos embodies a final culmination, a connection to enduring value, and is rational and just. But it is unclear whether Eastern religions capture what the cosmos actually is or project upon the cosmos our own deepest aspirations. We would like the cosmos to rule on strict moral deserts, to link us with enduring value, to offer a blissful final culmination to human life. Whether the cosmos reflects our deepest yearnings or is merely indifferent remains an open question. We yearn for Tolstoy's trinity; religions provide narratives to satisfy those hopes. Does that mean religion is true?

Western religions are much more individualistic than Eastern religions. Although the cosmos is unified, as part of the Supreme Being's grand design, human beings are individuals who do not suffer the cycle of rebirth. Tolstoy's trinity is affirmed, but without doctrines such as karma and multiple lives. Ultimate rationality and justice is embodied and dispensed by the Supreme Being: We each get one shot at life and are then evaluated by the Master Adjudicator.

Some contemporary philosophers, such as Irving Singer and Kurt Baier, insist that theism is no help in the quest for a meaningful life.[5] If meaning is preordained by a deity, the laws of nature, or both, then human beings are instruments or tools in a scheme not of their making. If our earthly tasks are assigned by outside agents, all life has a merely instrumental meaning. We ourselves were fashioned with a predetermined destiny. Our choices are only to celebrate the grand design in humble supplication to powers greater than ourselves or resist the divine plan. We are either toadies who curry favor out of fear or fools who risk eternal retribution.

This criticism of religion is unpersuasive. In religious accounts, the grand design is not merely a script imposed by a stronger force. The grand design exemplifies Truth, Goodness, and Reality themselves. We cannot simply go along with the drama tongue in cheek. Instead, we should internalize the norms of the divine plan, make them our own, and celebrate our connection with the ground of all being. We are mere instruments only if we are used. But we are not used if we cheerfully affirm a grand design that exudes the highest values. Human beings would be more than tools because of our free will: Through our choices, creativity, commitments, and actions we can make the divine plan our own. Western religions need not demand debasement of the self or a negative attitude toward the universe.

Eastern religions have a tougher but not impossible road to travel on these matters. Once people accept the Eastern understanding of self, the unity of the cosmos, the paramount value of transcendence, the doctrines of rebirth and karma, and the like, they can moderate suffering and realize their full potentialities in their moral and spiritual life. Eastern religions are a nonanthropomorphic way of connecting to value, meaning, and truth. Eastern religions need not be viewed as providing a merely instrumental purpose for human beings.

My limited defense of religion against an unfair form of philosophical attack must not be taken as a call to string up the revival tents, juice up the chorus, and pile on the testimonies. Religions can always be called into question.

First, no religion can be proved. Proofs for the existence of God are often energized by fear of an infinite regress, for example, a chain of causation and movement that never ends unless an unmoved mover or uncaused cause stops the chain. Infinite regresses terrify some philosophers because they provide no ultimate explanation of events on earth. But all such proofs, at best, can conclude only that there is an uncaused cause of some sort, not that the God of Judeo-Christianity or Allah of Islam is that first cause. Moreover, even the conclusion that there is an uncaused cause depends on eliminating, usually by logical fiat, the possibility of an infinite regress. Perhaps an infinite regress is the (non)explanation. Finally, the Supreme Being of Western religion can itself be viewed as an anthropomorphic infinite regress. Eternal and complete with no origin, the Supreme Being is every bit as mysterious an explanation of the cosmos as an infinite regress. Has religion substituted a living, eternal, infinite being for the infinite regress of causation and motion it feared? Insofar as a Supreme Being or Nature itself is a first cause it invites further questions: What is God's purpose in creating a meaningful world? Does a more ultimate purpose even than God's purposiveness exist? Theists might respond that as the ground of all being God would not be in a relationship with Truth, Goodness, Meaning, and the like. God would be identical to and the source of these values. But that identity and ground remain mysterious and beg the question against the nontheist.

In sum, proofs for the existence of God typically beg the question against the possibility of an infinite regress and, after concluding that an uncaused cause exists, affirm faith in a Supreme Being. Therefore, these exercises do not demonstrate the existence of a first being.

Second, scriptural accounts and religious experiences are likewise unreliable. The methodology of appealing to scriptures in sacred texts is questionable. Often, advocates take single scriptural passages as decisive for all moral cases that might relate to the passage. But there are grave difficulties in doing so. Questions about the original context in which the passage was used, about how the passage's context may have been shifted by later authors, and about how a scriptural passage relates to other passages on the same topic abound.

Much like the proclamations of the Delphic Oracle, the writings in sacred texts admit different interpretations. Such writings have a deep historical dimension; they arose at a time in a place under social circumstances. The existence of scriptures shows at best that certain people deeply believed certain things, including the existence of a Supreme Being, and interpreted certain events in certain ways in their time.

Religious experiences fare no better as demonstration of theism's truth. Having unusual experiences can be interpreted and can be accounted for in different ways. They provide little or no evidence for the existence of divinities. Even a visit from a seemingly powerful being, one who can perform extraordinary deeds beyond human efficacy, does not establish the qualities of the Western God. Is this powerful being a demon, a semi-god, or truly all-powerful, all-knowing, all-good?

Third, explanations other than the reality of gods can be offered for the prevalence of religious commitment. In the nineteenth century, the masters of suspicion undermined theism with relish. Karl Marx (1818–1883) called religion "opium for the masses," a way to divert the pain of proletariat life by focusing on a better world after death.[6] Part of the ideological superstructure that serves the interests of the dominant classes, religion distracts the disenfranchised from the misery of their social condition, forestalls revolutionary fervor, and reinforces prevailing economic systems. Marx, himself pursuing a quasi-religious grand redemption of the human race, argued that the functions religion serves will wither away once the communist paradise on earth is realized.

Sigmund Freud (1856–1939), although far from original on this issue, argued that we create gods, they do not create us.[7] We project our own deepest yearnings and fears on an indifferent universe, conjuring up various theisms to soften the human condition. Religion is thus an illusion that makes life palatable for many people.

Nietzsche viewed the creation of the major Western religions as the revenge of the herd.[8] The masses of human beings, resentful and fearful of those more noble and excellent, devise religion as a way of humbling their betters. Slogans such as "the meek will inherit the earth" and "the wealthy are as likely to pass through the gates of heaven as a camel is of passing through the eye of a needle" warm the cockles of the resentful masses and calm the haughtiness of the powerful. Religion, under this view, is a method born of ill motives to install and reinforce a particular system of values that glorifies equality, mediocrity, and social domesticity. Fueled by a lowest-common-denominator mentality, religion honors herd values to the detriment of potentially noble types. To ensure general compliance with these values, religion invents an all-powerful Supreme Being with strong retributive leanings: To fall out of line is to risk eternal suffering. Such an enforcer, who knows everything and can do anything, gives pause to even the most powerful on earth. Nietzsche concluded that the rise of science and the disaggregation of fervent religious conviction, the kind that truly animates everyday social life, showed that belief in God is no longer worthy. Human beings have created social conditions, including technological achievements, that undermine intense religious commitment. Priests, ministers, and rabbis now preside over the "death of God" as they orchestrate rituals that lack the power to energize daily life.

Fourth, the major religions invariably have tensions, ambiguities, and conflicts within their fundamental doctrines. The good news is that these frictions permit flexibility and adaptability to changing social circumstances. The bad news is that they diminish the clarity of the theistic message. Take the Christian notion of heaven. The state of eternal bliss is paramount in the theology because it is the final culmination of a meritorious life, the clear connection to Meaning, Truth, and Value, and the ultimate demonstration that the cosmos is rational and just. Heaven must conjure satisfactions that are understandable now. So the theology maintains that the bodies of those earning redemption shall be restored in a new, glorified form. Also, we retain our past histories, cleansed of imperfection and sinfulness. Thus we retain our affections for our backgrounds and contacts, and we have continuing knowledge and love of the created beings with whom we had relationships in our earthly lives. But heaven is nonmaterial and unchanging, so its crux is the intuitive apprehension of God as He is in Himself, and love. As a complete state, heaven permits our desirous spirits to attain eternal serenity.

From an earthly standpoint the notion of full actualization, having all one's potentials realized, is, happily, an impossibility. The process of life would end if human beings were somehow complete. If boredom is the shriek of unused capabilities can it also be the murmur of no more capabilities to use? Would heaven be boring after, say, the equivalent of five or six million years of apprehending the same?

None of this demonstrates logical error in the Christian notion of heaven. Surely it is reasonable to hold that there will be considerable mystery in describing and understanding a transcendent phenomenon in earthly terms. But the questions highlight the difficulty of even conceiving of what many take to be the highest human aspirations: the link with eternal Value, Meaning, and Rationality. Is the quest by its very nature outside the human condition?

Fifth, religious conviction may be taken as a matter of faith. But faith is not the absence of reason. Instead, faith is conviction and action not fully supportable by reason. Faith is not mysterious. Faith is required for life. Reason cannot establish itself. Even robust reliance on reason requires a certain faith. Faith, then, is not the opposite of reason, evidence, and probable belief. Religious faith is a type of, but does not define, faith. Religious faith is not created out of nothing. People who claim such faith can trace it back to a religious experience, acceptance of sacred texts, a particular socialization process, events in their lives from which it emerged, and the like. The basis of religious faith, then, is one or more of the sources already discussed. Religious faith, by definition, can neither be rationally proved nor disproved. But it does not follow that religious faith is immune from examination. The sources of faith are always subject to scrutiny. One cannot invoke religious faith as if it were a safe, unassailable oasis that ends discussion.

Nevertheless, Marx was incorrect in thinking that religious conviction would wither away once an ideal social scheme was realized. While religious conviction may well serve the functions Marx alleges, it also reflects a more enduring human concern: the search for meaning, understanding, and an antidote to finitude. Even in an ideal social scheme, human beings must struggle with their mortality and their need to connect with Tolstoy's trinity.

Tolstoy accepted a theistic assumption: Either God exists as the creator of meaning embedded in the universe or there is only chaos and meaninglessness. We may substitute Nature or the Absolute for God in some of the Eastern religions. This assumption holds sway over many people. Just as fear of an infinite regress compels many thinkers to embrace a first cause or unmoved mover, refusal to resign themselves to cosmic meaninglessness leads some thinkers, such as Tolstoy, to embrace theism.

Neither theists nor nonbelievers can rationally prove their claims or conclusively disprove the counterclaims of their opposites. Nonbelievers, though, will observe that technological and ideological developments in the twentieth and twenty-first centuries have radically intensified persistent human conflicts. Many find themselves alienated from the comforting, if often illusory, theistic certitudes of the past. Marx, Freud, and Nietzsche had earlier disaggregated the redeeming unassailability of religious meaning by pressing their suspicions that latent economic, psychological, and cultural motives underwrite, indeed create, religious conviction. Later, the rise of Fascism, Nazism, and Socialism amplified the risks inherent in state control of the individual and family. The explosive hegemony of instrumental reason and abstract systems of control facilitated a crisis of the spirit as anxiety transformed itself to addiction. Refined technology mocked itself by producing weapons that threaten a humanly inspired apocalypse. Lived experiences, especially of the body, are too often eclipsed by ersatz media-inspired substitutes: virtual realities, blatant commodifications, and images understood vicariously. The enormous increase in information finds no parallel in expanded wisdom. Too many of us seem unable to reconnect ourselves with or to re-create wholesome realities. The human search for meaning is caricatured by capitalist hucksterism, pop psychology, the sham transcendence of a drug culture, and craven flight from individual responsibility. Cynicism and thorough skepticism are falsely enshrined as insight. The citadel of the self is under siege.

Many people will forsake the religious solution for reasons good or bad. Some people will argue that if God exists then God would not insist on human beings following only one creed and set of rituals. Other people will not separate the historical record of Western religions from the belief in God. The institutions of organized religions will repel them. Utterly convinced of cosmic meaninglessness, the absence of any preordained or inherent purpose in the world, these critics of theism will still feel the urgency of Tolstoy's trinity. But new questions become compelling. Are the deepest human yearnings ignored by an indifferent cosmos? If the universe is inherently meaningless, can there be any meaning in life? Or can human beings forsake reliance on the gods and nature and create their own meaning?

## 4. COSMIC MEANINGLESSNESS

Shakespeare's *Macbeth*, Act 5, Scene 5, contains one of the clearest, most eloquent expressions of the sense of cosmic meaninglessness:

> Tomorrow, and tomorrow, and tomorrow
> Creeps in this petty pace from day to day
> To the last syllable of recorded time,
> And all our yesterdays have lighted fools
> The way to dusty death. Out, out, brief candle!
> Life's but a walking shadow, a poor player
> That struts and frets his hour upon the stage
> And then is heard no more. It is a tale
> Told by an idiot, full of sound and fury,
> Signifying nothing.[9]

One response to belief in cosmic meaninglessness and the rejection of religion is nihilism. First appearing in the mid-nineteenth century in Russia, "nihilism" bears numerous historical meanings.[10] Existential nihilism, vividly portrayed by Albert Camus (1913–1960), holds that no religious or philosophical system provides firm guidance for human life or assurances that values are adequately grounded. Human life is at its core meaningless because the cosmos is purposeless. Our recognition of this intensifies the absurd human condition: the confrontation between rational human beings and an indifferent universe. The world does not care about our hopes, fears, dreams, and experiences. While suicide is one possible response, it admits weakness and incapacity. A better response is human pride and rebellion, accompanied by human solidarity, which rejects despair in a self-conscious revolt against cosmic purposelessness. We should contemplate and defy our absurd situation in order to maximize life's intensity. Human beings give meaning to their existence not by eliminating the absurd, for that is impossible, but by refusing to yield meekly to its effects. Although the absurd prevents a fully satisfying existence, it does not prevent the creation of meaning through rebellious activity in the name of justice and human solidarity.

Passive nihilism, aspects of which appear in Schopenhauer, Buddhism, and Nietzsche's image of the last man, is a paralyzing, pessimistic inertia resulting from acknowledging inherent cosmic purposelessness. Passive nihilism is sometimes accompanied by the belief that life embodies no good, or that the path of least resistance and minimal effort is a prescribed response to the human condition: Avoiding suffering, striving for banal contentment and easy acceptance become paramount. Passive nihilism is more likely to produce a yearning to withdraw from the world, often in anticipation of a better afterlife.

Active nihilism, gleefully espoused by Nietzsche, accepts inherent cosmic purposelessness as the springboard to creative possibilities: reveling in radical contingency, embracing the human condition fully while recognizing its tragic dimensions, understanding the process of deconstruction, reimagination, and re-creation, and rejoicing in liberation from imposed values and meanings. Active nihilism places paramount value on this life.

The different moods nurtured by the forms of nihilism result from different reactions to the theistic assumption and to Tolstoy's trinity. The theistic assumption sets forth two alternatives: Either God exists as the creator of meaning embedded in the universe or there is only chaos and meaninglessness. Tolstoy's trinity is the yearning for a final culmination, a connection to enduring value, and a rational and just universe.

The most radical and unconvincing form of nihilism claims, paradoxically, to believe in nothing. It begins by warmly embracing the theistic assumption and deeply yearning for Tolstoy's trinity. After rejecting God's existence and the presence of embedded cosmic meaning, it concludes only chaos, emptiness, and triviality abound. A mood of despair follows as closely as darkness follows sunset. Existential and active nihilists reject the theistic assumption and have a more ambiguous relationship to Tolstoy's trinity. They may yearn for the trinity, but do not regard it as necessary for human meaning. A mood of liberation, a sense of anticipation, a return to earthly exhilarations may stoke the quest for humanly constructed meaning.

## 5. THE CONSTRUCTION OF CONTINGENT MEANING

Friedrich Nietzsche and Albert Camus offer the most compelling accounts of how human beings can construct meaning in their lives despite the background of inherent cosmic meaninglessness.

### A. Nietzsche

For Nietzsche, the meaning of life is not found in reason, but in the passions: in aspects of life that are of ultimate concern, our creations, devotion to worthwhile causes, and commitment to projects. Our instincts and drives create our meaning. Conscious thought can obscure our creativity.

The meaning of life, for Nietzsche, focuses on stylistic movement—graceful dancing, joyful creation, negotiating the processes of a world of flux with panache and vigor—instead of goal achievement. We cannot reach an ultimate goal. But we can develop through recurrent personal and institutional deconstruction, reimagination, and re-creation. Our exertion of our wills to power in the face of obstacles, with the knowledge of inherent cosmic meaninglessness, and with profound immersion in the immediacy of life, reflects and sustains our psychological health.

Personal and institutional overcomings will permit us to become who we are: radically conditional beings deeply implicated in a world of flux. By aspiring to live a life worthy of being repeated in all details infinitely, we joyously embrace life for what it is and regard it, and ourselves, as part of a grand aesthetic epic.

Whether self-mastery and self-perfection are the sole focus of the will to power, they are the prime concerns of Nietzsche's work. Neither state idolatry nor discredited supernatural images can provide human beings enduring consolations for their unresolvable existential crises. Instead, a new image of human beings is necessary.

Nietzsche promotes the individualism of the highest human types while understanding that values are initially established by people. Human beings create the value they embody by living experimentally and by nurturing an environment that propagates great people and high culture. Existence and the world are justified as an aesthetic phenomenon in that the highest artistic creations are great human beings themselves.

Nietzsche's new image of human beings is not projected for or achievable by all. His vision is an explicitly aristocratic ideal that is pitched only to the few capable of approximating it. Greatness and genius are fragile and vulnerable: They bring about their own destruction but arise stronger than ever.

The thrust of Nietzsche's thought is that we can formulate entirely new modes of evaluation that correspond to new, higher forms of life. The value of humanity is established by its highest exemplars and their creations. The higher human forms are extremely fragile and rare: Self-control, mastery of inclinations, resisting obstacles, experimentation, and forging a unified character require recurrent destruction and re-creation of self.

We can never transcend our conditionality and the lack of inherent meaning in the world of Becoming, but at least a few of us can loosen the limits of contingency, experience fully the multiplicity of our spirits, forge a coherent unity from our internal conflicts, and learn to overcome ourselves and our institutions: Theoretical insight can be turned to practical advantage.

Nietzsche's attitude of *amor fati* is not achieved through rational argument. Instead, it focuses on the rapture of being alive. *Amor fati* is an experience animated by faith, not cognitive discovery. *Amor fati* demands high energy and robust engagement. First, human beings have the freedom to order their interior life, their responses, to the thought of leading a life worthy of being repeated in every detail over and over again. Nietzsche's notion of eternal recurrence embodies this theme. While lower types adopt passive nihilism, higher types will embrace the entirety of life and view the lack of inherent cosmic meaning and infinite redemption as liberation from external authority. Even the Stoics recognized that nature could not control some things: our attitudes toward events in the world. Second, unlike the Stoics, Nietzsche glorifies the passions as robust manifestations of the will to power. To become who you are, to self-overcome, and to destroy, reimagine, and re-create require an active nihilism that elevates the present into a fated eternity. Third, higher types will recognize that passive nihilism or fatalism rests on the life-denying illusion that the "individual" is separate from the world. On the contrary, the thought of eternal recurrence underscores the individual's complete immersion in the world of Becoming: Cosmic fate is not external to us, it is us. Eternal recurrence is the test determining whether one truly loves life. Would you live the life you now lead, in all its details, over and over again? The test can make a difference in your life as you ask now and in the future: "Does this action merit infinite repetition? Am I becoming the kind of person whose life deserves to be lived repeatedly?" The thrust of the test is to affirm life in all its dimensions, to love that we are alive, to aspire to excellence. Instead of imputing a crude determinism to the acceptance of eternal recurrence, we can view acceptance as a free act: affirming the immediate moment, the present, willing its return and the return of every other "moment." By visualizing the present moment in terms of eternity, Nietzsche challenges us to embrace the ceaseless world of Becoming in which eternity does not freeze our choices but, instead, fulfills the present with endless possibility.

The core of truth in Nietzsche's eternal recurrence is that regrets about the past and postponements to the future deaden our spirit of adventure and renege on our commitment to continual self-creation. Thus, the eternal recurrence, in typical Nietzschean fashion, bears ambiguous tidings. For those of us clinging to the influences of religion and conventional morality, which have historically sought to marginalize the self, the thought of eternal recurrence will lead to despair and self-abandonment. For higher human types who can will the return of even the small, ugly, and petty, the thought of eternal recurrence facilitates self-mastery.

The texture and shadings of Nietzschean transcendence, eternality, and world creation are much different from religious versions. The focus is on this world, the premises are cosmic meaninglessness and a tragic view of life, the eternality is recurrent flux, and the transcendence is the process of destruction, reimagination, and re-creation. In sum, Nietzschean redemption is nothing more than a response to the lack of religious redemption, a message of affirmation to nudge away the nihilistic moment: Cosmic congratulations will not spring forth, but higher human types, who embody the proper attitudes, do not need any.

Nietzsche's grand individualism, however, is dangerous. Physicians understand that insecurity, a relentless striving for achievement, chronic impatience, intense competitiveness, and deep hostility increase bodily stress and that their presence is the best predictor of several diseases. These characteristics are much more likely to be embodied by people alienated from others than people intimately connected to others. The path to health, wisdom, and joy is reached by broadening one's boundaries and widening one's subjectivity.

Moral of the story: Our inner deconstructions, reimaginations, and re-creations must ultimately invigorate the quality of our participation in the external world. Otherwise, internal explorations are tepid exercises in abstraction and narcissism. Are Nietzschean relationships robust enough to ensure mental and physical health?

The slogan *"amor fati"* captures Nietzsche's highest value, a maximally positive attitude toward life. We should be drawn to life so powerfully that we celebrate life in all its dimensions, sufferings and joys alike. We should not seek to edit out tragedy or revise the past. For Nietzsche suffering does not have an antecedent negative value. The value of suffering or joy or any state in between is mostly up to us.[11] Influenced by aesthetic values, he advises us to evaluate our lives in their entireties. To edit out the pain from our life is to want to be a different person, which betrays a lack of love for our life and life generally. To desire to live our life as it has been, time and time again, is the psychological test. If we had full knowledge of our lives, only the robust will pass this test. The inner power that either attracts us or repels us from life is a person's measure. The greater the attractive power, the greater the person who embodies it. As his highest value, Nietzsche's *amor fati* is not derived from more basic reasons or rational argument. Those who are most strongly attracted to our world, the only world for Nietzsche, will find it most valuable.

If we embody Nietzsche's highest value then the question of life's meaning loses its force.[12] For Nietzsche, Tolstoy's problem was the loss of *amor fati*. Once lost, no rational argument or demonstration of objective meaningfulness suffices. The solution to the problem of the meaning of life is grounded in attitude not cognition.

Many of Nietzsche's specific pronouncements are unworthy of belief: the unabashed elitism that relegates the masses to serving the purposes of the highest human exemplars; the grand individualism that can turn too instinctively into narcissism; the warrior rhetoric that is too easily misunderstood as encouraging exploitation of "inferiors." Nor should his eternal recurrence doctrine be taken too seriously as a test of who qualifies as a higher human type. Last men might well affirm eternal recurrence if their effete lives mirrored their muted aspirations, while higher human types, if perfectionists, might well desire to edit out portions of their robustly meaningful, valuable lives.

The power of Nietzsche's thought lies not in his specific pronouncements, but in his broad themes: the inescapability of inner conflict; the perspectival nature of truth; the links between psychological types of human beings and their embrace of different truth-claims; the need to perceive reality from multiple perspectives; the connection between writing and life; the inability of language to capture life's complexity and fluidity; the human need to impose order and construct meaning on the world of Becoming; the salutary rhythms of deconstruction, reimagination, and re-creation; the need to recognize and welcome the tragedies and contingencies that constitute life; the call to luxuriate in the immediacy of life; and the deep gratitude embedded in his highest value, *amor fati*. Nietzsche, along with Camus, points us in the direction of constructing human meaning in a cosmos that is inherently meaningless.

## B. Camus

Camus resuscitates the ancient myth of Sisyphus. Condemned by the gods to push a huge rock to the top of a hill from which it fell down the other side, to be pushed again to the top from which it fell again, and so on forever, Sisyphus was doomed to futile, pointless, unrewarded labor.

Camus argues that human beings desperately crave inherent value, meaning, and rationality, but discover only a neutral, meaningless, indifferent cosmos. The enormous gap between human needs and an unresponsive universe is the crux of absurdity. Once we recognize the absence of a master plan and the absurdity of our existence, we underscore our own insignificance, our alienation, and our lack of ultimate hope. Our acts are ultimately futile. The absurd is not a philosophical concept, but a lived experience. Camus concludes that we cannot transcend or destroy the absurd, but we can forge and manifest our characters by our response to it.[13]

Three choices are available. We can seek the false consolations of religion. This strategy of denial permits us to pretend that human life is not absurd. Camus views this choice as inauthentic and weak: It seeks flight in fantasy as a distraction from robust confrontation with our fate. We can also commit suicide. But Camus views ultimate despair as cowardly: Peering into the profound void and feeling the hot breath of nothingness, we cravenly evade our fate by ending our lives.

Camus understands that most human beings continue to act on their preferences, values, and concerns despite a sense of cosmic meaninglessness, an awareness that no preordained or built-in meaning or value permeates our universe. Although Camus does not explicitly use this terminology, he implicitly understands the difference between viewing human lives from a cosmic perspective and viewing them from personal perspectives.

A *cosmic perspective* measures human life from the external vantage point of an indifferent observer, perhaps Nature itself. *Personal perspectives* evaluate human life from the internal vantage point of a person living his or her life. If nothing human matters from a cosmic perspective, we must still decide how to live and what to do.

Camus's preferred authentic response requires awareness of the absurd, living life in the face of our fate, affirming life through rebellion, maximizing life's intensity, and dying unreconciled. Sisyphus embodies the existential hero. He relentlessly confronts his fate, refuses to yield, denies psychological crutches, embraces no doomed hopes for release, and creates a fragile meaning through endless rebellion. Camus imagines Sisyphus "happy" as the "struggle itself toward the heights is enough to fill a man's heart."[14]

Camus's account oscillates between two descriptions of how human beings might create meaning in their lives. Both descriptions admit that adopting a cosmic perspective, looking at the whole of Sisyphus's task or the human task from the external vantage point of an indifferent world, provides only the bleak answer that life ultimately adds up to nothing. So we must develop personal perspectives that evaluate human life from the internal vantage point of people living it.

*Sisyphus as Cool Hand Luke.* Paul Newman played the lead role in the 1960s film, *Cool Hand Luke.* Luke is a victim of the brutality and sadistic discipline of his chain-gang wardens, but also of the indirect cruelty arising from the idolization of his fellow prisoners. He treats his jailors with defiance, endures their abuse, escapes only to be recaught, wins the admiration of his fellow prisoners, struggles mightily to maintain his pride and will, but is eventually hunted down and killed. This movie fits well much of Camus's description of one of Sisyphus's possibilities.

Camus advises Sisyphus to meet the gods of the myth with scorn and rebellion. He must condemn the gods for condemning him. Fueled by resentment and bravado, Sisyphus refuses to bend or to beg for relief. He cannot live within a cosmic perspective from which his life is insignificant, so Sisyphus revels in his hardness and endurance. He creates virtues out of contempt, pride, and strength. Like a stubborn army recruit sentenced to continually dig and fill the same hole in turn, Sisyphus's victory is in his refusal to seek the consolations of ordinary human beings. He will not admit defeat or yield. He will not ask his tormentors, whom he regards with disdain, for mercy: They can control his body but cannot influence his mind. Sisyphus lays a patina of defiance on extraordinary mental toughness. His attitude is a monument to the human spirit: authenticity leavened by indefatigability.

The image invokes mixed blessings. Some of us will admire Sisyphus's heroism and defiance as he distances himself from typical human reactions. He has proved himself superior to his peers and has denied the gods the added satisfaction of watching him writhe in misery. Other people will not embrace Sisyphus's self-styled martyrdom and victimization. Fueled by resentment, utterly detached from commitment beyond rebellion, intolerant of lesser responses, and keenly aware of his punishment, Sisyphus embodies a destructive romanticism.

Robert Solomon is deeply ambivalent about Camus's embrace of rebellion and scorn as an antidote to cosmic meaninglessness:

> There is something both beautiful and pathetic in [Camus's] quasi-rational, emphatically existential attitude. Shaking that puny fist at God or the gods is so poignantly human, so pointless, and at the same time meaningful. Of course, such behavior makes no conceivable difference to anything, except in our own attitudes . . . But what is beautiful and revealing about [Camus and other like-minded existentialists] is precisely their refusal either to dismiss [the philosophical question about the meaning of life] or to despair at the answer. They provoke an irresolvable tension . . . between our passionate commitments and our awareness that, nevertheless, our lives are ultimately not in our hands.[15]

Is Sisyphus a robust battler or is he a fugitive from life? Does the martyrdom of Sisyphus bear victory or does it confer additional power on the gods' decree? Sisyphus is, and his project does, all of these. Critics might insist that to assume this perspective is to reject life. But others will rejoin that we should never embrace the oppressor. And if cosmic meaninglessness reigns then life is an oppressor. All that remains is the refusal to yield.

*Sisyphus as Flowmeister*. Camus offers Sisyphus another possibility: to bask in the immediacy of his life, to engage in the process of living to the fullest extent, to immerse himself in the textures of experience. Sisyphus should avert his gaze from questions of what he is accomplishing by hurling himself into his task with gusto. He must pay close attention to the rock as it travels and to the textures of his journey. By luxuriating in the process of life and by living in the present, to the extent possible, Sisyphus makes the rock his own. He is so thoroughly involved in his task that the meaning of his life is single-minded engagement. From this perspective, Sisyphus is too busy and too fascinated with the wonders surrounding his journey to focus on contempt for the gods: "each atom of that stone, each mineral flake of that night filled mountain, in itself forms a world."[16]

Here Sisyphus brackets the cosmic perspective and forgets about his punishment. No longer fueled by resentment nor preoccupied with scorn of the gods, Sisyphus basks continually in the wonder of the moment. This image softens the condemnation of the gods by ignoring it. The gods' victory is diminished by its irrelevance to Sisyphus's life. Sisyphus appreciates his life and finds joy, even meaning. He rejects bitterness, refuses to view his world cynically, and chooses engagement.

The best experiences of flow, though, are episodic and unique. We cannot live our entire lives as flowmeisters even if we wanted to. The temporary loss of a sense of self, total immersion in the project at hand, and suspension of our awareness of time energize our spirits. At their best, flow experiences add complexity and nuance to our selves. The risk, however, is dehumanization through inadequate reflection. Bracketing the cosmic perspective, without a robust sense of past and future, and oblivious to other possibilities, Sisyphus as perpetually engaged flowmeister could become less human. Perhaps Sisyphus would be relatively happy, innocently contented, or simply too engaged to assess his condition. He, nevertheless, risks dehumanization as his givenness destroys his transcendence. Sisyphus works busily in his chains, but does not recognize how he remakes his context.

An important message lies at the heart of the image. Human beings too often project into the future while immersed in the everydayness and routines of life. We ignore the textures of the immediacy of life as we busily fulfill our daily schedules and fantasize about a better future. In the meantime much that is valuable in life seeps through our fingers. Sisyphus's obsession with the moment threatens his humanity, but maybe he has little choice given his fate. We have more freedom of focus. Even if total immersion in the flowmeister image is dehumanizing, a dose of it is healthy given the structure of our lives.

## 6. TELESCOPES AND SLINKY TOYS

Living robustly requires faith. Faith is not the opposite of reason, nor is it devoid of reason, nor is it distinctively religious. By "faith," I mean conviction and action not fully supportable by reason. Faith is necessary because human reason is limited. On fundamental questions of human existence reason is incapable of supplying a clear answer. Yet we must arrive at and act on positions on these questions. But faith is unsafe and uncertain. Faith is not won once and forever, but must be renewed. We can lose our faith.

Losing our faith in life involves seriously questioning life's meaning. When we question life's meaning seriously we are not entertaining an abstract, philosophical puzzle. Instead, we are psychologically and viscerally out of tune with life's rhythms. We feel that life lacks meaning. The causes of this feeling are varied. To name a few: loss of a loved one, failure of our major projects, onset of serious illness, clinical depression, disappointment that our successes leave us hollow, and philosophical paralysis.

Philosophical paralysis can result from preoccupation with the cosmic perspective. The process typically includes three stages. First, we reject religion and conclude that there is no meaning built into the cosmos ("cosmic meaninglessness"). Second, we undermine the importance of human life by viewing it from a wider context which contains and dwarfs human achievements. Typically, this involves ascending to the cosmic perspective and focusing on the impermanence, limitations, and ultimate insignificance of an individual life and human life taken as a whole. Third, we conclude that either human life is absurd or irredeemably futile. Once lost, there is no sure-fire way to regain faith. Psychologists struggle to reenergize clients suffering from the loss of a loved one, failure of major projects, onset of serious illness, clinical depression, and other disappointments. But philosophers must struggle with loss of faith caused by philosophical paralysis.

Psychological crisis occurs when we lose our ability to shift among perspectives, when the two major opposing vantage points press upon us with equal force, or when we are mired in the cosmic perspective. We are either paralyzed by an equilibrium of conflicting forces or we are radically disengaged from life. Our loss of will is fueled by a loss of faith. A sense of meaning is restored only if we again identify what we are doing with our own desires. False satisfactions may sustain a false sense of, but do not constitute, meaning. Meaning, then, cannot be purely a subjective matter: Believing that my life has meaning cannot guarantee that it does. Nor is meaning a purely objective matter. We are never in a neutral position to evaluate our perceptions and beliefs against the world as such. Our interpretations are within the realm of our experiences of the world, and we cannot transcend them to a point outside the world. We cannot appeal to an entirely atheoretical perception of pure, uninterpreted states of affairs. The realm of truth is within the realms of experience, reason, and emotion. Human beings do not have access to truth or knowledge outside those realms. Although no single, fixed position that could freeze truth-claims and sanctify interpretations once and forever is accessible to us, that does not imply that all interpretations or all perspectives are equally sound.

I may be connected to value, contribute to a wide network of relationships,

THE MEANING OF LIFE

and be deeply appreciated by my society, but if I lack the feelings, attitudes, intentions, and beliefs appropriate to my situation, my sense of meaninglessness will be acute. Tolstoy is a classic example. People may also accept that their lives are meaningful by the usual standards, yet feel that their lives are pointless. Such people have the correct set of beliefs about their situation but still lack the internal animation, the zest, necessary to experience their lives as meaningful. If a philosopher comes along and informs me that my life is objectively meaningful even though I sense it as subjectively meaningless, I am unlikely to jump for joy. I have lost my faith but kept my life.

Three strategies can soften the effects of philosophical paralysis and psychological crisis: (1) reinstating religious belief, (2) embracing pictorial symmetry, and (3) using the cosmic perspective for practical advantage.

1. *Reinstating religious belief.* If human beings could connect with an unlimited reality that is itself intrinsically meaningful, then our lives would be neither meaningless nor ungrounded. A sense of purpose would emerge from our freely chosen role in a grand epic or our eventual triumphant entrance into a grander, eternal world. Tolstoy regained his faith in life through this strategy.

2. *Pictorial symmetry.* Images emerging from the cosmic perspective necessarily shrink human achievements and life. As a view from afar, the cosmic vantage point renders its objects puny and insignificant. But pictorial accuracy requires symmetry, an adjustment for scale. A meaningful human life does not require what seems significant from the cosmic perspective, but requires only what is significant from a human perspective. Put differently: If human life seems puny from a cosmic perspective, then only puny meaning is required to close the gap of disproportionality between serious human effort and result.[17] Philosophical paralysis from preoccupation with the cosmic perspective results only from distortion: demanding massive, cosmically significant meaning to redeem human life.

3. *Using the cosmic perspective for practical advantage.* Instead of taking the cosmic perspective as another limitation on human experience, perhaps we can use it for practical advantage. By ascending in imagination to a larger context, we can usefully "put things in perspective." To lighten our suffering when we suffer grave loss, take ourselves and our projects too seriously, or feel overwhelmed, we can view our life from the cosmic perspective and shrink our problems. By moving artfully between the cosmic and human perspective and intermediary contexts,

perhaps we can maximize our triumphs and minimize our failures. Stepping back from what is happening and viewing as if from the outside, to be an observer of our own lives, to detach ourselves temporarily from events creatively uses the cosmic perspective.

The cosmic perspective, if used uncreatively, shrinks our lives, underscores the triviality of our projects, mocks our pretensions, and broadcasts our insignificance. Macbeth's soliloquy is the best literary summary of the horrors of immersion in the cosmic perspective. The personal perspective inflates our lives, amplifies the process and results of our projects, encourages our pretensions, and demands that we see ourselves as highly significant.

The vast discrepancy between the personal and cosmic perspectives can be bridged by intermediary perspectives. Global, national, communal, and familial perspectives, among others, are available. Part of the secret of life is to move artfully among these perspectives. Consider the expression "this too shall pass." Although having religious origins, the phrase is offered by even nontheists as a condolence.[18] The point of the offer is to ease suffering. As a positive reminder that the occasion for suffering is cosmically less important than it momentarily seems and that time moderates most pain, the phrase advises the sufferer to see the event from a broader perspective. Consider the expression, "Put it in perspective": The phrase is not offered because of its cognitive content that in a finite life all transitory things perish.

Imagine that your best friends have achieved an extraordinary goal which they have pursued with great effort for a long time. They have won the Nobel Prize, found true love, published their first book, accepted glorious jobs, or given birth to a greatly desired baby. Upon hearing this wonderful news, you tell them "this, too, shall pass." From a cognitive standpoint, the phrase is just as true now as in the case of the sufferer. But, unless we are classical Stoics, it is hideously inappropriate. Your friends would wonder about your motives. Are you trying to destroy their joy? Are you expressing your resentment, envy, or jealousy? Are you really their friend?

While the cognitive value of the expression is stable, its practical and moral values vary. Uttered as condolence, the phrase is often an appropriate attempt to lessen pain by broadening perspective. Uttered after great achievement, the phrase is an inappropriate attempt to trample joy by broadening perspective. By selecting perspectives for appropriate purposes we can soften the pinch of the absurd. I am not counseling a simpleminded use of perspectives: Utter "this, too, shall pass" at every tragedy, while giddily relishing and inflating every personal triumph. Tragedies should be met by an appropriate measure of grief and sorrow, but no more. Triumphs should be appreciated by an appropriate amount of joy and self-celebration, but no more. What is the appropriate measure? Finding the correct amount, like applying Aristotle's doctrine of the mean, is the province of people of practical wisdom. Individual differences in temperament and circumstance preclude a single, simple answer for everyone.

Once we are aware of the gap between cosmic and personal perspectives, it is unclear whether our situation is truly absurd. Living our lives in full light of the various perspectives from which they can be viewed need not produce any ridiculous incongruity, extreme irrationality, striking disharmony, or unrealistic pretension. Perhaps our situation is not absurd once we are able to adjust perspectives appropriately.

The idea that human life is absurd depends on our own pretensions. If we pretend that the cosmic perspective is illusory then our actions within the personal perspective may seem absurd because they take themselves to be more than they are. But this pretension is not inevitable. Once we reflect on the two perspectives and recognize their presence we can still act vigorously. We can act vitally within the personal perspective while later retreating to the cosmic vantage point to place our actions "in perspective." Doing so is neither absurd nor pretentious; it is living life fully, with faith and humility, combining engagement with reflection. Absurdity in the popular sense connotes incongruity, ridiculousness, or extreme silliness.

If we are deeply absorbed in a project, the cosmic perspective fades away, at least for the period of engagement. We do not simultaneously invest great energy, concern, and passion into a project and judge it ultimately pointless. We need not and typically do not claim our creations embody ultimate value even after the investment we have expended in the process of creation. No inflated claim exists for the cosmic perspective to return and debunk. Thus no necessary absurdity plagues human life. We can ignore the problem, unless we are already aware of it, or we can reconceive the problem creatively for practical advantage. What is for Camus and other theorists of absurdity a problem can be seen as another avenue for human possibility. By creatively transforming the problem into an opportunity, we exemplify the meaning in life the problem supposedly calls into question.

When considering life as a whole we should be wary of the images emerging from the cosmic perspective. Viewing human activity from the vast expanse of a cosmic perspective ungenerously shrinks our achievements. Just as viewing a building from afar with a telescope or taking a photo from a wide-angle lens renders the structure small and insignificant, so too placing human activity in a cosmic framework lures us into comparisons with Sisyphus. But fairness, perhaps pictorial accuracy, requires symmetry. We should not demand cosmic significance to redeem human lives that are being viewed from an otherworldly cosmic perspective. We would not measure the size of a building from a photo without adjusting for scale. Likewise, when minimizing human activity from a cosmic perspective we should recognize that a meaningful human life does not require what seems significant from that perspective. A meaningful human life requires what is significant from a human perspective. To think otherwise is like seeing a photo of a building and concluding the structure measures three inches by five inches.

Questions about the significance of death, the meaning or meaninglessness of life, and the importance or unimportance of our lives must be filtered through perspectives. But which is the better, even the supreme, perspective? To answer this question is to answer the other, more pressing questions of life and death.

My answer will disappoint those with a low tolerance for ambiguity, those overwhelmed by the imperatives of binary logic, and those appalled by conflict. My answer is that both the cosmic and personal perspectives, and those in between, are genuine. Neither can claim independent superiority over the other. Our choice of perspective, then, becomes crucial for our understanding and enjoyment of life. Life is like a telescope in that we can increase or decrease the magnification, adjust the focus, and view our lives from numerous vantage points. The most artistic and graceful among us travel lightly among the available perspectives, never seeing one as providing the only authentic answers to life's questions. Those of us who live the most meaningful, significant, valuable, and happy lives choose the perspective most appropriate for such lives more consistently than those who lead lives that seem less meaningful, significant, valuable, and happy. The presence of multiple perspectives at first blush increases the conflict, turmoil, and struggle within us. But it also offers opportunities for enriching our lives. Creatively using the cosmic, personal, and intermediary perspectives follows ancient wisdom: Nurture the most beneficial attitude given a situation.

Although harmony among perspectives is unavailable, thus rendering our lives both more tragic and comedic, the only alternatives are stunningly unappealing: full immersion in the personal perspective at the cost of reflection, or full immersion in the cosmic perspective at the cost of vibrancy. The lack of reflection transforms human life toward the bestial, while the lack of vibrancy paralyzes action and breeds clinical depression. Sartre offers better advice: We are condemned to our freedom.

The meaning of life is embedded in life itself, in our instincts and drives. Through our emotional life we experience the meaning in life. Through our reason we connect our lives to wider values that produce meaning. Creativity is not merely producing something somewhat original. Creativity is a self-examination and self-exploration that affects the creator. Creative activity involves self-transformation. But shifting perspectives is not an easy cure for our insecurities. We will still feel the hot breath of nothingness on our necks, and experience bafflement before darkness, anxiety when confronting the limits of rationality, surprise before the serendipity of the universe. Awe and wonder will never evaporate. But neither will dread and trembling.

Our lives are also like slinky toys. We bound from goal to goal as each satisfaction impels us to new imaginings and pursuits. Although we take time to savor our accomplishments, we are excited by the process and continue the quest. Nietzsche's deconstruction/reimagination/re-creation is the vivid exemplar of this propulsion. Although it can be reasonably criticized as not including sufficient respite and enough time to savor, Nietzsche's process nevertheless highlights the deficiencies of viewing life as a simple journey to a particular, fixed goal.

Creatively using perspectives is not a flight from life, but a method of squeezing the most out of it. The cosmic perspective is not a safe oasis outside of life, but a vantage point reflective human beings invariably greet. We are not editing out the hard parts of life, but interpreting them such that we retain our faith and rekindle our spirits.

## 7. MEANING AND SIGNIFICANCE

Would the cosmos be meaningful if it included no life? Imagine the stuff of the universe —planets, stars, sun, moon, and the like—continuing its regularity and pattern of motion. No consciousness, no projects, no interests, no nonmechanical relationships. Even if a Supreme Being created this lifeless universe for the Being's own amusement or as a show of creative power, it would not follow that the cosmos contained meaning, although it might provide meaning for its creator. A lifeless cosmos matters only if it matters to somebody. Now imagine that the cosmos includes animal, but not human life. Animals of severely limited consciousness might still be imagined as no more than living robots, programmed to act in ways by nature or their creator. Only animals of more robust consciousness, those to whom a degree of freedom and creativity might be imputed, can plausibly bring meaning to the cosmos. Higher life forms matter if they matter to themselves or to each other. If correct, this shows that meaning is tied to consciousness, freedom, and creativity. Even the higher animals may have only a portion of meaning: They act, but do they understand? Are they guided by their own convictions? The meaning of life, then, is not merely out there to be discovered. We must contribute to the cause. Our faith, our attitude, our ability to picture the world in a way compatible with the discovery and construction of meaning are paramount. The world insinuates itself upon us but cannot determine the purpose or meaning of our lives. Human choice and commitment illuminate, but do not create *ex nihilo*, the value of objects.

Will just any set of concerns and beliefs be enough for a meaningful life? It depends on how we understand "meaningful." If a life that has enough projects, interests, purposes, and commitments to energize its bearer's zest for and faith in life is meaningful, then almost any set of freely chosen, real concerns will do. Believing my life is meaningful is not enough. The activities that allegedly bring meaning must be appropriate to the experience, they must be real (not simulated through a virtual reality machine), not induced through external agency (imagine Sisyphus hypnotized by the gods into enjoying stone-pushing), or hallucinations (a person plagued by delusions that he is Napoleon). But the bar of a meaningful life is quite low. Once we factor out the impediments above, a life consisting largely of television-viewing or collecting pushpins may well be meaningful enough and fulfilling enough to be worth living. Better to continue watching *The Jerry Springer Show* and satisfy entertainment desires than to be dead. No one's life is only television viewing or collecting pushpins. Even minimally meaningful lives include relationships and connections to other projects.

As I have said, some lives are more meaningful than other lives. *Robustly meaningful lives*, the ones to which we aspire, embody interests, projects, purposes, and commitments that produce significance. A robustly meaningful life is significant, sometimes important, occasionally exemplary. We, typically, strive for our vision of a good life. Robustly meaningful lives, then, embody a much higher degree of meaning, zest, faith, and a richer network of interests and purposes than do minimally meaningful lives.

If a person is firmly convinced, as I am, that most lives are worth living, then to exclude minimally meaningful lives, in an act of Nietzschean imperialism, is to support a radical elitism. When we now talk of lives perhaps not worth living, those that are candidates for, say, justified voluntary euthanasia, we offer the permanently comatose, the terminally ill who are undergoing severe indignities, and those who are merely biologically alive but incapable of agency. The assumption is that these groups may no longer be able to form the interests, forge the commitments, and undertake the projects that brighten life. At least from a nonreligious perspective, such lives are no longer meaningful.

No objective criteria must be met for human beings to deserve to continue living other than, at most, that they are able to live more than a biological existence. We, therefore, recognize that lives are worth continuing and presumed to be minimally meaningful where great achievement is lacking. Meaningful lives, then, need not be significant, important, or valuable lives.

Some lives are robustly meaningful and valuable despite unattractive aspects. Pablo Picasso was a creative genius whose artistic significance and importance is incontestable. He was also a sexual predator, a pathetic father, and often unscrupulous. Still, his moral failings are far from those of a Hitler. We may argue that these shortcomings were offset by Picasso's promotion of aesthetic value and positive creative effect on thousands of people. His life may be viewed as *valuable*, in that his life considered as a whole was connected to cognitive and aesthetic value not offset by his moral failings; *significant*, in that his work influenced the lives of numerous other people in uncommon ways; and *important*, in that his life was significant enough to make a relatively enduring difference in the world.

I am not assuming that all values are commensurable, that if you create a great art piece you are allowed greater freedom to morally transgress. Our ranking of respective values is crucial. Nietzsche placed aesthetic and cognitive values above moral values. He was gravely suspicious of the origins and effects of the dominant morality of his time. Most people would probably place moral values well above other forms of values. We cannot add the effects of a life on each kind of value, arrive at an overall assessment, then conclude that life was or was not valuable as such. With Hitler and Picasso we can make rough assessments because Hitler is the paradigm of moral disvalue, while Picasso's moral shortcomings are not extraordinary.

Perhaps a life can be meaningless in itself, but still important and significant. Suppose a baby is afflicted with such grave disabilities that the baby has no more than a biological life. Someone who shortly after birth enters a permanently comatose state might be an example. If, because of exceptional circumstances, this infant has a great influence on numerous people, spurring them to noble, valuable acts, we could argue that the life was important, significant, and valuable, even though meaningless.

We might better say that the infant's life was not important, significant, and valuable, because the infant had no life beyond biological existence. The infant's agency, exercised in acts, choices, personality, and freedom, did not produce the positive response of others. To view such a life as important is inappropriate, even though the infant's existence generated a strong, positive response from other people. Yet, we could conjure less drastic cases in which a child did have limited agency which inspired others, where we would say that the life was important, significant, and valuable, although minimally meaningful at best.

If our actions fit into a reasonably coherent scheme, are not futile in that we can in principle achieve our goals or at least make valuable progress toward them, and have purposes within our life scheme, we have no good reason to think our lives are meaningless or that they are absurd. Even if life as a whole lacks inherent meaning, particular lives can range from minimally to robustly meaningful. Some lives, however, fail even to fulfill the criteria of minimal meaningfulness. Such lives are not worth living.

Still, a critic could argue that I have not explained why we should accept my account of meaning, according to which most human lives are meaningful, instead of an account that concludes most human lives are meaningless: "A few human lives are meaningful—those lives that are significant, important, and valuable—but most human lives are meaningless because they fall far short of that standard. So, yes, I will agree with you that Michelangelo, da Vinci, and their like forged meaningful lives, but disagree with you when you claim that most human lives are at least minimally meaningful."

Most accounts that conclude that all human lives are meaningless set the bar too high. The critic is claiming that to be meaningful a human life must be, in my terms, robustly meaningful, significant, important, and valuable. The critic charges that I set the bar for a meaningful human life too low.

My glib response is that agreeing with the critic is something like claiming that the only good baseball players were Joe DiMaggio, Babe Ruth, Hank Aaron, Willie Mays, Ted Williams, and their ilk: superstars or bust. Nietzsche might well have accepted this position, although even he would concede that the rest of us common folks could find value and meaning by serving the highest exemplars among us.

I am not claiming that my analysis captures the only way language must be used. By why demand so high a standard for meaningfulness when that is not required? Why assume that meaningful lives are a zero-sum game such that only a few human beings can attain the prize and most must fall short? The assumption that a meaningful life must be significant, important, and valuable consigns almost all of our lives to the dustbin of meaninglessness. Doing so, though, does not reflect common experience, is not required by logic, and does not correspond to social practices. If almost all human lives are antecedently doomed to meaninglessness, then the proper existential response to the gift of life is not gratitude but resentment.

In short, I cannot prove that the critic is misusing language, but I can advance good reasons why we should not purchase what the critic is hawking. The critic's position is a good example of using the cosmic perspective inartfully—in service of denigrating almost all human lives. If human beings construct meaning in their lives from the interests, projects, and purposes that flow from their agency, then describing a minimally meaningful life as I have is appropriate and salutary.

The best way to understand meaning in life is relationally. We gain meaning by connecting to and standing in a relationship with value, significance, and importance. As long as we are limited beings, we can always imagine beings or things of lesser limitations and bemoan our relative insignificance. We cannot guarantee wise and creative use of the cosmic perspective. The cosmic perspective is always available to bring us down, if we so choose. But why should we so choose?

Much of the meaning of life is in the process: imagining and dreaming, planning and organizing, integrating and striving. Time spent on matters of more enduring importance such as great music, classical drama, philosophical reflection, and intense personal relationships is often of greater importance than time spent on more mundane matters such as watching television programs with limited shelf life or engaging in meaningless small talk to pass time. This judgment stems from the transcendent nature of the more important matters, how they point to values and meaning beyond themselves. Loving and being loved, pursuit of truth, integrity, courage, the overcoming of obstacles, conscious self-creation, integration with a social network, all define the life of excellence more closely than material accumulation, social approval, and the quest for fame as self-validation. I am embarrassed to write this, though I do not embarrass easily. Cynics will judge this paragraph platitudinous and wince at my firm grasp of the obvious.

Meaningful lives require faith and love. We must adopt some form of Nietzsche's *amor fati*. We must love life and the world. We must give the world our fullest response. We must expand our subjectivity through connections and relationships. We will experience our lives as meaningful only if we present the requisite attitude to the world. To do all, or any, of this we must have faith. Reason cannot support our convictions and actions all the way down.

What comes first, faith in life or a sense of meaningfulness? Do we have faith in life because we already have a sense that our life is meaningful? Or is it the opposite? What happens if people meet all the criteria of a minimally meaningful life, except they feel their lives are meaningless? Are their lives meaningless and not worthwhile? Would they be better off dead? Can the cosmic and personal perspectives be manipulated as easily as I suggest?

I do not think faith in life and a sense of meaningfulness are related as cause and effect. Nor are they linked in an invariable temporal sequence. They are usually intertwined such that they are conceptually distinguishable but experientially joined. If people meet the criteria for a minimally meaningful life, yet they feel their lives are meaningless, we do not shoot them. We could have them view a season's worth of episodes of *The Anna Nicole Smith Show*. By comparison, their lives might look much better. Sarcasm aside, we have psychological counseling, philosophical therapy, and medical treatment available to reenergize our sense of meaning. Temporary bouts of an acute sense of meaninglessness are common. They often plague especially sensitive, reflective people. Using the cosmic and personal perspectives creatively can become a healthy habit that does not require self-conscious choice each time. Perhaps successful self-help books are exercises in adopting the appropriate attitude for different situations. Aristotle's advice to develop good habits is useful here.

Asking the question, "What might I regret on my deathbed?" helps us to establish priorities. I am unlikely to regret not having served an additional term on the Planning and Budget Committee. I cannot imagine my final gasp being, "If only I had bought a Bentley," or "My life would have been complete if I had met Donald Trump." I can imagine regretting not having written this book. By projecting to our grand finale we help learn what should be important to us now.

The search for meaning, emboldened by values that point to but never reach the eternal, is too often obscured by our lives of habit and diversion. We must learn to appreciate life as an endlessly dynamic process of change, not a fixed state. We must understand that a robustly meaningful, valuable life, married to a joyous or peaceful psychological condition that is earned, defines high aspirations. And then we must live.

## 8. DEATH

For those who reject the dualism of mind and body, and deny immortality, death terrorizes us because we fear nothingness, extinction, and deprivation, not because we anticipate a painful afterlife. Those things of value in life—

interpersonal relationships, projects, goals, aspirations, interests, and associations—end at death. And that is why death often seems so bad. Mere biological survival is not important to us. We do not hope for a permanent coma even if we are thereby kept biologically alive. A life completely lacking value and meaning would be a life not worth living, at least to the person in this condition. Death ensures, stipulating the rejection of dualism and the immortality thesis, that we are permanently deprived of the value, meaning, and good connected to our lives. While many of us also dread the process of dying and theists may fear eternal damnation, deprivation is the main reason we fear death and regard it as an evil.

Some deaths are more evil than others, even though the democracy of death commands we all die once. The evilness of a death is directly proportional to the actual and potential value of the life that has been terminated. Death is not always an evil because it is not always true that a meaningful and valuable life has ended. A meaningless and valueless life is one in which the kinds of activities and aspirations previously mentioned cannot be engaged in, nor is there a potentiality for future participation. If life itself, or a particular life, is not a good then its termination is not an evil. When our dearest projects are complete, our creative energies exhausted, and our higher human capabilities evaporating, death can be timely.

Although death is inevitable, this does not make the deprivation of life any less evil. Inevitability means the fact that we shall die is out of our control, but to acknowledge this need not make an occurrence any less evil. Suppose on every first Thursday all human beings would inevitably undergo severe stomach cramps, bleed profusely from the nose, and be afflicted with double vision: Would the inevitability of these ills make them less evil or painful or bad? The inevitability of death may mean that worrying about whether we will die is pointless, but that is about all it means.

Awareness of death is certainly relevant to a meaningful human life. Although I disagree with those who insist that immortality would necessarily bring boredom or disassociation from past identity,[19] I agree that mortality provides a clear context and coherency to our lives.

Heidegger argued that keen awareness of the ontological anxiety we confront in our death shakes us out of the everydayness of habit and diversion that dulls our sensibilities.[20] Our desperation can no longer be silenced. Received opinion, inherited social structures, and preexisting political institutions turn us toward stultifying conformity. But getting in touch with the anxiety spurred by impending nothingness turns us back toward authentic living. Learning to confront our death teaches us how to live as authentic individuals. The unspoken dictatorship of social conformity, the leveling tendencies of group-think, and the push and pull toward mediocrity require a strong antidote. The cost of being tranquilized is inauthenticity.

Heidegger tends to overdramatize the ontological anxiety of death and over-rates its unique role in an authentic life. But his main insights can be refashioned: Sharpening our awareness of death can be one path toward more robust and authentic living; confronting death is connected to learning how to live; and tranquilized immersion in the everydayness of habit and diversion dulls our spirits and dishonors the narrative of our life. A healthy attitude toward death includes fully recognizing its inevitability, refusing to live less energetically, constructing our projects in ways compatible with viewing ourselves as part of a long generational chain, pursuing ideals that affirm life's possibilities, maintaining a zest for the adventures, triumphs, and failures that constitute life, and appreciating the chance to be part of human history.

That slogan, "On their deathbeds people don't regret not having spent more time at the office," is useful because it gives us a sense of priorities. But the reason we, on our deathbeds, might regret failed relationships is that at that point we sense most sharply our isolation. We are about to die, we are scared, we are leaving the world, the others we know are staying, and some of us are terrorized by eternal damnation. We need comfort. Extra time at the office, watching another episode of *Murder, She Wrote* or *Walker, Texas Ranger*, completing the cement work on our front porch steps, going to the racetrack one more time: None of these actions provide that comfort. Nor does finishing another desperate book on human happiness. Comfort can be supplied only by those who share our fate or by a benevolent Supreme Being willing to forgive and forget. Or we suppose they are our final best hope. Who but an unrepentant philosopher such as Socrates could sit about calmly speculating about the immortality of the soul while awaiting the hemlock that would consume his life?

The way one dies, though, can make a difference, at times even be meaningful. The living appreciate it when a dying person is noble, humorous, and strong, instead of cowardly, bitter, and weak. But the living appreciate it because it diminishes their own fears of death and makes it easier to deal with the dying person: Just as during life, our companions can substitute bluster, easy smiles, lame bravado, and retread humor for the serious, intimate conversations about the meaning of life that make us so uncomfortable.

Suppose science developed to the point where it could accurately predict, barring fatal accidents, the date of our deaths. Would you want notice of the date of your death? Having that information would make it impossible to forget death on an everyday basis. The information would paralyze action. Imagine someone with a short-timer's calendar, crossing out each day, knowing the date of his or her death, as time creeps on its petty pace. Forgetting and bracketing may not be as inauthentic as Heidegger claims.

Most of us are not so obsessed with death that we have only the obituary pages to highlight our days. We are not merely in chains awaiting our turn. We have opportunities to pursue meaning and value. We are not consumed with our demise every waking moment. We attend to projects, interests, and relationships that animate our spirits and brighten our days. We do, however, watch the physical deterioration and deaths of loved ones, endure suffering, and inch closer to the turnstiles of doom with each passing hour.

Once more, we face the personal and cosmic perspectives. From a personal perspective, my death is the end, as long as we do not adopt theism, of the world. My consciousness is obliterated, the planets and heavenly bodies evaporate. From a cosmic perspective, my death is part of the process of change, allowing another person the time and space to enjoy or to suffer. My death itself is insignificant. An intermediary perspective would deny both extremes. My biological death need not toll the end of my biographical life, nor the end of those projects, meanings, and values upon which my life centered. While permanence is denied me, lingering influence is not.

Our attitude toward death deeply influences our possibilities for maximally affirming life. The end of our existence is less significant than the effects our knowledge of mortality has on the way we live. A life does amount to what a person does, but that need not fuel an inveterate striver's winner-takes-all mentality. Against Nietzsche, the possibility of a robustly meaningful life is not restricted only to the greatest among us.

A healthy, adequate awareness of death can energize meaningful activities. Human beings often take a romantic-heroic path in trying to transcend death by participating in projects that endure beyond their deaths. We achieve a fragile immortality by raising children, sharing grand political and social causes, creating new technological and communication networks, making artistic contributions, and the like. My writing this book, a text that will outlive its author, is an effort in that direction. We connect to value by extending beyond ourselves through relationships, projects, and creative endeavors upon which we stamp our identities. We can achieve a heroism that resists mortality by courageously struggling against a hard lot. An entire line of thinkers such as William James, Emerson, and Nietzsche sees the heroic quest as an attempt to transcend death by participating in projects of lasting worth.

Die at the right time . . . the death that consummates—a spur and a promise to the survivors. He that consummates his life dies his death victoriously, surrounded by those who hope and promise. . . . To die thus is best; second to this, however, is to die fighting and to squander a great soul . . . the free death which comes to me because I want it. . . . He who has a goal and an heir will want death at the right time for his goal and heir.[21]

We know, however, that we cannot transcend death, our projects do not last forever, the stamp of our identities smudges with time, and that for all but a few our footprints are trampled upon, then obliterated. But the experiences, the stream of processes, the struggles, defeats, and triumphs elevate our lives with meaning. The heroic quest may be a response to the terror of human vulnerability, limitation, and inevitable death. Perhaps an unearned narcissism fuels the journey. Perhaps human life is impossible to live robustly without illusions. Are you listening, philosophers? Do you nurture your own unacknowledged illusions? Perhaps religious commitment, instead of being the vehicle by which dominant classes solidify power, or by which the herd minimizes the glory of potential nobles, or by which human beings project their need for a Great Father, is an especially seductive narrative of the heroic quest for personal immortality.

We must choose and act in a partly self-forgetful way. A personal perspective allows us to luxuriate in the heroic quest by temporarily marginalizing explicit awareness of death. Yes, this can become inauthentic: We cannot live entirely in personal perspectives without yielding our reflective powers that elevate us from a purely animalistic life. But neither can we live entirely in a cosmic perspective that calls into question the justification of each conscious moment. The struggle to triumph over life's limitations, the hunt for ersatz immortality, the yearning for connection with value and meaning, render us noble in the face of our terror. Confronting the Grim Reaper at the moment of ultimate Truth can itself crown the meaningfulness of our lives, or not.

This is, perhaps, what Nietzsche meant in celebrating *amor fati* and disparaging the last man. Embracing life fully means accepting its tragic dimensions, including human limitation, individual estrangement, and inevitable death. A full acceptance of life and the surrounding world includes, for Nietzsche, the realization that prior to death our life has been fulfilling and is in need of no further acts to complete it. As the final curtain falls over our life, we savor the whole and wish only that it could be relived over and over, infinitely. Granted, this is a Nietzschean ideal, as death arrives on its own schedule and too often interrupts our best-hatched plans, but Nietzsche imagines a praiseworthy attitude toward death which sees mortality as neither necessary for a meaningful life nor necessarily depriving life of meaning. Mortality is our unchosen context, malleable within limits by our attitude.

Living with adequate recognition of mortality, yet responding zestfully, can vivify meaning in our lives and elevate death beyond meaningless termination. Mortality is our context, not necessarily our defeat. We need not glorify death, we need not pretend we do not fear death, but we should temper the Grim Reaper's victory by living and dying meaningfully.

The idea of biographical life revolves around human life as a narrative, a story. We are a series of stories in that we understand and identify ourselves through a chain of events, choices, actions, thoughts, and relationships. Our biographical lives, including value and meaning connected to our death and events thereafter, extend beyond our biological lives. The legacy of figures such as Jesus, Lincoln, Michelangelo, Mother Teresa, Jackie Robinson, and their like, bears meaning and value that transcend their deaths. And in some cases, such as Jesus, the way one dies brightens the legacy. The narrative of human lives often continues beyond our deaths. Many human beings recognize this by consciously nurturing legacies, images, creative works, children, and projects that flourish beyond their deaths. We are aware, however, that our projects cannot endure forever and we pursue them in that light. Death, then, does not supervene on life; it provides a context for life.

Admittedly, for most of us, our biographical story does not continue long after our deaths. Our fantasies to the contrary notwithstanding, we are not indispensable. At most, our departure would bring deep sorrow to those closest to us. Once those few who actually knew us and were influenced by us themselves die, most of us remain, at most, represented only by uncaptioned photos in web-covered albums stored in the corners of neglected attics. Most of our deaths will not be accompanied by massive displays of anxiety and gnashing of teeth. Beyond family, friends, and close associates, others will take note of our demise, perhaps attend a service, moan, "Too bad about Old Spike," or whisper, "No great loss," and get on with the mundane rhythms of life. Still, the question of what my future death means to me now is crucial. As Nietzsche insisted, the brio with which I live each moment of my life, the spirit of *amor fati*, is paramount. The meaning of my death hinges on the quality of my life. But we cannot maintain a lifelong giddiness. As we project toward the future we can, however, become more aware of the processes, not merely the outcomes, that constitute our lives. To make our activities more fulfilling, to focus our creative interest in the act of creation instead of only on the result, speeds us toward the Nietzschean ideal.

Leaving a rich legacy is not a way of achieving immortality, even though the advice "plant a tree, beget children, build a house, write a book" is sometimes taken in that vein. We are finished at death if no afterlife awaits us. But generating a legacy is a way of enriching the meaning of our lives now. Some of our projects should reach beyond our lifetimes. Guiding the next generation, creating something that has a life and identity outside of ourselves, transmitting a culture and heritage, attending to enduring yet finite projects, and influencing the future are not ways of halting the Grim Reaper, but they are paths to meaning. Although our biological lives expire, our biographical lives continue through such legacies. Again, this is not immortality, but it does mark a life well lived. Generating rich legacies energizes faith in life, binds us to something beyond ourselves, and nurtures meaning above narrow self-fulfillment.

Approaching our life and death in such a way may even ground the accurate, positive, self-appraisal of our lives that exudes worthwhile happiness. Should this not be enough to stoke the fires of our hearts and rekindle the sparks of our souls?

## NOTES

1. See, e.g., Robert Nozick, *Philosophical Explorations* (Cambridge, Mass: Harvard University Press, 1981), 571–572.

2. Leo Tolstoy, *My Confession*, trans. by Leo Wiener (London: J. M. Dent and Sons, 1905), 19–20.

3. John M. Koller, *Oriental Philosophies* (New York: Scribner and Sons, 1985).

4. See, e.g., *Catechism of the Catholic Church* (Mahwah, N.J.: Paulist Press, 1994).

5. Kurt Baier, "Threats of Futility," *Free Inquiry* 8:3 (Summer 1988): 47–53; Irving Singer, *Meaning in Life* (New York: The Free Press, 1992), ch. 1 and 3.

6. Karl Marx, *Karl Marx: Selected Writings*, ed. David McLellan (Oxford: Oxford University Press, 1977).

7. Sigmund Freud, *The Future of an Illusion*, trans. James Strachey (New York: W. W. Norton & Co., 1961).

8. Friedrich Nietzsche, *Beyond Good and Evil*, trans. Walter Kaufmann (New York: Vintage Books, 1966); and *On the Genealogy of Morals*, trans. Walter Kaufmann and R. J. Hollingdale (New York: Vintage Books, 1967).

9. William Shakespeare, *Macbeth*, Act 5, Scene 5, in *Complete Works of Shakespeare*, ed. Stanley Wells and Gary Taylor (Oxford: Oxford University Press 1988), 997–998.

THE MEANING OF LIFE

10. See, e.g., Albert Camus, *The Rebel* (New York: Vintage Books, 1956); Keith Ansell-Pearson, *An Introduction to Nietzsche as Political Thinker* (Cambridge, England: Cambridge University Press, 1994), 39, 200–201.

11. Nietzsche, "On the Thousand and One Goals," in *Thus Spoke Zarathustra*, in *The Portable Nietzsche*, trans. Walter Kaufmann (New York: Viking Press, 1954).

12. Nietzsche, "The Problem of Socrates," sec. 2 in *Twilight of the Idols*, in *The Portable Nietzsche*.

13. Albert Camus, *The Myth of Sisyphus*, trans. Justin O'Brien (New York: Vintage Books, 1991); and *The Rebel* (New York: Vintage Books, 1956).

14. Camus, *The Myth of Sisyphus*, 123.

15. Robert C. Solomon, *The Joy of Philosophy* (New York: Oxford University Press, 1999), 117.

16. Camus, *The Myth of Sisyphus*, 123.

17. See, e.g., Thomas Nagel, "The Absurd," *The Journal of Philosophy*, 21 October 1971: 716–727.

18. See, e.g., Matthew 5:18; Matthew 24:34–35; Mark 13:30–31; Luke 16:17; Luke 21:32–33; I Corinthians 13:10; Hebrews 12:27.

19. Raymond Angelo Belliotti, *What is the Meaning of Human Life?* (Amsterdam, Netherlands: Editions Rodopi, 2001), 140–144.

20. Martin Heidegger, *Being and Time*, trans. John Macquarrie and Edward Robinson (New York: Harper & Row, 1962), sec. 50–53.

21. Nietzsche, "On Free Death," in *Thus Spoke Zarathustra*.

# BIBLIOGRAPHY

Ansell-Pearson, Keith. *An Introduction to Nietzsche as Political Thinker*. Cambridge, England: Cambridge University Press, 1994.

Aquinas, St. Thomas. *Treatise on Happiness*. Translated by John A. Oesterle. Notre Dame, Indiana: University of Notre Dame Press, 1983.

Aristotle. *Nicomachean Ethics*. Translated by W. D. Ross, revised by J. L. Ackrill and J. O. Urmson. Oxford: Oxford University Press, 1980.

Augustine, St. *City of God*, in *Fathers of the Church*. Translated by Gerald G. Walsh, Daniel J. Honan, and Grace Monahan. Washington, DC: The Catholic University of America Press, 1952.

Baier, Kurt. *The Meaning of Life*. The Inaugural Lecture at Canberra University College. Canberra: The Australian National University, 1957.

————. "Threats of Futility," *Free Inquiry* 8:3 (Summer 1988), pp. 47–53.

Barrow, Robin. *Happiness and Schooling*. New York: St. Martin's Press, 1980.

Baumeister, Roy F. *Meanings of Life*. New York: The Guilford Press, 1991.

Belliotti, Raymond Angelo. *Good Sex*. Lawrence, Kansas: University Press of Kansas, 1993.

————. *Seeking Identity*. Lawrence, Kansas: University Press of Kansas, 1995.

————. *Stalking Nietzsche*. Westport, Conn.: Greenwood Press, 1998.

————. *What is the Meaning of Human Life?* Amsterdam, Netherlands: Editions Rodopi, 2001.

Bentham, Jeremy. *A Fragment on Government and the Principles of Morals and Legislation*. Oxford: Basil Blackwell, 1948.

Berkeley, George. *Three Dialogues Between Hylas and Philonous* in *The Works of George Berkeley*, 4 vols. Edited by A. C. Fraser. London: J. M. Dent and Sons, 1901.

Berlin, Isaiah. *The Roots of Romanticism*. Princeton: Princeton University Press, 1999.

Bernstein, Richard J. *Beyond Objectivism and Relativism*. Philadelphia: University of Pennsylvania Press, 1983.

Brothers, Dr. Joyce. "You Can Lead A More Joyful Life," *Parade Magazine*, October 15, 2000, 6–8.

Camus, Albert. *The Rebel*. New York: Vintage Books, 1956.

———. *The Myth of Sisyphus*. Translated by Justin O'Brien. New York: Vintage Books, 1991.

Cicero, Marcus Tullius. *De Fato*. Translated by H. Rackham. Cambridge, Mass.: Harvard University Press, 1933.

Covey, Stephen R., A. Roger Merrill, and Rebecca R. Merrill. *First Things First*. New York: Simon & Schuster, 1992.

Csikszentmihalyi, Mihaly. *Flow*. New York: Harper & Row Publishers, 1990.

Diogenes Laertius. *Lives of the Eminent Philosophers*. Translated by R. D. Hicks. Cambridge, Mass.: Harvard University Press, 1931.

Edwards, Paul. "Life, Meaning and Value of," in *The Encyclopedia of Philosophy*, Vol. 4. New York: Macmillan Co., 1967.

Epictetus. *Encheiridion*. Translated by W. A. Oldfather. Cambridge, Mass.: Harvard University Press, 1928.

———. *The Discourses as Reported by Arrian, the Manual, and Fragments*. Translated by W. A. Oldfather. Cambridge, Mass.: Harvard University Press, 1961.

Epicurus. "Letter to Menoeceus," in *The Stoic and Epicurean Philosophers*. Translated by C. F. Bailey. Edited by Whitney J. Oates. New York: The Modern Library, 1940.

Feldman, Fred. *Confrontations With The Reaper*. New York: Oxford University Press, 1992.

Finnis, John. "Practical Reasoning, Human Goods, and the End of Man," *Proceedings of the American Catholic Philosophical Association* 58 (1985): 23–36.

Foster, Rick, and Greg Hicks. *How We Choose to Be Happy*. New York: Penguin Putnam, Inc., 1999.

Frankl, Viktor E. *Man's Search For Meaning*. New York: Simon & Schuster Inc., 1959.

Freud, Sigmund. *The Future of an Illusion*. Translated by James Strachey. New York: W. W. Norton & Co., 1961.

Gabay, Jonathan, ed. *The Meaning of Life*. London: Virgin Books, 1995.

Gilson, Etienne. *The Christian Philosophy of St. Thomas Aquinas*. Translated by L. K. Shook. New York: Random House, 1956.

Goldstein, Irwin. "Happiness," *International Philosophical Quarterly* 13 (1973): 523–534.

Griffin, James. *Well-Being*. Oxford: Clarendon Press, 1986.

Guignon, Charles, ed. *The Good Life*. Indianapolis, Ind.: Hackett Publishing Co. Inc., 1999.

Hartshorne, Charles. "Outlines of a Philosophy of Nature." *Personalist* 39 (Fall 1958): 380–391.

Hegel, Georg W. F. *The Philosophy of Right*. Translated by T. M. Knox. Oxford: Clarendon Press, 1942.

———. *The Phenomenology of Mind*. Translated by J. B. Baillie. New York: Harper & Row, 1967.

Heidegger, Martin. *Being and Time*. Translated by John Macquarrie and Edward Robinson. New York: Harper & Row, 1962.

Hudson, Deal W. *Happiness and the Limits of Satisfaction*. Lanham, Maryland: Rowman & Littlefield Publishers, Inc., 1996.

Joske, W. D. "Philosophy and the Meaning of Life," *Australasian Journal of Philosophy* 52:2 (1974): 93–104.

Kant, Immanuel. *Fundamental Principles of the Metaphysic of Morals* in *Kant's Critique of Practical Reason and Other Works on the Theory of Ethics*. Translated by Thomas Kingsmill Abbott. London: Longmans, Green Publishers, 1879.

———. *Critique of Practical Reason and Other Works on the Theory of Ethics*. Translated by Thomas Kingsmill Abbott. London: Longmans, Green Publishers, 1926.

———. "Transcendental Doctrine of Method," in *Critique of Pure Reason*. Translated by J. M. D. Meiklejohn. New York: John Wiley, 1943.

Kaufmann, Walter. *The Faith of a Heretic*. New York: Anchor Books, 1963.

Kekes, John. "Happiness," *Mind* 91 (July 1982): 358–376.

———. *The Examined Life*. University Park, Penn.: The Pennsylvania State University Press, 1992.

Kingwell, Mark. *In Pursuit of Happiness*. New York: Crown Publishers, 1998.

Kohl, Marvin. "Meaning of Life and Happiness: A Preliminary Outline," *Dialectics and Humanism* 4 (1981): 39–43.

Koller, John M. *Oriental Philosophies*. New York: Scribner and Sons, 1985.

Korsch, Karl. *Three Essays on Marxism*. London: Pluto Press, 1971.

Kotre, John. *Make It Count: How To Generate A Legacy That Gives Meaning To Your Life*. New York: The Free Press, 1999.

Kraut, Richard. "Two Conceptions of Happiness," *The Philosophical Review* 88 (April 1979): 167–197.

Lane, Robert E. "The Road Not Taken: Friendship, Consumerism, and Happiness," *Critical Review* 8 (1994): 521–554.

Lu, Luo. "Personal or Environmental Causes of Happiness," *The Journal of Social Psychology* 139:1 (1999): 79–90.

Lu, Luo and Jian Bin Shih, "Sources of Happiness," *The Journal of Social Psychology* 137:2 (1997): 181–187.

Lucretius. "On the Nature of Things," in *The Stoic and Epicurean Philosophers*. Translated by H. A. J. Munro. Edited by Whitney J. Oates. New York: The Modern Library, 1940.

Lykken, Dr. David. *Happiness*. New York: St. Martin's Press, 1999.

Maritain, Jacques. *Moral Philosophy*. London: Geoffrey Bles, 1964.

Marx, Karl. *Selected Writings*. Edited by David McLellan. Oxford: Oxford University Press, 1977.

Matson, Wallace I. *A New History of Philosophy*, Vol. I. New York: Harcourt Brace Jovanovich, Inc., 1987.

McFall, Lynne. "Happiness, Rationality, and Individual Ideals," *Review of Metaphysics* 38 (March 1984): 595–613.

————. *Happiness*. New York: Peter Lang, 1989.

McGill, V. J. *The Idea of Happiness*. New York: Frederick A. Praeger Publishers, 1967.

Mill, John Stuart. "Utilitarianism," in *Utilitarianism, Liberty and Representative Government*. New York: E. P. Dutton, 1944.

————. *Autobiography*. Edited by J. M. Robson. Toronto: University of Toronto Press, 1981.

Moorhead, Hugh S., ed. *The Meaning of Life*. Chicago: Chicago Review Press, 1988.

Morris, William, ed. *The American Heritage Dictionary of The English Language*. Boston, Mass.: Houghton Mifflin Company, 1969.

Myers, David G. *The Pursuit of Happiness*. New York: Avon Books, Inc., 1992.

Nagel, Thomas. "The Absurd," *The Journal of Philosophy*, 21 October 1971: 716–727.

————. *The View from Nowhere*. Oxford: Oxford University Press, 1986.

Nietzsche, Friedrich. *Thus Spoke Zarathustra*. Translated by Walter Kaufmann in *The Portable Nietzsche*. New York: Viking Press, 1954.

————. *Twilight of the Idols*. Translated by Walter Kaufmann in *The Portable Nietzsche*. New York: Viking Press, 1954.

————. *Beyond Good and Evil*. Translated by Walter Kaufmann. New York: Vintage Books, 1966.

————. *The Birth of Tragedy*. Translated by Walter Kaufmann. New York: Random House, 1967.

————. *The Gay Science*. Translated by Walter Kaufmann. New York: Random House, 1967.

————. *Ecce Homo*. Translated by Walter Kaufmann and R. J. Hollingdale. New York: Random House, 1967.

————. *On the Genealogy of Morals*. Translated by Walter Kaufmann and R. J. Hollingdale. New York: Vintage Books, 1967.

Niven, David. *The 100 Simple Secrets of Happy People*. New York: HarperCollins Publishers, 2000.

Nozick, Robert. *Anarchy, State, and Utopia*. New York: Basic Books, 1974.

————. *Philosophical Explanations*. Cambridge, Mass.: Harvard University Press, 1981.

Pears, Iain. *An Instance of the Fingerpost*. New York: Riverhead Books, 1998.

Pieper, Josef. *Happiness and Contemplation*. Translated by Richard and Clara Winston. New York: Pantheon Press, 1958.

Plato. *The Dialogues of Plato*. 2 vols. Translated by B. Jowett. New York: Random House, 1920.

————. *Phaedo*. Translated by David Gallop. Oxford: Oxford University Press, 1993.

Plotinus. *Enneads*. Vol. I. Translated by A. H. Armstrong. Cambridge, Mass.: Harvard University Press, 1966.

Rosenberg, Jay. *Thinking Clearly about Death*. Englewood Cliffs, N.J.: Prentice-Hall, Inc., 1983.

Russell, Bertrand. *Principles of Social Reconstruction*. London: Allen & Unwin Publishers, 1916.

———. *The Conquest of Happiness*. London: Horace Liveright Publishers, Inc., 1958.

Sanders, Steven, and David Cheney, eds. *The Meaning of Life*. Englewood Cliffs, N.J.: Prentice Hall, 1980.

Sartre, Jean-Paul. *Being and Nothingness*. Translated by Hazel E. Barnes. New York: Philosophical Library, 1966.

———. *No Exit and Three Other Plays*. New York: Vintage Books, 1989.

Schopenhauer, Arthur. *The World as Will and Idea*. Translated by R. B. Haldane and J. Kemp. London: Routledge & Kegan Paul, 1948.

Second Vatican Ecumenical Council. *Catechism of the Catholic Church*. Mahwah, N.J.: Paulist Press, 1994.

Seligman, Martin E. P. *Authentic Happiness*. New York: The Free Press, 2002.

Shakespeare, William. *Macbeth* in *Complete Works of Shakespeare*. Edited by Stanley Wells and Gary Taylor. Oxford: Oxford University Press, 1988.

Singer, Irving. *Meaning in Life*. New York: The Free Press, 1982.

———. *The Harmony of Nature and Spirit*. Baltimore, Md.: Johns Hopkins University Press, 1996.

Solomon, Robert C. *The Joy of Philosophy*. New York: Oxford University Press, 1999.

Stones, M. J., Thomas Hadjistavropoulos, Holly Tuuko, and Albert Kozma. "Happiness Has Traitlike and Statelike Properties," *Social Indicators Research* 36 (1995): 129–144.

Taylor, Richard. *Good and Evil*. New York: The Macmillan Co., 1970.

———. "The Meaning of Human Existence," in *Values in Conflict*. Edited by Burton Leiser. New York: The Macmillan Co., 1981

———. "Time and Life's Meaning," *Review of Metaphysics* 40 (June 1987): 675–680.

———. "The Meaning of Life," *Philosophy Now* 24 (Summer 1999): 13–14.

Theron, Stephen. "Happiness and Transcendent Happiness," *Religious Studies* 21 (September 1985): 349–367.

Tolstoy, Leon. *My Confession*. Translated by Leo Wiener. London: J. M. Dent and Sons, 1905.

Veenhoven, Ruut. *Conditions of Happiness*. Dordrecht, Holland: Reidel Publishers, 1984.

———. "Is Happiness a Trait?" *Social Indicators Research* 33 (1994): 101–160.

Von Wright, G. H. *The Varieties of Goodness*. London: Routledge & Kegan Paul, 1963.

Wilson, John. "Happiness," *Analysis* 29 (January, 1968): 13–21.

# INDEX

# ABOUT THE AUTHOR

**Raymond Angelo Belliotti** is Distinguished Teaching Professor and Chairperson of Philosophy at the State University of New York at Fredonia. He received his undergraduate degree from Union College in 1970, after which he was conscripted into the United States Army, where he served three years in military intelligence units during the Vietnam War. Upon his discharge, he enrolled at the University of Miami where he earned his master of arts degree in 1976 and doctorate in 1977. After teaching stints at Florida International University and Virginia Commonwealth University, he entered Harvard University as a law student and teaching Fellow. After receiving a juris doctorate from Harvard Law School, he practiced law in New York City with the firm of Barrett Smith Schapiro Simon & Armstrong. In 1984, he joined the faculty at Fredonia.

Belliotti is the author of five other books: *Justifying Law* (1992), *Good Sex* (1993), *Seeking Identity* (1995), *Stalking Nietzsche* (1998), and *What is the Meaning of Human Life?* (2001). *Good Sex* was later translated into Korean and published in Asia. He has also published fifty-five articles and twenty-five reviews in the areas of ethics, jurisprudence, sexual morality, medicine, politics, education, feminism, sports, Marxism, and legal ethics. These essays have appeared in scholarly journals based in Australia, Canada, Great Britain, Italy, Mexico, South Africa, Sweden, and the United States. Belliotti has also made numerous presentations at philosophical conferences, including the 18th World Congress of Philosophy in England, and has been honored as a featured lecturer on the Queen Elizabeth II ocean liner.

While at SUNY Fredonia he has served extensively on campus committees, as the chairperson of the College Senate, and as director of general education. For six years he was faculty advisor to the undergraduate club, the Philosophical Society, and he has served that function for Il Circolo

Italiano. Belliotti has been the recipient of the SUNY Chancellor's Award for Excellence in Teaching, the William T. Hagan Young Scholar/Artist Award, the Kasling Lecture Award for Excellence in Research and Scholarship, and the SUNY Foundation Research and Scholarship Recognition Award.